# A Manner of Speaking

## Successful Presentations for Work and Life

**Second Edition**

R. Michael Bokeno
Edward C. Brewer
William D. Cole
Crystal Rae Coel Coleman
Stephen A. Cox
Camisha Pierce Duffy
Sheryl D. Lidzy
Barbara K. Malinauskas
Lou Davidson Tillson
*Murray State University*

**KENDALL/HUNT PUBLISHING COMPANY**
4050 Westmark Drive          Dubuque, Iowa 52002

# Contents

# Acknowledgements

We would like to acknowledge the contributions of Kate Reeves of Wrather West Kentucky Museum for providing the auditorium backdrop for many of the photographs in this text. Additionally, we appreciate the countless contributions of the many students who gave their time and effort in assisting with the editing and photography for this text. Finally, we would like to acknowledge the faculty of the Organizational Communication Department for their countless reviews and cooperation in making this second edition better than the original.

# A Manner of Speaking

*Successful Presentations
for Work and Life*

# 1

# History of Public Speaking

## CHAPTER PREVIEW

| 1 | The relevance of history |
| 2 | The influence of classical rhetoric |
| 3 | Contemporary influences on public speaking |

Speaking is something all of us do. Indeed, a typical point of conversation in a beginning speech class concerns the idea that "since we all know how to speak, why take this class?" Unfortunately, such comments usually reflect the attitude that the study of public speaking is unnecessary, irrelevant, or worse, easy. Quite the contrary. It is precisely "because speaking is humanity's most common form of communication," writes Minnick, that "it is not surprising that people have spent considerable time and effort studying the process."[1] Specifically, the study of public speaking, also called rhetoric, oratory, and oral argument,[2] spans about 2,500 years. This chapter offers a sense of the historical significance of public speaking. Throughout its 2,500 year history—from its classical heritage in ancient Greece to the present—public speaking has been viewed as both a noble art and a questionable art. An understanding of the ways in which rhetoric has been viewed historically will facilitate a deeper appreciation for the skills of public speaking, which constitute the remainder of this text.

## Greek Influence

The history of public speaking began with the ancient Greeks in the fifth century B.C. In Greece at this time, a new democratic form of government was being instituted. One of the goals of this new government was to return parcels of land that had been confiscated by the previous government to their rightful owners. As a result of the long years of tyranny that preceded the new government, no one really knew who owned certain parcels of land; that is, various individuals were presenting claims to the same piece of property. A man by the name of Corax realized that if someone was to win the title to the piece of land in question, that person must establish a more believable or plausible case than his opponent. Corax outlined a set of rules designed to aid in the arguing of one's legal case. These rules, as Corax

developed them, focused on how to show probability. That is, between two arguments or propositions, one is more likely to be true than the other. With his ideas concerning probability, Corax began the study of communication with a clear emphasis on persuasion, or rhetoric.

An interesting aspect of Greek life in this new democracy was that every free male citizen was expected to take part in public discussions. That is, part of being a Greek citizen in this new democracy was to participate in public oratory concerning political and legal matters, as well as public ceremonies. Citizen participation in the legislative assembly helped establish government policy. Also, citizens could not hire lawyers to represent them in legal disputes. Rather, citizens had to plead their own cases in front of a legal assembly or jury. In addition, citizens were called upon to speak at public social gatherings, to celebrate a recent battlefield victory, to praise a particular leader, or to eulogize an important person. Thus, the degree to which a Greek citizen could speak effectively had a great influence on his political standing and social success.

## Sophists

But what about those who did not have the ability to speak persuasively or argue effectively? This need for training and education in oral presentation—rhetoric—was filled by a group called "sophists." The **Sophists** were "teachers of wisdom" who traveled from place to place and offered their educational services for a fee. Sophists claimed to be able to teach anyone about virtually any subject matter, including rhetoric, grammar, art, architecture, mathematics, poetry, literature, etc. But, in addition, sophists often concentrated on "proving opposites," or proving both sides of an argument or issue. This activity focused attention on the lack of certainty or absolute truth in communication situations; both sides of most issues do have some amount

3

of plausibility. Unfortunately, the sophist's emphasis on proving both sides of an issue, combined with their philosophy which denied certain truth, eventually caused "sophistry" to become suspect and to decline gradually in importance in the early fourth century B.C. Their enthusiasm for arguing both sides of an issue may have been pursued for "sport"—or at least, with little thought for ethics in communication. Sophists were also accused of using **rhetoric** simply to flatter, impress, or even mislead others. It is due in part to the abuses of the sophists that the term "rhetoric," even today, seems negative or undesirable to some, as reflected in statements such as, "we want more action and less rhetoric," or "that's mere political rhetoric." Finally, the sophist's methods sometimes came back to haunt them.

According to one ancient story, Tisias, a student of Corax, accused Corax of providing worthless instruction and refused to pay his fee. Corax then filed suit for the payment. Classical scholar James J. Murphy reports that the court postponed the decision indefinitely.[3]

## Sophist-icated!

**Corax:** *You must pay me if you win the case, because that would prove the worth of my lessons. If you lose the case, you must pay me also, for the court will force you to do so. In either case, you pay.*

**Tisias:** *I will pay nothing, because if I lose the case it would prove that your instruction was worthless. If I win, however, the court will absolve me from paying. In either case, I will not pay.*

In some senses, today's professional arguers—lawyers—might be seen as the contemporary counterpart of the ancient sophists. Though today's lawyers usually choose to specialize as either prosecutors or defense lawyers, and although they are usually more ethical, their education and training certainly requires that they know how to argue both sides of a question.

In direct opposition to the sophistic view of communication as a method for proving all sorts of "truth," Socrates and his famous pupil, Plato, looked at communication as a way of proving THE TRUTH. Plato had little use for formal speeches. In the Platonic dialogues, the character "Socrates" molded the skills of questioning, discussing, and defining into what he called "dialectic": Communi-

cation as a philosophical method of determining Truth. In other words, dialectic "involves the use of dialogue to ascertain the truth of an opinion through questioning."[4] This form of communication resembled an interview or group discussion more than persuasive speaking. In his later works, however, Plato came to appreciate the role of speeches and more formal rhetoric in leading others to the Truth, once Truth has been established by means of the dialectical method. Hence, Plato's primary concern was with the pursuit of truth and knowledge through questioning, and the dissemination of this knowledge through the practice of rhetoric.

One of Plato's students, Aristotle, collected material from other thinkers—both Plato and the sophists—integrated some ideas of his own, and developed the framework used by many teachers of speech and communication today. Unlike his teacher, Aristotle realized that most matters of human concern were questions of probable truth instead of certainty. But unlike the "anything goes" view of sophists, Aristotle held to the ethical view that rhetoric should try to uphold probable truth. Aristotle noted three specific functions of rhetoric: (1) to teach ordinary people in a way suitable to a popular audience, (2) to analyze both sides of a question, and (3) to enable an individual to defend himself from verbal attack. Aristotle's perspective, then, was of rhetoric as a practical art and a moral art, and this perspective remains a solid foundation for the study of public speaking today.

The contributions to communication study that were made during the Roman period cannot be stressed too strongly. The surviving accounts or reported writings of individuals such as Cicero and Quintilian contributed insights to what we now call classical rhetoric. To Cicero, we attribute the idea that the speaker should be conversant on an incredibly wide variety of subjects; to Quintilian we attribute the famous notion that the perfect speaker was "the good man speaking well."

While the ancient Greek and Roman periods were characterized by great gains in rhetorical theory, the Middle Ages were equally characterized by the lack of such development. One major exception to this was the new role of rhetoric as perceived by practitioners. To classical scholars, rhetoric was important in three spheres of human interaction: in the law courts (much like Corax), in the legislative assemblies, and in the public forums and social/public gatherings and celebrations. In the Middle Ages, the role or rhetoric was expanded to include sermonizing from the pulpits and letter writing generally.

While there were few theoretical advances, rhetoric was viewed as what the religious leader did or what the head of state said in letters to other dignitaries or the public.

In the seventeenth and eighteenth centuries, the study of rhetoric or persuasive communication began to reach such levels of importance that this period—along with the classical period—would become known as the second of three great periods of communication study.

## Four Schools of Thoughts

This time of theory development is divisible into the contributions of four great schools of thought: the **neoclassic**, the **epistemologist**, the **belletristic**, and the **elocutionist**. The "neoclassic" scholars were perhaps best represented by Jonathan Swift and Alexander Pope who sought, in their various ways, to return to the rhetoric of the classical scholars; hence their title, the new classicists.

Also important to the student wishing to understand advances in rhetorical theory were the "**epistemologists**." Guided by people like Francis Bacon, George Campbell, and Richard Whately, epistemology—the scientific study or theory of knowledge—was seen as related to rhetoric. Discussions of what science had to do with rhetoric and what rhetoric had to do with science created a tremendously exciting period in the development of rhetorical theory.

Equally interesting was the thinking of the "**Belletristic**" scholars who sought to cement the relationship between literature and rhetoric. Men such as Hugh Blair and Adam Smith described how the study of literature—"beautiful letters"—could aid the development of oral as well as written communication. The link between literature and rhetoric continues even today with "rhetoric" being a common topic in both academic departments of English and departments of communication. Perhaps more commonly known than the work of the neoclassicists, the epistemologists, or the belletristic scholars was the work of the "elocutionists."

In contrast to the other three major groups of the seventeenth century, the **elocutionists** sought to confine the study of rhetoric or communication to the realm of what we could call "speech performance." These writers and practitioners felt that the most important factors in communication included graceful gesture and the correct facial expression. Elaborate schemes and training techniques were devised so that the student could create the precise movement, gesture, and facial expression that would convey his or her thought. So important was the "delivery" of the speech that little thought was given to whether the speaker really had anything to say. And, if it is true that little important theory was developed during this period, it is equally true that the heritage of the elocutionists lives on: beginning students will sometimes believe—incorrectly—that the study of communication is simply the study of excessive and dramatic gestures and expressions.

## Twentieth Century/ Contemporary Perspectives

With the excesses of the elocutionists so pronounced, it is little wonder that the twentieth century—the third great period of communication thought—brought whole new perspectives to the study of communication. Literary theorist **I.A. Richards** was crucial to the development of communication studies by insisting that for too long the study of rhetoric was simply the study of persuasion; the task of informative speaking—of having an audience simply understand the speaker—was, in his view, at least as important. **Richard Weaver** contributed to a re-awakening of the concern for ethics in communication. Every speech, he reasoned, attempted to have an audience make choices; the speaker, therefore, was ethically responsible for what choices the audience made. Literary theorist **Kenneth Burke** contributed much to the sociological understanding of communication. Armed with the works of Freud, classical rhetoricians, Marxist political theory, and contemporary sociology, Burke explained that the process of persuasion was basically a matter of "identification." That is, to the extent that the speaker could create bonds of similarity

between himself or herself and an audience, he or she would be a successful speaker. Contemporary epistemologist **Stephen Toulmin** re-evaluated "logic" and created a new approach to the study of argumentation—an approach which virtually revolutionized how the study of argumentation and communication has developed. His emphasis upon audience belief instead of formal logic was a milestone in the development of communication study.

## Diverse Contributions to Communication Thought

The fact that Burke, Weaver, and Richards were from the field of "English" and that Toulmin was a philosopher indicate the great "borrowing" that accounts for much of the contemporary study of communication. The study of communication in the twentieth century also borrowed heavily from experimental and empirical studies that have arisen since the late 1920s. Insights and research from psychology, sociology, anthropology, political science, and linguistics have all been important to the development of communication thought. The research undertaken by communication scholars—as well as that borrowed from other fields—has created a wealth of information about the human process of communication.

This brief survey of the history of public speaking and communication reveals how the basic public speaking course has its roots in 2,500 years of thinking about logic, people, argumentation, literary style, truth-seeking, ethics, informative speaking, persuasion, group interaction, and the need to understand and to be understood. It is the basic course in communication, more than other courses, which serves as an introduction to the insights and skills relevant to all these concerns.

## Applying the Chapter

1. What surprised you about the origins of public speaking?

_____

_____

_____

2. Who were the Sophists and what impact did they have on public speaking?

_____

_____

_____

3. What contributions to public speaking did each group make:

   a. Romans: _____

   _____

   b. Greeks: _____

   _____

4. What are the three (3) functions of rhetoric?

   (1) _____

   (2) _____

   (3) _____

5. How are these functions apparent in public speaking today? (Use examples of speeches you've heard.)

_____

_____

_____

# History of Public Speaking

# Think about It . . .

1. The contemporary world is often referred to as being without "anchors" or stable foundations for determining the truth of anything. Who is best equipped to operate effectively in such a world: Plato, Aristotle or the Sophists? Who does the world need more? Who could it do best without?

2. Watch TV news or other "informative" programs for an evening or two. Identify a speaker you see— in some sort of public speaking context—that would fit into each of the following groups. Tell why.

Speaker . . .

Most like . . .

_____

_____

_____

_____

_____

_____

_____

_____

_____

_____

| Plato |
| Aristotle |
| Sophists |
| Cicero |
| Quintilian |
| Neoclassicists |
| Belletrists |
| Epistemologists |
| Elocutionists |
| Contemporary Theorists |

## Notes

1. Wayne C. Minnick, *Pubic Speaking* (Boston: Houghton Mifflin Company, 1983), p. 2.
2. Ibid.
3. James J. Murphy, *A Synoptic History of Classical Rhetoric* (New York: Random House, 1972), p. 7.
4. Ibid, p. 17.

# 2 Getting Started with Confidence

## CHAPTER PREVIEW

| 1 | Why do I need to know how to speak in public? |
| 2 | Why do I get so anxious? |
| 3 | How can I manage my public speaking anxiety? |
| 4 | How do I get started? |

> Nothing in life is to be feared. It is only to be understood.
>
> ⁓Marie Curie

## Why Public Speaking Is Like Riding a Bicycle

*Do you remember when you learned how to ride a bicycle? You weren't born with that ability . . . someone had to encourage you, push you, teach you. You probably began on a tricycle. I had an oversized red one that I proudly pedaled down the street to the post office with my mother each afternoon. It didn't require much skill. I just had to make sure I stopped pedaling when my mother stopped walking so I wouldn't ride up on her heels, which really annoyed her!*

*When I was 5 or 6 my parents bought me my first bicycle. It was a beauty . . . mirror-finished chrome and metallic blue paint, with handlebar streamers and a shiny blue and white, banana-shaped seat that sparkled in the sunlight. One of the most vivid childhood memories I have is of the day my dad took off the training wheels. My heart, pounding out a deafening rhythm in my chest, partially blocked out the frightened voice in my mind, which was whispering, "you can't do this . . . you're going to wreck . . . the other kids will see you and laugh when you fall . . . all of your friends can do it, but you'll never learn how . . . ."*

*Nonetheless, my dad shouted words of encouragement above the sound of my thundering heart, gave me a final shove, and I was off. I pedaled with all the speed a 5 year old could muster, forgot about the bass drum in my chest, and successfully, albeit a bit wobbly at first, flew down Oakwood Avenue, demonstrating my newfound independence to the other kids in the neighborhood. Skinned knees and bruised elbows were forgotten as my father ran along-side me, coaching, "You can do it . . . keep pedaling . . . that's it . . . balance . . . balance . . . keep pedaling . . . you're doing it . . . you're doing it . . . keep pedaling . . . I TOLD YOU YOU COULD DO IT!"*

Delivering a speech or making a presentation is similar to riding a bicycle. You aren't born with the ability to deliver a speech. You aren't even born with the ability to articulate words or speak in complete sentences. You have to learn how, just like you had to learn how to ride a bicycle. Along the way, you might have begun with the most simplistic delivery method (remember reading book reports aloud in elementary school, barely speaking loud enough for the teacher to hear and NEVER glancing up from your notebook?). Perhaps you've moved up to the bicycle with training wheels. You've made other presentations and taken some delivery risks, perhaps added more dynamic vocal inflection or better eye contact. Some of you might have taken a public speaking class in high school or competed on a forensics team. Now, however, you're in college and preparing for your professional lives. It's time to remove the training wheels altogether. It's going to require a lot of practice, but you can do it. You'll have to learn how to balance content with delivery and how to support your ideas with facts and examples . . . but you can do it! You'll have to learn how to organize your thoughts and present them creatively . . . but you can do it! You'll have to practice, practice, practice, but you CAN do it!

This chapter will help you approach public speaking with confidence, with a "can-do" attitude. The remaining chapters will teach you specific techniques and strategies for creating successful presentations for work and life. So hop on, let's get started. It's going to be a great ride!

## Why Do I Need to Know How to Speak in Public?

Riding a bicycle is challenging and fun. It fosters independence and can take you places that you couldn't get to otherwise. Public speaking is much the same. Being able to share your ideas with others, or persuade a group to agree with your point of view, or entertain an audience with a good story are presentation experiences every one of you is likely to encounter throughout your life. Being able to speak effectively is empowering and rewarding.

What do you expect to be doing in the future? Working for a major corporation or a non-profit organization? Raising a family? Participating in civic organizations? Teaching Sunday School? Going into the family business? Volunteering at a local school or hospital? Regardless of which path you walk down, good communication skills will be instrumental in helping you achieve your goals.

Employers consistently identify communication skills as a basic requirement. As a matter of fact, communication competence is necessary for your academic and personal success and helps to facilitate upward mobility and professional achievement![1]

Students enrolled in an introductory public speaking class were asked to identify the types of communication they anticipated engaging in based upon their major area of study and future career plans. Take a look at their list and highlight any that might match up with your course of study and future plans:

- Delivering platoon commands and orders
- Holding press conferences
- Delivering classroom lectures
- Presenting ideas to a school board
- Making speeches during band concerts
- Speaking to a curriculum committee about the importance of music in public schools
- Making presentations to college campus organizations
- Describing processes to clients
- Reporting to my supervisor
- Persuading companies to buy my product

- Persuading an organization to fund a project
- Informing groups about particular medical procedures
- Presenting legal arguments
- Delivering commencement addresses
- Speaking to Parent-Teacher Associations
- Making informal presentations on special occasions
- Recruiting organizational members
- Speaking at faculty meetings
- Making presentations at school programs
- Speaking to parents on "parents' night" at my school
- Leading meetings of professional organizations
- Selling a product or a service
- Leading staff meetings at work
- Presenting ideas to international clients or employees
- Presenting research findings
- Defending conservation efforts to the public
- Addressing employees
- Giving a talk at church
- Making progress reports at work
- Telling stories to young children
- Motivating athletes
- Lobbying politicians
- Conducting training seminars
- _____
- _____
- _____

Most of you will have to make presentations in other classes during your college studies. Most of you (if you haven't done so already) will engage in public speaking activities on the job, in social groups, or in civic organizations.

Unfortunately, most of us, as we prepare to enter the professional workforce, are still wearing our training wheels! We need to develop and fine-tune our public speaking skills in order to move ahead. Research indicates that job applicants lack effective communication skills in job interviews.[2] Further, once newly hired graduates actually succeed in entering the workforce, their strong academic skills don't compensate for their lack of "communication skills and the ability to work in teams and with people from diverse backgrounds."[3] One study of 1,000 human resource managers found that communication skills, specifically skills of listening, oral communication (both public and interpersonal), written communication, and the trait of enthusiasm, were

the most valued in the contemporary job-entry market.[4] The Department of Labor, in its study of American workforce competencies for 2000 and beyond, concluded that "Tomorrow's workers will have to listen and speak well enough to explain schedules and procedures, communicate with customers, work in teams, understand customer concerns . . . probe for hidden meanings, teach others, and solve problems."[5]

Bottom line: you need to be a competent communicator. At this point, you may be convinced of the need to develop your communication skills, but still apprehensive about doing so. The next section of this chapter will help explain why so many people are apprehensive (o.k., downright scared!) about public speaking and provide some ideas to help you manage that anxiety.

have been written about the subject, and it's been labeled in myriad ways: bashfulness, timidity, stage fright, shyness, reticence, (un)willingness to communicate, presentational anxiety, communication apprehension, social anxiety. Regardless of what it's called, most of us recognize the symptoms. Do any of these sound familiar to you?

- Pounding or racing heart
- Hot flashes
- Clammy or sweaty hands
- Dry mouth
- Butterflies in the stomach
- Nausea
- Breathlessness
- Trembling
- Muscle tension
- Shaky voice
- Blushing

## ■ Why Do I Get So Anxious?

Removing the training wheels, in a manner of speaking, means moving beyond the way you've always done things. Removing the training wheels means stepping outside of your comfort zone and taking creative, yet calculated, risks. Emeril might say removing the training wheels is like, *"BAM! Kicking it up a notch!"* The training wheels have to go because employers are telling us that they interfere with, even prevent, success in the workplace.

But why does removing the training wheels make me so nervous? Why are so many people anxious about public speaking? Hundreds of articles

What symptoms of public speaking anxiety do you experience? How do you handle them?

_____

_____

_____

_____

_____

_____

All of these "symptoms" are physiological in nature and stem from what Harvard physiologist, Walter B. Cannon initially described in the early 1900s as the "fight or flight response." He determined that when an animal is faced with a physical threat to its survival, it is faced with two options: fight off the attacker or flee from the threat. Either option requires the body to prepare for intense activity in order to respond to the threat. The brain initiates 1,400 different responses, including dumping adrenaline into the bloodstream,[6] producing an increase in heart rate, blood pressure, muscle tension, and breathing rate. Interestingly, Cannon's research indicated that an animal would not differentiate between a real threat and a perceived threat. For example, an attacking dog and a movie depicting a vicious dog could elicit the same physiological response in a kitten exposed to both. In either case, the mind would stimulate the body to prepare to run away from, or to fight its way out of, the threatening situation.[7]

What does the "fight or flight response" have to do with public speaking anxiety? Many people view public speaking as a threatening situation. They may be afraid that they will make mistakes or stumble, be evaluated negatively by the audience, or reveal insufficient public speaking skills. For some, the stress is so profound that they postpone enrolling in a required 100-level, basic public speak-

ing class until the last semester of their senior year! Hopefully, they decide that completing the course is less of a threat than not graduating from college, so they enroll and "fight" their way through the assignments. Others repeatedly enroll in the class, but "flee" (drop) it before the first speaking assignment.

Research, however, suggests that it is "normal to experience a fairly high degree of anxiety about public speaking."[8] You are probably familiar with the results of a nation-wide survey in which adults reported that speaking before a group was their greatest fear, surprisingly ranking higher than death![9] It has been estimated that over 70 percent of the general population experiences communication apprehension in the public speaking context.[10]

> One of the fears that I have about public speaking is that of going completely blank and losing all my train of thought right in the middle of my speech.
>
> — Aaron

The anxiety that you feel, caused by your brain's perception of a threat, mobilizes your body for the fight or flight response. Too much adrenaline can interfere with your ability to deliver a speech by causing the symptoms listed earlier. Too little adrenaline can result in a "flat," uninspiring

| Symptom | Cause |
|---|---|
| Pounding or racing heart, hot flashes | Breathing rate increases and the heart supplies more blood to the lungs to absorb the extra oxygen. Blood flow may increase 300% to 400%.[11] |
| Perspiration | Blood flow is diverted away from the skin to support the heart and muscle tissues, resulting in cool, clammy, sweaty skin.[11] |
| Dry mouth | Fluids are diverted from nonessential locations, resulting in dry mouth and difficulty talking, or even swallowing.[11] |
| Butterflies or nausea | Digestive activity shuts down.[11] |
| Breathlessness | Breathing rate increases, causing the breathing to become more shallow.[12] |
| Trembling or muscle tension | Extra energy is diverted to the muscles. If it is not worked out through physical activity, it results in muscle tightness, cramps, or feeling "shaky." |
| Shaky voice | Muscles in the throat may tighten or spasm, and when combined with breathlessness and/or dry mouth, causes shaking vocal delivery. |
| Blushing | Blood vessels in the face (and sometimes throat and chest) are prompted to open wide, which floods the skin in these areas with blood.[13] |

presentation that fails to engage your audience members' attention. A reasonable amount of this "adrenaline rush" can actually improve your public speaking performance by stimulating creativity and adding energy and enthusiasm to it, much as it enables an athlete to succeed in his or her sport. Just like the children's story about Goldilocks and the three bears, a moderate amount of adrenaline is "just right" in most public speaking situations.

> I am becoming much more relaxed and confident with each speech I give. The more I practice, the better I get. Also, I am starting to get to know my classmates, and this makes me much more comfortable in front of them.
>
> ⌐ Hagan

## TIP

For more information on all aspects of stress and how it affects the human body, visit The American Institute of Stress On-Line at http://www.stress.org.

## Four Ways to Manage My Public Speaking Anxiety

> That the birds of worry and care fly above your head, this you cannot change, but that they build nests in your hair, this you can prevent.
>
> ⌐ Chinese proverb

Tips for handling stress are as varied as suggestions for stopping the hiccups! The best strategy for you

depends upon the reason or reasons why you get anxious about public speaking in the first place!

The following are "tried and true" anxiety-reducing strategies and are guaranteed to work better than the ineffectual suggestion to "imagine the audience naked." Frankly, envisioning that kind of image in the middle of a speech might cause even more problems!

### Skills Training

For some students, public speaking anxiety occurs because they have never been taught how to deliver a formal speech. If that describes you, then the introduction to public speaking class is the best place for you to be right now! This class will teach you how to select a speech topic, organize your thoughts, develop support for your ideas, and present them dynamically. Feel free to read ahead in the textbook. Talk to friends who have already completed the class. Surf the internet for ideas. Most importantly, practice, practice, practice! But remember, practice doesn't make perfect, it makes permanent. Perfect practice makes perfect.

> When I practice my speeches, I sometimes practice in front of the mirror. Other times I say my speech to my roommate or to my mom or boyfriend over the phone. It sounds silly, but it works. I practice especially any words and phrases that I wish to emphasize.
>
> ⌐ Ashley

### Deep Breathing

A former acting coach taught me to use this method before theatrical productions to help reduce my stage fright. I've been passing the technique on to

| If you're anxious because . . . | then focus on: |
|---|---|
| ■ you lack experience . . . . . . . . . . . . . . . . . . . . . . . . . . . . | skills training |
| ■ you anticipate performing poorly . . . . . . . . . . . . . . . . | skills training and positive self-talk |
| ■ your body seems to go into overdrive . . . . . . . . . . . . . | deep breathing exercises and imagery |
| ■ you tend to blow the public speaking experience out of proportion (e.g., I'll die if I have to give a speech!) . . . . . . . . . . . . . . . . . . . . . . . . . . . . . . . . . . | positive self-talk and reframing |

public speaking students for the past 20 years—it really helps! First, close your eyes and focus on your breathing. Breathe in through your nose and out through your mouth. Inhale and exhale as deeply and slowly as is comfortable for you. As you breathe begin to focus on the number "1." Say it and visualize it in your mind. Practice for at least three to five minutes. This strategy works because engaging in deep breathing triggers a relaxation response in your body. Concentrating on the number "1" helps you to become more mentally focused, less distracted by the noises and events going on around you and the stressful feelings going on inside of you. As you practice this strategy, your mind and body learn to respond with feelings of relaxation more readily. After you have mastered this technique, try doing it while waiting for your turn to deliver a speech in class.

## Imagery

After completing the deep breathing exercise described above, consider engaging in an imaging exercise. This isn't an opportunity for you to "visit your happy place," as some might suggest. Instead, it's an opportunity for you to "pre-wire" your brain for success. While your mind and body are relaxed, envision yourself successfully delivering a speech. Include all of the sensory details to make the scene vivid in your mind's eye. *See yourself confidently walking to the front of the classroom—take note of the clothes you are wearing. Notice how you carefully organize your notes on the podium. See yourself look out at your audience, smiling as you make eye contact with your classmates. Picture how you will begin your introduction. Hear yourself speaking enthusiastically.* In other words, create a complete and detailed mental scenario of you delivering an A+ speech! Try to engage in this imaging exercise at least once a day for a week before you deliver a speech in class.

Major James Nesmeth was a prisoner of war in North Vietnam for seven years. During that time he was imprisoned in a cage that was approximately four and one-half feet high and five feet long. Because he was almost exclusively in solitary confinement, he knew that he needed something to occupy his mind to prevent him from going insane. So he played golf. He visualized himself playing 18 holes a day. *"He experienced everything to the last detail. He saw himself dressed in his golfing clothes. He smelled the fragrance of the trees and the freshly trimmed grass. He experienced the weather conditions—windy spring days, overcast winter days, and sunny summer mornings. In his imagination, every detail of the tee, the individual blades of grass, the trees, the singing birds, the scampering squirrels and the lay of the course became totally real. He felt the grip of the club in his hands. He instructed himself as he practiced smoothing out his down-swing and the follow-through on his shot. Then he watched the ball arc down the exact center of the fairway, bounce a couple of times and roll to the exact spot he had selected, all in his mind . . . . Not a detail was omitted. Not once did he ever miss a shot, never a hook or a slice, never missed a putt."* Before his imposed hiatus from golf, Major Nesmeth had been a weekend golfer, shooting in the mid- to low-nineties. After his release from seven years of solitary confinement and playing golf only in his mind's eye, he returned to the game and discovered that he had shaved 20 strokes from his average![14]

If positive imagery can help a prisoner of war in solitary confinement improve his golf game, surely it can aid you in decreasing your public speaking anxiety and assist you in improving your presentational skills!

## Reframing

This strategy helps you to redefine your thoughts and create more positive, or, at the very least, neu-

---

In English, "crisis" is a negative, stressful word for most people. If you hear that someone is having a crisis, you don't say, "Hey, that's great. Can I come over? I'll bring pretzels and beer and we'll have a crisis together." You're more likely to say, "Gee, I'm sorry to hear that. I hope things work out. Let me know if I can help."

危机 But in Chinese, the word crisis is written with two characters and each stands for a different concept: the first for "danger," the second for "opportunity." So while the English word, "crisis," has a negative connotation, in Chinese it invites you to see both the down side and an up side. It doesn't deny the negative. But it suggests a positive aspect as well. It encourages you to reframe the situation—to acknowledge the downside, but also to explore the possibilities and opportunities . . .

David M. Posen, M.D.[15]

tral labels for stressful situations. The assumption here is that if you don't label or define the event as stressful, then your mind and, hence, your body won't undergo the fight or flight response because they won't be experiencing stress. For example, if you describe a public speaking situation as scary, your mind tells you that you are frightened and your body goes into fight or flight mode. If, however, you label the same public speaking situation as challenging, your mind tells you that you are energized and excited and your body can function at a heightened pace, but not an abnormal one!

Another way to reframe a stressful situation is to simultaneously acknowledge negative aspects and actively seek out positive elements of the same event.

> *Public speaking is intimidating, but it is not life-threatening.*

> *Public speaking makes me nervous, but I know I can write a good speech.*

> *I have never delivered a formal speech before, but I know I'm a good storyteller.*

## Positive Self-Talk

As a child, I was terribly afraid of the dentist and managed to survive my visits to his office by talking myself through it: *you can do this; it will be over with in the same amount of time it would take to watch an episode of Gilligan's Island; other people do this, you can, too*. Without realizing what I was doing, I was replacing my fearful and self-defeating thoughts with positive messages.

Sometimes we let our minds talk us into feeling nervous or more frightened than a situation truly warrants. You might recall getting worked up over an upcoming examination only to discover that it was really a piece of cake. All of that needless worrying caused you to feel more and more anxious. Left unchecked, it could have even prevented you from studying and actually led to a failing grade on the exam (i.e., negative self-fulfilling prophecy). Your thought process influenced your feelings of anxiety. With positive self-talk, we reverse the process. We send ourselves coping messages that help to decrease our anxiety instead of increase it. We create positive self-fulfilling prophecies! To engage in positive self-talk, complete the following:

## Applying the Chapter

1. Describe a public speaking situation that makes you feel anxious. Be sure to describe what you think makes you feel anxious about this particular event. (For example, first speech assignment, don't know classmates, speech is graded).

   _____

2. Describe your thoughts about this particular public speaking situation. Anxiety-producing thoughts are examples of your negative self-talk (e.g., you might think, "What could I possibly talk about for three to five minutes that others would be interested in?" or "I just know I'll lose my train of thought and start stumbling.").

   _____

   _____

   _____

   _____

   _____

   _____

   _____

   _____

3. Create positive self-talk messages to replace your negative thoughts. For example:

| Negative | Positive |
|---|---|
| 1. *What could I possibly talk about for three to five minutes that others would be interested in?* | 1. *I have a lot of ideas that would be of interest to others.* |
| 2. *I just know I'll lose my train of thought and start stumbling.* | 2. *I can stay focused and speak fluently for 3-5 minutes. I've done it in lots of other situations.* |

Negative                                          Positive

_____

_____

_____

_____

_____

4. Practice thinking positively! Each time you catch yourself engaging in negative self-talk, quickly change your thinking. Replace the self-destructive thought with a positive message. You might even consider putting a loose rubber band around your wrist and snapping it each time you catch yourself engaging in negative self-talk. The idea is not necessarily to inflict pain, but to provide you with an attention-getting, physical reminder to stop your negative thinking and replace it with positive self-talk!

While the strategies for minimizing your anxiety are the tools you need to take off your public speaking training wheels, the remaining section of this chapter will introduce you to techniques you can use to actually get on your "two-wheeler" and ride with confidence.

## How Do I Get Started?

Do not underestimate how much time it takes to prepare a good speech.

⌒ Tisha

You understand the importance of effective public speaking. You recognize various symptoms of public speaking anxiety. You know how to combat the proverbial butterflies. But how do you actually get started?

Many times students experience "speaker's block" when they hear their instructor make a speech assignment. Since the hardest part of preparing a speech is taking the first step and selecting a topic, it would be a good idea for you to create an inventory of your interests and experiences.

## Applying the Chapter

Instructions: Generate possible responses for each category.

1. **Memorable experiences** (once-in-a-lifetime events, embarrassing moments, emotional experiences, trips or vacations, turning points in your life, work-related events)

_____

_____

_____

_____

_____

_____

2. **Personal beliefs** (family, religion, politics, education)

_____

_____

_____

_____

_____

_____

3. **Hobbies and activities** (past, current, potential)

_____

_____

_____

_____

_____

_____

4. **Unique qualities** (personality traits, physical abilities, quirky characteristics, "gifts")

_____

_____

_____

_____

_____

_____

5. **Ambitions** (future plans, dream trip, career aspirations)

_____

_____

_____

_____

_____

_____

6. **Heroes and heroines** (real and fictional individuals)

_____

_____

_____

_____

_____

_____

7. **Pets** (current, past, "would love to have...")

_____

_____

_____

_____

_____

_____

"Would you tell me, please, which way I ought to go from here?"
(Alice speaks to Cheshire Cat)

"That depends a good deal on where you want to get to," said the Cat.

"I don't much care where—" said Alice.

"Then it doesn't matter which way you go," said the Cat.

"—so long as I get somewhere," Alice added as an explanation.

"Oh, you're sure to do that," said the Cat, "if you only walk long enough."[16]

From *Alice's Adventures in Wonderland*
By Lewis Carroll

When your instructor assigns a speech, you can easily review your list for potential topics. While this inventory may not always yield a topic appropriate for a particular speech assignment, it is a great place to begin.

Avoid "speaker's block" by reviewing your personal inventory for potential speech topics. If one of your entries fits the speech assignment, you are ready develop it further.

To get started on a speech, you have to know where "you ought to go," because, as Alice learned during her adventures, the destination greatly influences the path you take to get there. When you prepare a speech, you have to know where "you ought to go" with it. Are your remarks designed to inform, persuade, or entertain? Almost all speeches will pursue one of these three **general goals.** Does that mean that persuasive speeches can't simultaneously inform or entertain? No, but each speech will generally emphasize one of the three goals.

Once you know the general goal of your speech, you will need to select a specific topic. (Always consult your instructor to see if any speech topics are ill-advised for a particular assignment). We suggest you choose a topic that you are knowledgeable about and/or a topic that you feel strongly committed to for some reason. Being knowledgeable about the topic enhances your credibility as a speaker and builds your confidence. Being committed to the topic enables you to speak with conviction and passion. The more knowledgeable and committed you are to your topic, the more likely you are to hold your audience's attention, and the less likely you are to experience public speaking anxiety.

Listed below are three speech topics. Briefly describe how one speech topic could be developed into each of the three general speech goals.

> While preparing for my first speech I was wondering what topic would be interesting enough to keep my audience watching me, not the clock.
>
> ⁓ Gregory

## Topic 1: *Cruises*

To Inform: _____

_____

To Persuade: _____

_____

To Entertain: _____

_____

_____

## Topic 2: *Credit Cards*

To Inform: _____

_____

To Persuade: _____

_____

To Entertain: _____

_____

## Topic 3: *Ceremonies*

To Inform: _____

_____

To Persuade: _____

_____

To Entertain: _____

_____

Now that you understand the general goal of a speech, let us move on to the specific objective and thesis statement. The specific objective is an infinitive phrase that identifies both the general goal and the particular topic of your speech. The thesis statement is a declarative sentence that includes and summarizes the main points of the speech. Most of the speeches you develop for your public speaking class will have two to five main points. In the following example, the thesis statement indicates there are four main points for this informative speech on Chicago.[17]

| | |
|---|---|
| **Topic:** | Chicago |
| **General Goal:** | To inform |
| **Specific Objective:** | To inform my audience about the reasons for vacationing in Chicago, Illinois. |
| **Thesis Statement:** | Chicago offers a wide variety of entertainment that appeals to art, sports, historical, and shopping enthusiasts. |
| **Main Points:** | 1. Chicago offers a wide variety of entertainment that appeals to art enthusiasts. |
| | 2. Chicago offers a wide variety of entertainment that appeals to sports enthusiasts. |
| | 3. Chicago offers a wide variety of entertainment that appeals to historical enthusiasts. |
| | 4. Chicago offers a wide variety of entertainment that appeals to shopping enthusiasts. |

Revisit the speech topics you developed earlier. Select the three topics you generated for the informative general goal and create appropriate specific objectives and thesis statements for them. Identify the main points suggested by each thesis statement.

**1. General Goal:** To inform

**Specific Objective:** To inform my audience about _____

_____

_____

**Thesis Statement:** _____

_____

_____

**Main Points:** _____

_____

_____

_____

_____

_____

_____

**2. General Goal:** To inform

**Specific Objective:** To inform my audience about _____

_____

_____

**Thesis Statement:** _____

_____

_____

**Main Points:** _____

_____

_____

_____

_____

_____

**3. General Goal:** To inform

**Specific Objective:** To inform my audience about _____

_____

_____

**Thesis Statement:** _____

_____

_____

**Main Points:** _____

_____

_____

_____

_____

_____

## Ethically Speaking

Brainstorming exercises are great ways to begin or broaden a speech. An ethical speaker knows, however, that the appropriate follow-up to any brainstorming activity is research.

Sometimes it's difficult to create thesis statements. You have a speech topic in mind, but you are not sure how to develop it. There are several strategies you can use to help generate main points. These strategies include cubing, journalistic writing, and webbing.

### Cubing

Cubing is a brainstorming exercise that encourages you to explore six different aspects of a given topic.

To understand how this strategy works, consider the following exercise. Select an item from your living room or dormitory room (e.g., your computer or cell phone). Look at your object very carefully for a couple of minutes, making detailed observations before you engage in the following timed writing exercise. Write for one minute about what you see as you look at one side of your object. Do not lift your pen or pencil from you paper; rather, force yourself to write nonstop for the entire time. Do not worry about how neat or grammatically correct your writing is. The goal is to record as much detail as possible during the time allocated. When the minute is up, turn the object (or move to a different vantage point if the object is too large for you to move easily) and continue the writing exercise, describing in detail what you see on this side of the object. Keep turning the object (remember to look at the top and underside, if possible) until you have thoroughly described six different sides of the item.

# Cubing Exercise 1

Look around this classroom and approach it as you would the computer or cell phone. Spend one to two minutes describing each wall, the floor, and the ceiling as "sides" of the room.

Side 1:

Side 2:

Side 3:

Side 4:


Side 5:


Side 6:

# Cubing Exercise 2

Now that you have completed two cubing practice rounds using a physical object and this classroom, try the technique again using an idea you have for an informative speech. Revisit your personal inventory if you are having a difficult time selecting a speech topic. This time force yourself to write for at least three minutes on a different side, or aspect, of your topic. It is important for you to push yourself to think of different approaches and not stop when the "easy" ideas seem to run out. Remember, the goal of cubing is variety and volume. You want to create as many potential discussion points about as many different aspects of your topic as possible! This strategy may help you identify new avenues for your topic or enable you to generate examples that will add depth to your speech.

Informative Speech Topic

Side 1:

Side 2:

Side 3:

Side 4:

Side 5:

Side 6:

Once you have completed the cubing exercise in the activities section for this chapter, review what you have written. What jumps off of the page at you? What strikes you as attention getting? What can you group together? Do you see any themes emerging from what you've recorded? What examples could you further develop into supporting stories?

## ▨ Journalistic Writing

Another strategy that may help you generate main points for a speech assignment is commonly used by journalists. When writers develop stories for the newspaper, they must cover certain basic points for the reader: Who, What, When, Where, Why, and How? You can use this strategy to identify the basic points of your speech topic, to suggest the most interesting parts of the topic, or even to reveal the part of the topic you know the most (or the least!) about.

**Example:** Tae Kwan Do (Hobbies and Activities)

**Who:** Who created this form of martial art? Who are famous Tae Kwan Do martial artists? Who teaches lessons locally?

**What:** What is Tae Kwan Do? How does it differ from karate or judo? What goes on at a Tae Kwan Do tournament or competition? What do the different belt colors mean? What are the uniforms called? What is the school called?

**When:** When was it developed? When did it become an olympic sport?

**Where:** Where did it originate? Where is it practiced throughout the world? Where is it taught locally?

**Why:** Why did Tae Kwan Do develop originally? Why is Tae Kwan Do good for you? Why is the Korean language used during lessons?

**How:** How can you learn Tae Kwan Do? How old do you need to be? How do you become a blackbelt? How are lessons taught?

Revisit the topic you used for the earlier cubing exercise or select a new one from your personal inventory. Develop that topic as fully as you can using the journalistic writing technique. Try to create at least three questions for each basic point identified below:

**Topic:**

**Who:**

**What:**

**When:**

**Where:**

**Why:**

**How:**

Once you have completed the journalistic writing exercise, review what you have written. If you were writing for a newspaper, you would want to include basic information (who, what, when, where, why, and how) to provide a solid foundation, but you would also want to include new or novel information to keep the reader interested.

Review the questions you developed. Which ones do you think your audience would already know the answers to? Which ones do you think they might be most interested in? Which ones do you know the most about? Which ones would you have to investigate further?

### Webbing

A third strategy for creating main points for a speech is taught in literature and creative writing classes. Webbing asks you to select a topic, then simultaneously generate and organize related subtopics (or main points).

In a literature course, webbing could enable the reader to identify the characters, setting, and plot of a short story and to visualize the interrelationships between all of them. In a creative writing class or a speech class, webbing can be used to create a framework, rather than to analyze an existing story. In this instance, you graphically portray what you know about a chosen (or assigned) topic and the connections between the various elements. You can use this strategy to identify the main points of your speech topic, to illustrate relationships between the main points, and to indicate if your main points are balanced or developed equitably.

To begin weaving a web, select a speech topic and record it in the middle of a piece of paper. (We suggest you use printer paper instead of lined, writing paper for this exercise). Identify 3, 4, or 5 related subtopics and record them around your speech topic. Begin brainstorming additional information that supports, clarifies, or otherwise explains the subtopics. Use circles to group subpoints and lines to illustrate interrelationships, as demonstrated in the example below.

**Example:** Trip to Ireland (Ambitions—Dream Trip)

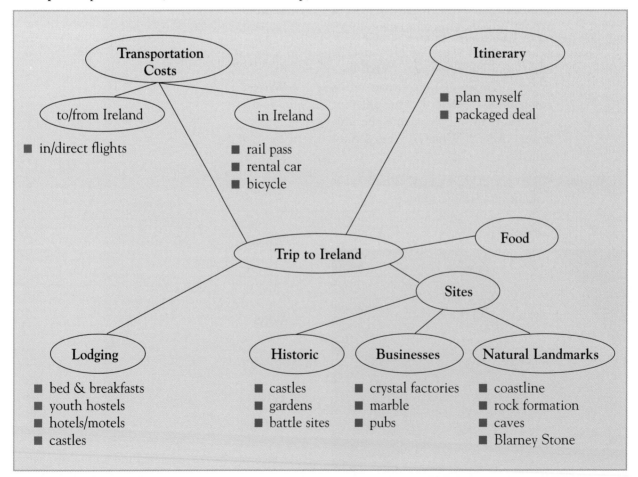

# Webbing Exercise

Revisit the topic you used for the earlier cubing exercise or journalistic writing, or select a new one from your personal inventory. Develop the topic as fully as you can using the webbing technique. Try to create as many elements or characteristics as you can for each subpoint identified in your web.

Once you have completed the webbing exercise, review what you created. Can you tell what your main points are? In terms of supporting elements or characteristics, are the points balanced? Which ones need additional research? Do any of the ideas overlap? How are they related? Can you use the connections between the points to create transitions in your speech?

At this time, you, unlike Alice in Wonderland in the earlier excerpt, have developed strategies that will guide you where "you ought to go." You should have a pretty good idea about how to get started on a speech. You know you must begin with one of three general speaking goals: to inform, to persuade, or to entertain. You know that the next step is to create a specific objective statement (remember it is written as an infinitive phrase) (e.g., to inform my audience about the most economical cruises tailored for college students). Finally, you have used three different strategies to create potential main points for a speech topic. The cubing exercise helped you to explore six unique aspects of a speech idea. Journalistic writing encouraged you to cover the basics of your speech topic by developing the who, what, when, where, why, and how questions. Finally, the webbing technique asked you to graphically illustrate the interrelationships of your main points. "At this rate," the Cheshire Cat might claim, "You are sure to get where you want to go."

## Final Thoughts

CONGRATULATIONS! The training wheels are off. I told you you could do it! You may still be a bit wobbly or feel a little unsure of yourself, but the rest of this textbook will help you cruise through the toughest of speaking assignments. You realize that a little anxiety will actually enhance your speech delivery. You know how to develop specific objectives and thesis statements. You are able to use three different strategies to identify main points and generate supporting elements. These skills, coupled with your "can-do" attitude, mean you no longer need the training wheels!

This chapter has explored the answers to four questions: Why do I need to know how to speak in public? Why do I get so anxious? How can I manage my public speaking anxiety? How do I get started? The next chapter will help you provide a solid foundation for your speeches through research, supporting material, and audience analysis. The ride is not over yet. There is much more to be discovered and developed. While most of us do not need to know how to ride a bicycle like Lance Armstrong, or deliver a speech like Martin Luther King, Jr., mastering the basics of either activity can be rewarding and empowering throughout your life.

### Ethically Speaking

Because "file speeches" are easily obtained on many campuses or readily found on the internet, you may be tempted to "borrow" someone else's work for your public speaking class. Granted, using these speeches saves you time and effort. But if you do, you are acting unethically and engaging in plagiarism, or intellectual theft. When you plagiarize, you present another person's written or spoken ideas as if they were your own. You steal. Crafting your own speech, however, enables you to speak with more conviction (because you are presenting ideas you believe in), with more enthusiasm (because you are presenting ideas you feel strongly about), and with more confidence (because you are presenting ideas that belong to you).

# ACTIVITIES

# Getting Started with Confidence

# Building Community and Reducing Communication Apprehension: A Case Study Approach[18]

## *Public Speaking 101: A Case Study*

**Directions:** Read the case study and answer the questions below. Be prepared to discuss your responses.

It was the first day of graded speeches in Public Speaking 101. Scott, the football team captain and a 4.0 student, was nearing the end of his speech on the use of steroids in high school athletics. He efficiently reviewed his main points and concluded his speech with a poignant story about a teenager who died because he wanted to play football as best as he possibly could, even if that meant taking drugs to do so.

"...Jason Robinson died in pursuit of excellence. There is no need for other youngsters to follow in his footsteps to an early grave."

His words ended on a quiet note and his classmates tentatively began to applaud before breaking out into a loud ovation. Breathing a sigh of relief, Scott gathered his notecards from the podium and began walking back to his desk in the third row of the classroom. His classmates were obviously impressed.

"Way to go, man! Where'd you learn to talk like that?"

"Geez, I'm glad I don't have to go next."

"Was that a true story or did you just make it all up?"

I asked the students to write down their comments on Scott's presentation while I finished writing my own evaluation. A couple of minutes passed and students began talking among themselves. I checked my sign-up sheet to see who would be delivering the next speech. It was Lisa. My heart went out to the timid girl sitting two seats away from me. Lisa had registered for my section of Public Speaking 101 last semester, but had dropped it before she had to make any oral presentations in the class. I knew she was nervous—probably more so than any of the other students. As she dropped her stack of 4x6 notecards and busily tried to reorganize them, a niggling little voice spoke in my mind, "Maybe you should have touched base with her last week to see if she was ready for the assignment." And then the voice of reason and practicality spoke up, "You don't have time to spoon feed every scared student."

"OK, Lisa. You're up next," I said in what I hoped was an encouraging tone of voice.

A petite, blonde girl wearing wire-rimmed glasses and clasping notecards, stood, took a few audible gulps of air, and walked toward the front of the classroom. Twenty-seven pairs of eyes looked in her direction. Lisa cleared her throat and placed the notecards on the podium as the class had been instructed to do. Her hands immediately grabbed onto the edge of the podium in a white-knuckled, death grip. A flush slowly inched its way from her chest to her throat. As her cheeks turned a blotchy, fire-engine red, she cleared her throat again and began to talk in a faltering, timid voice.

"My speech is on ... why children who commit violent crimes . . . should be tried as adults in the court system," she stumbled. "There are three reasons why children who commit violent crimes should have to face adult penalties for their actions..."

Lisa got off to a rough start. "How many times had I told the class not to introduce a speech with 'my speech is on' or 'today I want to talk about'," I asked myself. "Where was the clever attention getter no speech should be without?"

She continued, "The first reason why children who commit violent crimes should be tried as adults is because . . ." Lisa fumbled through her preview. As she arranged her notecards, one fell off the podium and slid under a nearby desk. No one else seemed to notice—except Lisa. She appeared to freeze in time as she apparently wondered whether to retrieve the card or try to continue without it. Her eyes looked scared and wild, like an animal caught by surprise in car headlights on a dark road.... Several seconds passed before Lisa decided what to do. . . . As she stepped out from behind the podium she bumped into it and the rest of the cards fluttered to the floor. That mishap was the proverbial last straw. With a dumbstruck expression on her face, Lisa abandoned her search for the lost notecard, turned, and ran out of the room. Tears of frustration and embarrassment already stained her blotchy cheeks. The classroom was uncomfortably quiet except for the haunting sound of Lisa's footsteps running down the tile hallway. With a sinking feeling in my stomach, I looked away from the empty doorway and faced twenty-seven pairs of eyes looking at me.

1.  What might have caused Lisa to feel/react the way she did?

2.  Pretend you were one of her classmates. How would you have felt?

3.  What was the instructor's reaction? How could s/he have prevented Lisa from "falling apart?"

4.  What could Lisa have done to prevent reacting the way she did?

5.  What advice can you give Lisa to help her prepare for the next speech assignment?

6.  How can the instructor and/or the students show support for Lisa when she returns to class?

# Personal Report of Public Speaking Anxiety (PRPSA)[19]

**Instructions:** This instrument is composed of 34 statements concerning feelings about communicating with other people. Work quickly; just record your first impression. Indicate the degree to which the statements apply to you by marking whether you:

**1=Strongly Agree**
**2=Agree**
**3=Are Undecided**
**4=Disagree**
**5=Strongly Disagree**

_____ 1. While preparing for giving a speech, I feel tense and nervous.

_____ 2. I feel tense when I see the words *speech* and *public speech* on a course outline.

_____ 3. My thoughts become confused and jumbled when I am giving a speech.

_____ 4. Right after giving a speech I feel that I have had a pleasant experience.

_____ 5. I get anxious when I think about a speech coming up.

_____ 6. I have no fear of giving a speech.

_____ 7. Although I am nervous just before starting a speech, I soon settle down after starting and feel calm and comfortable.

_____ 8. I look forward to giving a speech.

_____ 9. When the instructor announces a speaking assignment in class, I can feel myself getting tense.

_____ 10. My hands tremble when I am giving a speech.

_____ 11. I feel relaxed while giving a speech.

_____ 12. I enjoy preparing for a speech.

_____ 13. I am in constant fear of forgetting what I prepared to say.

_____ 14. I get anxious if someone asks me something about my topic that I do not know.

_____ 15. I face the prospect of giving a speech with confidence.

_____ 16. I feel that I am in complete possession of myself while giving a speech.

_____ 17. My mind is clear when giving a speech.

_____ 18. I do not dread giving a speech.

_____ 19. I perspire just before starting a speech.

_____ 20. My heart beats very fast just as I start a speech.

_____ 21. I experience considerable anxiety while sitting in the room just before my speech starts.

_____ 22. Certain parts of my body feel very tense and rigid while giving a speech.

_____ 23. Realizing that only a little time remains in a speech makes me very tense and anxious.

_____ 24. While giving a speech I can control my feelings of tension and stress.

_____ 25. I breathe faster just before starting a speech.

_____ 26. I feel comfortable and relaxed in the hour or so just before giving a speech.

_____ 27. I do poorer on speeches because I am anxious.

_____ 28. I feel anxious when the teacher announces the date of a speaking assignment.

_____ 29. When I make a mistake while giving a speech, I find it hard to concentrate on the parts that follow.

_____ 30. During an important speech I experience a feeling of helplessness building up inside of me.

_____ 31. I have trouble falling asleep the night before a speech.

_____ 32. My heart beats very fast while I present a speech.

_____ 33. I feel anxious while waiting to give my speech.

_____ 34. While giving a speech, I get so nervous I forget facts I really know.

To determine your score on the PRPSA, complete the following steps:

1. Add the scores for items 1, 2, 3, 5, 9, 10, 13, 14, 19, 20, 21, 22, 23, 25, 27, 28, 29, 30, 31, 32, 33, and 34.

2. Add the scores for items 4, 6, 7, 8, 11, 12, 15, 16, 17, 18, 24, and 26.

3. Complete the following formula:

$$PRPSA = 132 - (\text{total from step one}) + (\text{total from step two})$$

Your score should range between 34 and 170. If your score is below 34 or above 170, you have made a mistake in computing the score.

| SCORES BETWEEN | INDICATE |
|---|---|
| 34 and 84 | Low anxiety about public speaking (5%) |
| 85 and 92 | Moderately low level of anxiety about public speaking (5%) |
| 93 and 110 | Moderate anxiety in most public speaking situations (20%) |
| 111 and 119 | Moderately high level of anxiety about public speaking (30%) |
| 120 and 170 | Very high level of anxiety about public speaking (40%) |

*MOST people score in the moderate to high categories!

**Note:** Complete one of these forms at the beginning of the semester and one after your final speech. Compare your total scores as well as your responses to individual items.

# References

1. Morreale, S., Osborn, M., & Pearson, J. (2000). Why communication is important: A rationale for the centrality of the study of communication. *Journal of the Association for Communication Administration, 29* (1), 1-25.

2. Peterson, M. (1997). Personnel interviewers' perceptions of the importance and adequacy of applicants' communication skills. *Communication Education, 46,* 287-291.

3. Graduates are not prepared to work in business. (1997, June). *Association Trends,* p. 4.

4. Winsor, J., Curtis, D., & Stephens, R. (1997). National preferences in business and communication education: A survey update. *Journal of the Association for Communication Administration, 3,* p. 170-179.

5. U.S. Department of Labor. (1992). What work requires of schools: A SCANS report for America 2000. *Economic Development Review, 10,* p. 16-19.

6. Stress: The silent killer. (2002). Retrieved August 10, 2003, from http://www.holisticonline.com/stress/stress_GAS.htm

7. Allen, R. P. (1983). *Human stress: Its nature and control.* NY: Macmillan Publishing Company, p.8.

8. Richmond, V. P., & McCroskey, J. C. (1985). *Communication apprehension, avoidance, and effectiveness.* Scottsdale, AZ: Gorsuch Scarisbrick, p. 35.

9. Berliner, B. (1992). *The book of answers.* NY: Simon and Schuster, p.15.

10. Richmond, V. P., & McCroskey, J. C. (1985). *Communication apprehension, avoidance, and effectiveness.* Scottsdale, AZ: Gorsuch Scarisbrick, p. 36.

11. Reuters Health. (2001). *What is stress?* Retrieved July 29, 2003, from http://www.reutershealth.com/wellconnected/doc31.html

12. Oxford Brookes Medical Centre. (1999). *Managing stress.* Retrieved July 29, 2003, from http://www.brookes.ac.uk/student/services/health/stress.html

13. Better Health Channel. (2002). *Blushing explained.* Retrieved July 29, 2003, from http://www.betterhealth.vic.gov.au/bhcv2/bhcarticles.nsf/pages/Blushing_explained?

14. 18 holes in his mind. (1995). In J. Canfield, & M. Hansen (Eds.), *A 2nd Helping of Chicken Soup for the Soul.* Deerfield Beach, FL: Health Communications, Inc., p. 235-236

15. Posen, D. (n.d.). *Tips and techniques for dealing with stress.* Retrieved July 18, 2003, from http://www.davidposen.com/pages/tips/tips11.html

16. Carroll, L. (1884). *Alice's adventure in wonderland* (The Millenium Fulcrum Edition 3.0.). [Electronic version]. Retrieved on August 18, 2003, from http://www2.cs.cmu.edu/People/rgs/alice-table.html

17. Seay, R. (2003). *Informative speech outline for COM 161.* Unpublished manuscript, Murray State University, Murray, KY

18. Tillson, L. D. (1995, Summer). Building community and reducing communication apprehension: A case study approach. *The Speech Communication Teacher,* 9(4), pp.4-5.

19. Richmond, V. P., & McCroskey, J. C. (1985). *Communication apprehension, avoidance, and effectiveness.* Scottsdale, AZ: Gorsuch Scarisbrick, p. 113-114.

# 3

# Building the Foundation of Your Presentation

## CHAPTER PREVIEW

**1** The relationship between audience adaptation, audience analysis, and research

**2** Conducting audience analysis with research

**3** How ethos, logos, and pathos relate to the research process

**4** Why research is the key to building an effective presentation

**5** Using research to support ideas in a presentation

**6** Enhancing speaker credibility through research

**7** Resources for research

> There are no bad speech topics . . . just bad ways of developing them.
>
> ⏤Dr. Jim Gibson, University of Missouri-Columbia

Don't forget this principle! Any topic can be made to seem "exciting" or made to seem "boring." It's your choice. It all depends on how you choose to develop your presentation.

When delivering a presentation, we all want to make a good impression. Unfortunately, most people try to find a topic they believe the audience will find "exciting" or "interesting." Let's face it, 90 percent of all topics you can think of would bore most people. What is "exciting" about deodorant, car tires, carpeting, or breakfast cereal? For most of us, NOTHING! But advertisers find ways to make each of these products interesting and desirable to consumers. You too can take any product, process, problem, service, or issue and find a way to hold the audience's attention, extend their knowledge, and convince them that you are right. By using a variety of images, examples, facts, stories, and testimony, you can build an exciting, interesting, and effective presentation.

When making presentations, you never want to bore the audience by only telling them what they already know or by being so sophisticated or technical that the audience loses interest. While you cannot prepare a presentation that satisfies all the members, the goal is to extend the knowledge of the majority of audience members.

## How to Conduct an Audience Analysis

When people first meet, they begin asking each other questions and telling about themselves to help reduce the initial uncertainty of the situation.[1] Similarly, the audience analysis allows you to size-up your audience so you have some idea about who they are, what they are like, and how they will respond. This information will make you a more confident, well-prepared speaker. Here are some of the basic questions you want answered about your audience.

## Three Areas of Audience Analysis

An audience analysis includes: (1) a **demographic analysis,** (2) a **situational analysis,** and (3) an **attitudinal analysis.** Let's start with the goals of the demographic analysis.

### Demographic Analysis

A demographic analysis is a descriptive summary of the audience's objective characteristics or traits. Descriptive characteristics you may need to measure include the age, income level, rank, race, gender, and/or educational level of your audience members. For example, delivering a presentation to a room of 20-year-old men is very different than presenting to a room full of 60-year-old women. While we cannot say all men think one way and all women think another, evaluate which of your examples, facts, or illustrations may be gender biased and which would appeal to both genders. Similarly, you need to present a more sophisticated and well-supported presentation to a highly educated audience (e.g., lawyers). However, you would need to use less sophisticated and technical language with a minimally educated audience (e.g., 6th graders). If you were delivering a presentation on Medicare benefits, it would be important to know how many Republicans, how many Democrats, and how many medical professionals are in your audience. Other topics may have more relevance to audience members' religious backgrounds, ethnic or racial heritage, and/or marital status.

Combined, these demographics can help you select the most appropriate content based on the audience's similarities and differences. By identifying and measuring these important demographic traits, you can begin to understand the types of people you will be addressing and which strategies will be most effective with your unique audience. Here is a summary of some "demographics" that may have relevance to your presentation topic.

## TIPS

**Demographic questions to ask yourself**

- Gender—What percentage of my audience is female and what percentage is male?

- Age—What age groups are represented in my audience?

- Educational Level—What educational levels are represented in my audience?

- Group Affiliations—What political, religious, social, and/or professional groups are represented in my audience?

- Socio-cultural Background—What social and cultural backgrounds are represented in my audience (e.g., members' country or state of origin, economic background, ethnic or racial heritage, and/or marital status)?

### Situational Analysis

Always carefully consider the situation or setting in which you will be presenting. Consider the situational variables of presenting at a large church on a Sunday morning. This situation would call for a different delivery style and content than presenting at the Monday morning departmental meeting at work. Likewise, the occasion of an *employee orientation meeting* would have very different situational demands than presenting at a *retirement ceremony*. Here is a brief list of some key situational variables you should consider and adapt to when delivering a presentation.

## TIPS

**Situational questions to ask yourself**

- Time—Time-of-day, day-of-the-week, month-of-the-year? How long can I speak?

- Place—Will I present indoors or outdoors? Will I speak sitting or standing? What seating will the audience have available? How large is the room, how bright or dim is the lighting, and will there be a microphone and podium? What visual/audio equipment will be available? What sources of noise or distractions may be present?

- Size of the Audience—How many people will be in the audience?

- Context of the Presentation—What is the occasion of the presentation? What recent presentations has the audience heard? What recent events have occurred that may influence the audience's thinking?

### Attitudinal Analysis

An **attitudinal analysis** is the most important step in analyzing your audience. An attitudinal analysis is an assessment of your audience's general disposition (e.g., attitudes, beliefs, and values) and knowledge level of your topic. While it is important to understand your audience's demographic characteristics (e.g., age and gender) and the situation in which you'll be presenting, your most important insights come from analyzing your audience's attitudes, behaviors, and knowledge level. Understanding what your audience likes, values, believes, and desires allows you to create a presentation that is easy to listen to and retain. By effectively adapting your content to their lives, needs, hopes, habits, etc., you have the best chance of delivering a clear, interesting, and credible presentation. Here are some of the key issues you'll want to examine in your attitudinal analysis.

---

**TIPS**

**Attitudinal questions to ask yourself**

■ Habits and behaviors—What related habits and behaviors do audience members practice?

■ Knowledge—How much knowledge do audience members have of my topic?

■ Attitudes—What likes and dislikes (or preference) do audience members have related to my topic?

■ Values—How much importance does my audience place on issues or things related to my topic?

■ Beliefs—What does my audience think to be true or untrue related to my topic?

■ Ethics—What related behaviors or actions do audience members believe to be right or wrong?

■ Motivations—What motivates the members of my audience? What needs and desires do they have (e.g., the need for power, success, love, creativity, or recognition)?

---

## ▓ Where Do I Get Demographic, Situational, and Attitudinal Information?

Now that you understand the type of information you want to gather in an audience analysis, the next issue is finding the demographic, situational, and attitudinal information you need. But, where do you look? Audience analysis information can be gathered through several different sources:

1. *Ask the person who invited or gave you permission to present.* He/she will be familiar with the situation, the demographic composition, and some of the attitudes/beliefs/etc. of your audience.

2. *Ask someone who has presented to this audience in the past.* Past speakers can give you insight into the type of audience members you will be addressing, the situation, and how they reacted to previous presentations.

3. *Talk to individuals who will be members of your audience.* When possible, talk to individuals who are members of your future audience. They can give you first-hand information about the speaking setting, the audience members, and their dispositions. These individuals can give you great insights into the wants, needs, and knowledge levels represented in your audience.

4. *Read published information about your audience.* Suppose you were presenting at a manufacturing tradeshow or the annual meeting of a national organization. Newspaper articles, internet websites, and company/organizational publications are often valuable sources for information about the type of individuals who are members of these organizations or work in these industries.

5. *Survey members of your audience.* A written survey is the best method for gathering demographic and attitudinal information from your audience. It allows you to ask specific questions about your audience's behaviors, dispositions, beliefs, and knowledge. While this is a common practice in the public speaking classroom, having the opportunity to distribute a survey to the employees of an organization or members of a community group is rarely possible. Typically, you would not have a chance to do such before a sales presentation, business meeting, or presentation to a local organization.

## ▓ *Advice for Creating Audience Analysis Surveys*

If you do have the opportunity to develop and administer a written survey of your audience's demographic and attitudinal data, there are three types of questions you can use to gather information: (1) **closed-ended questions**, (2) **scale questions,** and (3) **open-ended questions.** First, **closed-ended** (or fixed-alternative) questions provide respondents with options from which they can select the appropriate answer. Examples of closed-ended questions include true/false, agree/disagree, or multiple-choice questions (e.g., Circle one: Male or Female or Check one: Democrat____, Republican____, Independent____). Second, **scale questions** measure the respondents' impressions or reactions to a question or statement. If you wanted to measure the audience's feelings about current economic conditions, you could propose a statement (e.g., "The economy will be stronger one year from today") and have respondents rate their reactions (strongly disagree—1—2—3—4—5—strongly agree). Finally, open-ended questions do not provide options from which respondents select answers. **Open-ended questions** allow respondents to freely answer questions in their own words. Open-ended questions can provide great insight into the dispositions, beliefs, and actions of the audience (e.g., "If you did vote in the last presidential election, explain the most important factors influencing your voting decision." "What qualities are you looking for in our next U.S. President?" "If you did not vote in the last presidential election, please explain why you did not.").

Clearly, these three types of questions produce different types of useful data. The key is to select the best combination of these questions to reveal important information about your audience's demographic and attitudinal traits. Here are some helpful guidelines to keep in mind when creating an audience analysis survey.

1. *Keep them brief.* The survey should be brief enough that an audience member can complete it in 5-10 minutes. Remember that closed-ended questions take the least amount of time and open-ended questions take the most time to answer.

2. *Ask clear, unambiguous questions.* Vague questions produce vague answers. Specific questions will provide more helpful information. For example, "How should society punish criminals?" is too vague. Providing questions about specific crimes will elicit clearer insight into respondents' beliefs about "appropriate punishments for criminals."

3. *Carefully plan and pretest to ensure your survey will elicit the desired information.* It is a great idea to ask a few friends to complete the survey before you distribute it to audience members. Based on their feedback, you can determine if questions need to be revised, added, or deleted, and if the survey questionnaire is an appropriate length.

## ▥ Building Your Case and Selling Your Ideas

Conducting research is the key to building a solid presentation. Just as a lawyer works to create a convincing courtroom case, you also must build an "iron-clad" argument (i.e., an argument that cannot easily be damaged or destroyed). In a criminal case, prosecuting lawyers must present enough compelling evidence to convince a jury or judge that the defendant is guilty beyond a reasonable doubt. If successful at presenting the right evidence in the right way, the prosecuting lawyer wins a conviction and the defendant is punished. What is the difference between an acquittal and a conviction? *Answer: the quality and combination of evidence and ideas presented in the courtroom.*

Likewise, when a sales representative goes to sell a product or service, the customer will always have a number of reasons not to buy (e.g., "It's too expensive . . . I don't need it . . . I buy from a different company . . . I don't know you"). A sales representative must convince the customer of the value, benefits, and advantages of his/her product or service. If the customer does not buy into the sales presentation, then no business is conducted and they go away empty handed. What is the difference between a successful and an unsuccessful sales presentation? *Answer: the quality and combination of evidence and ideas presented to the customer.*

Every speaker has the same goals as the lawyer and the sales representative. Speakers want to win over the hearts and minds of their audience by delivering the very best presentation. For this reason, you must conduct research to find the best combination of supporting materials to build a solid foundation for your presentation.

## ▥ Conducting Research

You should now understand that by analyzing your audience and the speaking situation, you will have information to guide how you create the foundation of your presentation. As stated earlier, to give your presentation a *solid foundation,* you must find credible,

logical, and interesting supporting materials. After all, a presentation's "foundation" must be solid if you are going to be an effective speaker . . . to win over the audience, sell a product, win a conviction, etc. The following will review both the sources of supporting materials and the different types of support you will want to consider using in your presentation.

### Where Do I Research My Topic?

Building a solid presentation requires that you find a wide variety of supporting materials from a wide variety of sources. To create an accurate and credible presentation, find a vast number of expert opinions, examples, news reports, and/or facts to support your presentation. If your presentation were based on information taken from only two websites or from three newspaper articles, your presentation would be very biased, underdeveloped, and poorly supported. Therefore, let's examine some of the various sources from which you can gather supporting materials for your presentation.

- Library
- Internet and Search Engines
- Corporate and Organizational Information
- Mass Media and Real People

### Library

**The best resource in any library is a librarian.** Librarians love to search for information! They have extensive training and experience in how to help you find information from around the world. Realize that a library is not a *warehouse* for books.

Rather, today's library is a *gateway* to valuable information that is stored both on-site and across the globe. Conducting research is like a "treasure hunt" and librarians possess the "map" to the "world of information." Librarians don't know what you'll find but they know where you should look to find related information. With the help of librarians, you can make the most of three key library resources: (1) library catalogs, (2) interlibrary loans, and (3) indexes and databases.

LIBRARY CATALOGS. Today, most libraries use electronic catalogs to list the books, journal titles, newspapers, microforms, videotapes, CDs, etc. owned by the library. These electronic catalogs generally allow you to search by author, subject, and/or title of the work and provide the location within the library to find these resources. The variety of resources available through your library is extensive: dictionaries, yearbooks, encyclopedias, thesauruses, newspapers, anthologies, bibliographies, biographies, directories, catalogs, atlases, textbooks, government documents, journals, histories, genealogies, magazines, theoretical manuscripts, manuals, films, music, scientific reports, corporate/financial reports, fiction, and more! All of these resources may be potential sources for information on your topic located through the library catalog.

However, all libraries are limited in what they can afford to purchase. It may be necessary to search the catalogs of other community, university, state (e.g., Kentucky Virtual Library, http://www.kyvl.org), or national libraries (e.g., The Library of Congress, http://www.lcweb.loc.gov). Your library's homepage and/or librarians can assist you in locating the Internet homepages and electronic catalogs of these libraries.

INTERLIBRARY LOAN. Because your library has a limited collection of books, journals, newspapers, reports, CDs, etc., your library may offer "interlibrary loan" services. If you find citations to resources not locally available, the interlibrary loan staff can borrow these articles, books, reports, etc, owned by other libraries for your use. Be sure to check with your library to see if there are additional costs associated with borrowing the desired materials from other libraries.

INDEXES AND DATABASES. While there are still numerous *print* indexes and databases being published, searching through electronic indexes and databases is quick and convenient. These password-protected indexes and databases (e.g., EBSCOHost, FirstSearch, Infotrac, and PsycINFO) allow library patrons to search through a variety of information sources (e.g., journal articles, book chapters, news reports, conference papers, government documents, corporate and financial reports). These indexes and databases allow you to find and sort through the most recent articles, reports, book chapters, etc, related to your topic. Electronic searches provide the citation (e.g., author, date, source, page numbers, etc.) and often provide a brief abstract of the information. Some databases provide the citation plus the fulltext, allowing you to read through or print the entire document.

Your library subscribes to these indexes and databases which have annual fees ranging from several hundred to tens-of-thousands of dollars per year. Keep in mind that all databases are limited due to the costs associated with publishing and indexing. Publishers sell to libraries direct access to their information or they sell it to database companies who then index and store full text versions of the information. Not every helpful resource will be listed in every index. For example, EBSCOHost will index thousands of the most respected and widely circulated journals, but you won't find all the journals indexed that relate to your topic. Also, electronic indexes and databases start with the most recent information and gradually add earlier information over time. For example, you may be able to find a 1995 article from *Fortune*, but the same database may not list *Fortune* articles published prior to 1990. Be sure to check on the limitations of any index or database when conducting research. Due to limitations in electronic databases, a traditional "print" index may be the best source for information. Librarians can guide you through this maze of indexes and databases.

### The Internet and Search Engines

The Internet is the information superhighway! This resource has changed the way the world communicates, shares information, markets products, promotes ideas, and entertains itself. We turn to the Internet for the latest information, news, opinions, and trends. The Internet is also a tremendous vehicle for democracy, allowing anyone with access to participate in sharing opinions and ideas. Clearly,

the Internet has the potential to greatly enhance the quantity and quality of information you find to support your presentation.

Like any trip on a superhighway, you should know where you want to go and how to get there safely. The challenge of the Internet is to find accurate, unbiased information from credible sources. Because there are no regulations on Internet postings, people and organizations are virtually unlimited on the opinions and information they can choose to include on their sites. You have to carefully evaluate the credibility and accuracy of that information. You will need to determine the author of the information, when the information was posted, and if it may be biased due to the sponsorship or organizational affiliation of the website.

Keep in mind that all Internet search engines (e.g., Yahoo, http://www.yahoo.com, or Excite, http://www.excite.com) will have strengths and weaknesses. Search engines will have the most popular topical areas divided into subject areas (e.g., news, entertainment, travel, business, sports, health), but each uses different processes for finding, prioritizing, and listing results. Finding the best information often depends on which search engine you use with which key words (or combinations of key words). Your best bet is to use a variety of search engines and related key words as you begin your Internet research. The search engines will take you to the free information posted by organizations, individuals, companies, etc.; however, some of the best information may cost you money to access.

### Corporate and Organizational Information

While corporate and organizational information may be found through the library's catalog, indexes, and databases, you may need to go directly to these corporations and/or organizations for information. Although organizations or corporations are obviously biased, they are very valuable sources of publications and resources that may not make it into your local library. Corporations and organizations often have individuals or entire departments (e.g., Public Relations or Public Affairs) devoted to generating and distributing information about the goals, successes, and actions of the company or organization. Looking through the company's or organization's homepage can often provide you access to a wide variety of information. By finding their mailing addresses, phone numbers, or websites, it is also possible to request that particular types of information are sent to you. Annual reports, position papers, press releases, informational videotapes, fact sheets, and other types of published materials are generally available upon request.

To balance the bias of the information provided by the corporation or organization, you may ask their competitors and customers their observations and opinions. For example, competitors can provide additional information about the competitive environment, how the companies perceive one another, and the key strengths and weaknesses of each. Likewise, customers can tell us their impressions of how well the organization or company lives up to their mission, why they use the company or organization, and specific examples or stories about the company or organization that your audience may find interesting.

### ▌ *Mass-Media and Real People*

So far you can turn to the library, the Internet, and the company/organization for information. However, a couple other sources may also aid your research efforts. First, don't forget other forms of mass-media and entertainment as potential information sources: television news, documentaries, radio broadcasts, speeches, concerts, special reports, films, plays, sporting events, music, talk shows, educational programs, television comedies, dramas, cartoons, billboards, advertisements, how-to shows, reality shows, etc. All of these are full of examples, stories, statistics, illustrations, and facts that can be used to help support your presentation.

Second, interviewing "real people" who have special knowledge or experience related to your topic may help your presentation (e.g., local experts, your neighbors, business owners, or your friends). Your community includes medical professionals, educators, lawyers, ministers, managers, bankers, technicians, government officials, business owners, and a host of other "experts" who can provide you information. If you are giving a persuasive presentation on the need to update highway infrastructure, interview the local "experts" on road and bridge conditions (e.g., the owner of a local paving company or the director of the county highway department). If you are giving a presentation on small business development, interview the president of the local Chamber of Commerce. Likewise, do not

overlook interviewing your neighbors and friends. While we may not know them personally, the fact that you do and they have related experience or knowledge makes them an ideal resource. For example, if you are giving a presentation on cancer prevention and you share the story of your neighbor who's spouse died of cancer, the reality and credibility of your presentation dramatically increases. Remember, local experts, neighbors, and friends are all valuable sources of support.

---

### TIPS

**When conducting research interviews**

■ Interview last—Do your other research first so you know exactly what information you hope to get from the interviewees.

■ Sell them on the interview—Tell them why you want to interview them and what type of questions you will ask.

■ Time limit—Tell them how much time the interview will take.

■ Recording the interview—If you want to record the interview, ask permission first.

■ Don't improvise—Formulate a short set of clear interview questions.

■ Take the list of interview questions with you.

■ Take thorough notes during the interview and review your notes to add missing details after the interview.

■ Respect anonymity—If they ask to remain anonymous, do not identify them by name.

---

### ▌ What Types of Supporting Material Could I Use?

When looking for types of supporting materials, follow the principle of "The more the merrier!" The more types of support (e.g., definitions, facts, examples, statistics, opinions, and stories), the more "building blocks" you'll have with which to construct your foundation. But remember, you'll be selecting the most appropriate building blocks based on your audience analysis. Therefore, some supporting materials you find will work and other information would be inappropriate for your audience. This is why the greater the variety of supporting materials, the better presentation you can potentially construct. Let's quickly review a variety of helpful forms of supporting materials.

1. **Facts and examples.** Everyone wants to hear concrete facts and examples. If you were making a presentation on dieting, giving examples of new laws that regulate these facilities is a concrete way to support your presentation. Saying, "My neighbor lost 15 pounds in three months by eliminating fried food from his diet" would be a concrete fact the audience can understand. The more vivid and specific the facts and examples, the easier it will be for your audience to understand and retain your ideas.

2. **Explanations.** Explanations get beyond the simple, fact of *what* something is to specifying the *how and why* something works. For example, it is not sufficient to say to a customer, "My company's products will save you money and time." The customer will want to hear *how and why* it will save both money and time. Audience members would want to know *why* eliminating fried food from their diet is the key to losing weight. Saying, "Research states that fried foods are bad for your health" is a good start, but individuals want to know *how bad it is* and *why it is bad.* Explanations help create deeper understanding by describing the relationships and connections between causes and effects.

3. **Analogies.** An analogy is either a literal comparison or a figurative comparison between two

things. To draw a comparison between two laws, towns, people, or events would be a literal analogy (e.g., "Last year's hurricane season was the same as the 1995 season. They both had mild, wet summers followed by turbulent August and September weather patterns."). However, a figurative analogy draws comparisons between two dissimilar things to highlight unexpected similarities (e.g., "It was a disaster! Last year's hurricane season was as unpredictable as a room full of 7th grade boys.").

4. **Definitions.** A definition, either from a dictionary or in your own words, helps to provide clarification and a common starting point from which to educate your audience. Abstract terms and technical jargon often need to be defined for audience members. For example, if you were going to give a presentation on "The American Dream" or "The Challenge of Stem Cell Research," either of these phrases would need to be clearly defined to ensure the audience members shared a common point of reference to understand your presentation.

5. **Opinions and testimonies.** An opinion or testimony is a statement of the experiences, beliefs, or feelings of an individual. Brief opinions or more developed testimonies can be taken from either literary figures (e.g., a quote from a character in fiction . . . Tom Sawyer, Scarlet O'Hara, Mickey Mouse), experts (e.g., statements from historical or current experts on a subject), or even from your peers and friends. Citing the opinions or testimonies of literary figures, respected experts, and/or your peers is a memorable, effective, and credible way to support your presentation.

6. **Stories.** Everyone loves a good story. If you say to an audience full of adults, "Let me tell you a story," they will all begin listening as if they were children back in elementary school. People will rarely listen to 30 minutes of facts, examples, definitions, and statistics without losing interest. However, 30 minutes of "storytelling" is sure to keep them engaged (just like a 30 minute episode of your favorite television show). We are all familiar with the basic structure of a story—a situation, characters, conflict, dramatic climax, and a resolution of the problem leading to some insight about life. Likewise, stories can help you frame the introduction of

your presentation, help illustrate key ideas in the body of your presentation, and assist you in concluding the presentation. When looking for relevant stories, you are free to draw from your personal life and experiences, factual stories about others you may or may not know, or fictional stories to illustrate a point (but always let the audience know it is fictitious). Clearly, good stories, either brief or thoroughly developed, can add life to your presentation by making your topic vivid, engaging, and memorable.

7. ***Statistics and numbers.*** As you can now see, statistics and numbers are only one form of supporting material. The use of statistics and numbers tends to bring an air of credibility and objectivity to your presentation. For example, saying that "Four out of five dentists recommend chewing sugar-free gum" sounds impressive. However, how many dentists did they survey? You may also be able to find four dentists to say that the amount of sugar in chewing gum is so small that it makes no difference what type of gum people chew. If you blindly claim "the numbers speak for themselves" or use too many numbers, your audience is likely to become confused and is not likely to believe you. Here is a set of guidelines to assist you in the use of statistics and numbers.

   a. *Less is best when using statistics and numbers. Using too many statistics will overwhelm, confuse, and bore your audience.*

   b. *Round off statistics and numbers. Telling the audience that "632,014 U.S. children were born last year in poverty," is too confusing. It is best to say, "over 600,000." It is better to say, "75 percent of all our customers . . . " rather than saying "Exactly 73.67 percent of our customers . . . ." Numbers that are rounded off, without being "misrepresented," are easier to retain and are more effective.*

   c. *Interpret statistics for the audience. Because numbers don't speak for themselves, your job is to interpret statistics for your audience. For example, a 25 percent payroll tax increase sounds huge! How much is "a 25 percent payroll tax increase" in real dollars per taxpayer? If a 25 percent tax increase resulted in an extra $50 dollars, per taxpayer, per year that sounds much more reasonable than if a 25 percent increase*

resulted in an extra $500 in annual taxes per taxpayer. Find ways to make these statistics understandable and relevant to the audience.

   d. *Use representative, reliable statistics and numbers. Using earthquake statistics from California would not apply to an audience from Kentucky. Be sure to check if your statistics are representative of all cases or apply to only to specific groups, areas, or industries. Furthermore, you must check to see if the statistics are from a reliable source. The National Inquirer may not provide as reliable economic data as would The Wall Street Journal.*

   e. *Use visual aids to show statistics and numbers. A picture truly is worth a thousand words when it comes to statistics and numbers. Due to the complexity of numbers and statistical data, visuals will help you display your numbers more*

## ETHICS: Am I telling the truth?

The ethical dilemma of conducting research is to ensure that you have thoroughly researched the topic, accurately interpreted that information, truthfully represented these ideas, and cited the sources from which you gathered it. Telling "the truth, the whole truth, and nothing but the truth" is the outcome of good research. To help ensure you are being ethical, ask yourself . . .

- Am I taking supporting materials out of context?

- Am I exaggerating or misrepresenting facts?

- Am I using single facts or examples to make sweeping generalizations?

- Am I finding enough relevant information to fully represent my topic?

- Am I citing the sources of my supporting materials?

- Am I omitting important information the audience should know to make an informed decision?

- Am I presenting all sides of the issue?

*clearly, increase your audience's understanding, and increase audience retention of numerical information.*

### Which Supporting Materials Should I Use?

Where the previous section followed the principle of "the more the merrier," your new dilemma will be sorting through your collection of supporting material to select the very best supporting materials. At this point, you now need to adopt the philosophy that, "Less is best!" Provide enough foundation and support to fit the audience and situation but don't try to include all that you have found. In fact, you will only be using a small percentage of everything you discovered. You are transitioning from an extensive understanding of *"what could be said"* to a more focused and refined sense of *"what should be said."*

Here is a list of criteria to use when selecting which sources and types of supporting materials to include in your presentation.

---

## TIPS

**Criteria for selecting supporting materials . . .**

■ How relevant is your supporting material to your purpose and main ideas?

■ How vivid and interesting is your supporting material?

■ How appropriate is your supporting material for your audience?

■ How difficult will it be to explain your supporting material to this audience?

■ How timely is the supporting material? Is it too dated or is it timeless?

■ How credible and reliable is the source of your supporting material?

■ How biased is the source of your support?

■ How accurate is your supporting material?

■ How representative is the supporting material? Does it apply generally or is it a limited example? Is it consistent with other supporting materials?

---

## Building Main Ideas and Citing Sources

One of the major questions new students of public address have is, "How do I include all this supporting material and cite sources in my presentation?" Remember that you need to cite the sources of your material to enhance your credibility. Keep in mind that not every fact, definition, example, statistic, and story must be fully cited with source, year, page, etc. Writing the outline of a presentation is not the same as writing a well-supported and appropriately cited essay. However, you must include enough supporting materials and cite enough sources to create a credible, understandable, and interesting presentation.

The following four-step process will illustrate how to integrate supporting materials and cite sources in order to create a solid presentation.

### Four Steps of Building Main Ideas and Citing Sources[2]

I. State your main idea

II. Cite your source(s)

III. Present supporting material
**Repeat steps II and III until the main idea is sufficiently proven**

IV. *Restate main idea*

As you can see, the first step is to clearly state your main idea. Once the main idea is sufficiently introduced, you can begin citing sources and presenting supporting materials. Keep in mind that every piece of support may not need a citation. It can also be that some citations are vague reference to the sources (e.g., "Other recent news reports have confirmed that new treatments for the disease are being tested.") other times you can skip citing a source. However, the audience will begin questioning your ideas if they feel you are making too many statements without citing credible sources. Once enough supporting material and credible sources are established to prove your main idea, it is then time to repeat and summarize the main idea one final time before moving onto the next main point. Look at the following example of how a speaker could integrate each of these steps into building a well-developed main idea.

**(I. Main idea)** The first step to improving our state's economy is to get more adults to attend and graduate from college. **(III. Support)** We can all agree that the highest paying jobs generally require the most advanced training, such as jobs in engineering, medicine, finance, or law. Unfortunately, our state is not producing enough college graduates to work in these high-paying career fields. **(II. Source)** Daryl Denham, State Commissioner for Higher Education, **(III. Support)** reported that less than 25 percent of the state's high school seniors applied to attend a college and technical school last year. A recent **(II. Source)** *Time* article **(III. Support)** reported that over half of all new U.S. jobs require some college or technical training. How can our state's economy improve with so few citizens prepared for these jobs? Sadly, **(II. Source)** the 2000 U.S. Census reported that **(III. Support)** our state ranked 47th in the nation in "adults with college degrees" and 45th in the nation in "per-capita income." **(III. Support)** Contrast our numbers with Missouri, which ranked 28th in "college degrees" and 26th in "per-capita income" or Indiana, which ranked 22nd in "college degrees" and 25th in "per-capita income." **(IV. Restate Main Idea)** The relationship between a state's percentage of college educated adults and the income level of its citizens is strong. If our state's economy is going to improve, we must get more adults to pursue higher education.

## ■ Adapting Your Presentation to Your Audience

Who is more important? (select one)

Yourself _____ Others _____

While you are in the midst of preparing your presentation, it is very easy to see yourself as the most important element in this process. After all, you are the one who has brainstormed the topic, determined a purpose, and crafted a specific theme for the speech. You're the one constructing it, you're the one doing the research to support your ideas, and ultimately, you're the one delivering it. It's yours.

Although it is easy to understand your role this way, it is more helpful to understand that the presentation you are constructing is for the benefit of someone else—a little like a gift you are presenting to someone. Did you ever receive a gift you didn't want, like, or need? While you may have said, "Thank you," did you also wonder if the gift-giver had you in mind at all when choosing or making it? Did the person give you the gift you wanted, liked, or needed, or the one he/she wanted to give?

Even though it cannot be accomplished all the time, we should always work to place the needs of others ahead of our own desires. Good spouses, parents, employees, and bosses conduct themselves in such a way to make "others" feel important and appreciated. Successful companies develop products that are customized to meet the unique desires of consumers (e.g., automobiles are produced in a wide variety of styles, classes, and colors to satisfy different consumers).

## ■ Three Types of Credibility

You must establish your credibility as an audience centered speaker. There are three types of credibility: **initial, derived,** and **terminal.** Initial credibility involves anything you do from researching up to your introduction for your speech. Derived involves anything you do during the speech (vidual aids, delivery, content, etc.). Terminal involves your conclusion and how you handle questions from the audience as well as heading to your seat. Can you imagine the impact of falling on your way back to your seat? What type of credibility might you categorize your appearance?

### ▌ *Adapting Your Ethos, Logos, and Pathos*

Your audience is the "consumer" of your ideas. Not all speakers are equally effective at getting audiences to consume presentations because some fail to adapt their message to meet the needs of audience members. In the 4th century B.C., Aristotle taught that speakers create effective (e.g., "easy to consume") presentations by adapting three elements: **Ethos, Logos,** and **Pathos.**

■ Ethos: The character and credibility of the speaker.

■ Logos: The logical appeals in the presentation (e.g., evidence, facts, or reasoning).

■ Pathos: The emotional appeals in the presentation (e.g., appeals to love, pride, or power).

You will conduct research to enhance the ethos (credibility), logos (logic), and pathos (emotion) of your presentation. Let's first look at why ethos, or credibility, is so important.

### Oprah, Jerry Springer, and Your Credibility

Students often ask, "Why should I conduct research? Isn't my personal opinion and experience enough?" The answer: NO. We live in the age of the talkshow: *Oprah, Jerry Springer,* and many others. These television shows prove one thing; everyone has an opinion and a story. Whatever opinion or experience you have, someone else has a different opinion or experience. Your opinions and experiences are a great start, but they are not enough to convince the audience that you are a credible speaker.

Begin establishing your credibility by telling of your experience, knowledge, training, and/or credentials. However, if the goal is to create an "ironclad" argument, you will need the help of others. You need to discover other evidence to support your opinions and experiences. For example, find others who have written about their similar experiences, find documented facts that confirm your observations, and/or share the testimony of others who agree with your views. Citing the source or author of facts you share with the audience builds your credibility. For example, suppose you're giving a presentation on body piercing and you share a quote from a local tattoo/piercing artist. The credibility of that person makes your presentation seem more believable. Similarly, if *Oprah* had an episode on body piercing, sharing a quote from one of Oprah's guests would add further credibility to your speech. Whatever you can do to boost your ethos/credibility will aid your effectiveness as a speaker.

### Overcoming the Audience's Skepticism, Confusion, and Apathy

We often assume that our audience is highly motivated and interested in listening to our presentation. Unfortunately, every audience has members who fall into one of three categories:

■ The **Skeptics**—people who don't believe your message.

■ The **Confused**—people who don't understand your message.

■ The **Apathetic**—people who don't care about your message.

*How do we overcome these problems? How do we get everyone to believe, understand, and care?*

By conducting an audience analysis, you can custom build your presentation to fit your audience's unique characteristics. Audience analysis allows you to strategically select the best combination of credible fact, logical arguments, and engaging ideas. The *Skeptics* doubt because they don't believe you or your ideas are credible (i.e., poor ethos). The *Confused* don't understand because your facts or ideas are unclear (i.e., poor logos). The *Apathetic* don't care because you have not stirred their interest by relating your content to their lives (i.e., poor pathos). By analyzing your audience and discovering appropriate research, you will have the tools to build a solid presentation that is credible, clear, and interesting to your audience.

## TIPS

**Ways to enhance your credibility**

- Speak of your personal experience and learned knowledge.

- Express awareness of and concern for the consequences of your information and ideas.

- Use direct eye contact and smile.

- Reference your positions of authority within organizations or the community.

- Speak with enthusiasm, conviction, and sincerity.

- Establish common ground with the audience by expressing points-of-view with which the audience can identify.

- Support your speech with engaging facts and testimony from respected sources.

- Make the audience aware of any similarities between your background, beliefs, values, and attitudes and their own.

- Establish goodwill for the audience. Demonstrate that you really and truly desire to provide benefits to your audience.

- Demonstrate open-mindedness by respecting points-of-view contrary to your own.

## Conclusion

Clearly, there is a foundation for a good presentation. The previous pages reviewed a number of key ideas essential for building a solid foundation for a presentation.

- You must be an audience-centered speaker rather than a self-centered speaker.

- You must realize that a solid presentation is credible (ethos), clear (logos), and interesting (pathos).

- You must conduct three types of analyses to properly adapt your presentation: a demographic analysis, situational analysis, and an attitudinal analysis.

- You must realize that finding supporting materials may require you to gather library resources, Internet information, corporate/organizational resources, mass-media and entertainment sources, and interviews of people.

- You must use more than just statistics and numbers to support your presentation. You should also gather facts, examples, analogies, explanations, definitions, opinions/testimonies, and stories as forms of potential supporting materials.

- You must carefully evaluate which supporting materials can be used and which will not facilitate building a solid presentation.

- You must intentionally and purposefully integrate supporting materials and cite related sources to show the audience that you have effectively developed a credible, logical, and interesting presentation.

Regardless if your goal is to sell your product, motivate your workers, win a court case, or persuade citizens to vote, you must first lay a solid foundation for your presentation. Clearly, good research is the key to creating a solid presentation in every speaking situation.

# ACTIVITIES

# Building the Foundation of Your Presentation

# Increasing Speaker Credibility

1. One hurdle for the beginning speaker is to increase his or her credibility. In small groups, first create a list of 10 speech topics the entire group considers to be "good" topics. Look back at the "Tips" box in the chapter that described ways to enhance your personal credibility. For each topic, discuss the "collective credibility" your group possesses for each of these topics (e.g., knowledge level, related experiences, social or professional affiliations, enthusiasm, etc.).

## Ten Speech Topics

1.

2.

3.

4.

5.

6.

7.

8.

9.

10.

2. By this time you should know who is the most and least credible speakers related to these ten speech topics. Decide which group member has the "most speaker credibility" related to one of your ten topics (e.g., "Ann has the most credibility on the topic of architectural design."). Likewise, select the one group member who seems to have the "least speaker credibility" related to a second topic (e.g., "Doug has the least amount of credibility on the topic of pledging a sorority.").

■ As a group, brainstorm about how the **"high credibility"** member can go about further a) establishing and b) enhancing his/her credibility on his/her topic. Be as specific as possible. Record your ideas:

■ As a group, brainstorm about how the **"low credibility"** member can go about a) establishing and b) enhancing his/her credibility on his/her topic. Be as specific as possible. Record your ideas:

# Investigating Demographic Variables

A demographic analysis allows you to gather information about the descriptive traits and objective characteristics of your audience (age, gender, cultural background, etc.).

As a class, develop a demographic survey to determine the characteristics represented by all your classmates. Look back at the section on demographic analysis to determine what demographic traits could be measured in the classroom. Generate as many as possible demographic questions listing them on the board or on a flip-chart. Have one member record the answers for the entire class and display the statistical results of the survey (e.g., total students = 25; males 10 (40%), females 15 (60%) . . . etc.). Have the entire class share their opinions about the following questions:

■ What generalizations can be made about how the audience would think or act?

■ What speech topics do you think would be well received by this audience?

■ What topics would be most difficult or challenging to relate to this audience?

Answering below, explain how should you adapt your next speech topic to fit the audience's demographic traits and characteristics.

_____

_____

_____

_____

_____

_____

_____

_____

_____

_____

_____

_____

_____

_____

_____

_____

# Developing Scale Questions

The "attitudinal analysis" helps you determine the audience's dispositions, beliefs, and values related to your topic. One way of measuring the intensity of those dispositions, beliefs, and values is through the use of scale questions (e.g., scales ranging from "strongly agree" to "strongly disagree," "very likely" to "very unlikely," "very important" to "very important" etc.). For each of the following purpose statements, formulate **two related scale questions** that would provide you unique and valuable insight into the audience's attitude, beliefs, values, etc.

■ To inform my audience about the four steps to protecting themselves against identity theft.

■ To inform my audience about the process of sewage treatment.

■ To persuade my audience to become parents through adopting children.

■ To persuade my audience to stop drinking carbonated soft-drinks.

■ To persuade my audience to subscribe to the *Wall Street Journal*.

# Developing Open-Ended Questions

Open-ended questions allow audience members to provide answers to questions in their own words. Effectively phrased, open-ended questions can give you the most insight into their feelings, wishes, behaviors, and thoughts. Returning to the same topics in question #3, develop **two open-ended questions** for each of the following specific purpose statements. Keep in mind that you need to develop questions that go beyond information already provided in closed-ended or scale questions.

■ To inform my audience about the four steps to protecting themselves against identity theft.

■ To inform my audience about the process of sewage treatment.

■ To persuade my audience to become parents through adopting children.

■ To persuade my audience to stop drinking carbonated soft-drinks.

■ To persuade my audience to subscribe to the *Wall Street Journal.*

# Audience Analysis Surveys

The following audience analysis surveys have several mistakes or weaknesses. Identify what is wrong with each and suggest corrections.

---

### Exercise and Health

1. How do you feel about your current health and amount of daily exercise?

2. What type of health problems do you associate with a lack of exercise?

3. How important is it to you to live a long life?

   a. Very Important

   b. Important

   c. 50/50

   d. Little Importance

   e. Not Important

4. In your opinion, list the main reasons that people do not exercise daily?

---

### Retirement

1. What is your name?

2. What is your age?

3. What is your ideal job?

4. How much money do you hope to be earning 5 years after graduation?
   $20-30,000_____     $30-40,000_____     $40-50,000_____     $50,000+_____

5. At what age do you plan on retiring?

6. How much money do you save each year towards retirement?

7. Rate how you feel about the following:

   | Home | "Very Important" | 1—2—3—4—5—6 | "Very Unimportant" |
   |---|---|---|---|
   | Children | "Very Important" | 1—2—3—4—5—6 | "Very Unimportant" |
   | Success | "Very Important" | 1—2—3—4—5—6 | "Very Unimportant" |
   | Family | "Very Important" | 1—2—3—4—5—6 | "Very Unimportant" |
   | Community | "Very Important" | 1—2—3—4—5—6 | "Very Unimportant" |
   | Recreation | "Very Important" | 1—2—3—4—5—6 | "Very Unimportant" |
   | Friends | "Very Important" | 1—2—3—4—5—6 | "Very Unimportant" |

# Gathering Supporting Materials

To create a logical, interesting, and credible presentation, you must gather a variety of supporting materials beyond those readily available through your own personal knowledge and experiences.

What is the topic of your next presentation? _____

1. Log onto the library main homepage and locate the list of available electronic "indexes and databases." Using one of these indexes/databases, locate a full-text journal article (one where the entire article could be printed or downloaded) related to your topic. You may need to read the description of each database to determine which would be of greatest help related to your topic.

   Name of the database/index used: _____

   Keyword(s) used to find the article: _____

   Write the bibliographic citation of the source of this article:

   _____

   _____

2. Use the electronic library catalog (e.g., RACERTRAC) to find one resource (print or audio/visual) on your topic available in the library. Use either a "Keyword" search or a "Subject" search. Provide the following information:

   Call number: _____

   Author: _____

   Title: _____

   Publisher and date: _____

3. Using an index or database, find one "periodic article" (e.g., newspaper, magazine, or scholarly journal—not a book) related to your topic that is not available in your library. Go to the library reference desk or the library homepage to find the Interlibrary Loan (ILL) form. Fill out the request for the article and attach the form to this assignment. DO NOT PROCESS an ILL form unless you really need the article.

   Name of the DATABASE used to find the article: _____

   Title of article: _____

   Author: _____

   Title of periodical: _____

   Volume: _____ Date: _____ Pages: _____

4.  Using the Internet, locate one web resource or site related to your topic. Write the name of the site and the URL (Uniform Resource Locator) of the site:

Name: _____

http://_____

Using the Internet, locate the homepage of an organization, corporation, or government agency that would provide information for your topic. Write the name of the organization/corporation, their mailing address, and the URL of the site:

Name: _____

Mailing address:_____

http://_____

5.  Identify the names of three potential interviewees that could provide you additional information about your subject. Explain why they would be helpful sources of information.

Name: _____

Name: _____

Name: _____

# Variety of Supporting Material

Clearly, a wide variety of supporting materials can be used to support any speech. This chapter reviewed seven types of supporting materials: facts/examples, explanations, analogies, definitions, opinions/testimonies, stories, and statistics/numbers.

1. Using your library catalog, periodical databases, or the Internet, locate the text of a speech. Go through this speech locating at least one example of each type of supporting material. Attach a copy of the speech where you have *highlighted* and *labeled* the speech text to show each of the seven types of supporting materials. Indicate if any of the seven types of support are not present in your speech's content.

    From the speech, provide one example of each of those seven types of supporting materials:

    Facts/examples: _____

    Explanations: _____

    Analogies: _____

    Definitions: _____

    Opinions/testimonies: _____

    Stories: _____

    Statistics/numbers: _____

2. Using the same speech, evaluate how well the speaker supported his/her presentation. Review the "tips" on the "criteria for evaluating supporting materials" and the information on the effective use of statistics. Also, look at the four steps of "building main ideas and citing sources." Apply all these guidelines to evaluating the speech content. Type a two-page critique where you evaluate how well he/she followed these guidelines and supported his/her presentation. Give examples of both the strengths and weaknesses of the speech. How could the speaker have improved his/her speech content? What did you learn about creating a solid presentation by analyzing this speech?

# Notes

1. Berger, C. & Calabrese, R. (1975). Some explorations in initial interaction and beyond: Toward a developmental theory of interpersonal communication. *Human Communication Research, 1*, 99-112.

2. Bebee, S. A. & Beebe, S. J. (1994). *Public speaking: An audience-centered approach*. (2nd ed.) Englewood Cliffs, NJ: Prentice Hall.

# 4 Designing the Blueprint for Your Speech

## CHAPTER PREVIEW

| 1 | Patterns of organization |
| 2 | Integrating support material |
| 3 | Verbal connectives |
| 4 | Types of outlines |
| 5 | Rules for outlining |

> Every discourse ought to be put together like a living creature, with a body of its own, so as to be neither without head nor without feet, but to have both a middle and extremities described proportionately to each other and to the whole.
>
> ⌐ Plato

You have completed your research, gathered your materials, and now it is time to arrange that information in such a way that it is not only clear to your audience but suitable for your delivery as well. YOU NEED A BLUEPRINT. Just as a contractor, building a house, needs an architect's blueprint to determine where to pour the concrete for the foundation, where to construct the walls, and where to install the wiring, so must speakers organize their ideas in a responsible and reasonable manner. In this chapter we will address designing a blueprint for the effective speaker. This blueprint includes *organizing and outlining* the material for your speech.

For some, public speaking is a stressful situation. It demands courage to stand up in front of a group of peers to share your thoughts and ideas. For others, the fear of public speaking is not so much the concern, but rather the critical thinking and the amount of time for preparation it takes to be effective. For everyone, however, public speaking is somewhat like peeling a banana. The act of pulling back the banana's peel can expose the firm, edible flesh of the fruit as well as reveal possible undesirable, soft, or brown spots. As you deliver your presentation, your speaking strengths as well as your inadequacies are clearly made public. To reduce the exposure of "brown spots" or inadequacies, however, effective speakers *organize* their material. Just organizing your material with the aid of a blueprint or a plan can reduce your fears, enhance your confidence, and establish your credibility.

## ▌ Create a Speech Creature

This creature illustration implies that the speech needs a head, an **introduction,** in which the speaker reveals to the audience the blueprint. This introduction composes about 10 to 20 percent of the speech, gets the audience's attention, familiarizes the speaker with the audience, establishes the speaker's credibility, and leads smoothly into the body. The **body** is where "you tell 'em'" and includes the main ideas of your topic. Based on the specific purpose of the speech, these main ideas can be organized in specific ways that will influence the "shape" of the creature's body and comprise about 70 percent of the presentation. (We will discuss these shapes in more depth later in the chapter.) Finally, the creature must have feet, the **conclusion,** where the speaker reviews or summarizes the main points of the body (tell 'em what you told 'em), and with a strong final statement brings the speech to a resounding finish.

> It's bad enough that I have to deliver this speech in the first place; now you want me to spend time creating a creature and organizing it. Why can't I just get up and talk?

Obviously you *can* just get up and talk. But effective speakers understand and appreciate the essential need for organization for both audience and speaker. Aristotle emphasized, and we continue to believe, that public speaking is an **audience-centered activity.** Noted speech teachers Steven and Susan Beebe write that hearing a speech "is a 'one-time-only' experience for the audience, therefore, organization is critical. The audience cannot go back and read."[1] Consequently, you organize initially for the benefit of your audience.

Another way of understanding the importance of organization is that you are taking the audience on a trip, a verbal adventure of ideas. You are informing them. Or perhaps this journey entails convincing them to take a particular fork in the road. You are persuading them. In either case, to accomplish your goal, you need your audience to be

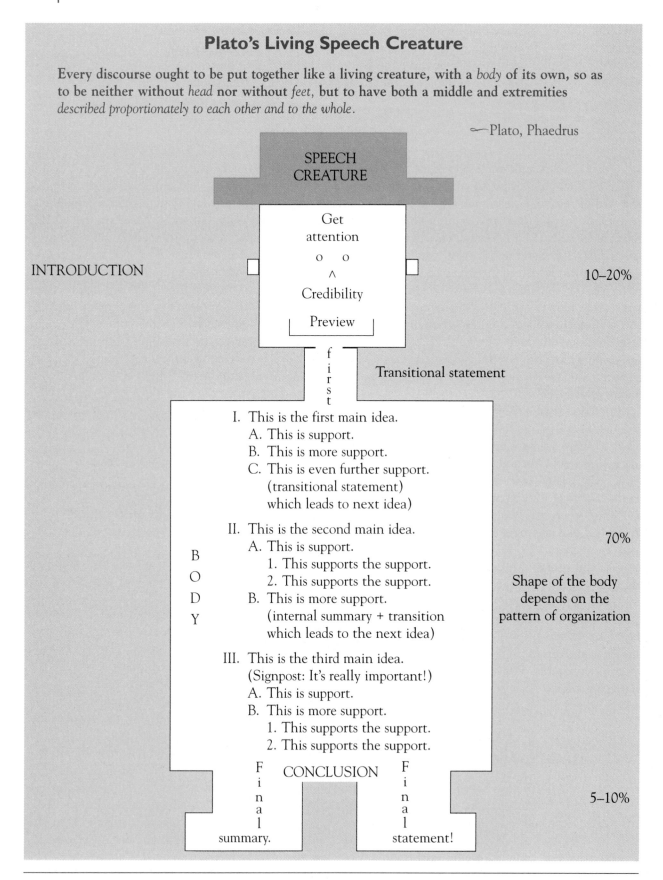

**FIGURE 4.1** Plato's Speech Creature

focused and stay with you throughout the entire trip. That demands that you play tourist guide along the way and follow a prescribed itinerary. Explain clearly to your listeners where you're going and why, the purpose of your trip, what stops you'll make, what sights you'll see and where you'll spend the night. This organization enables the audience to listen with greater ease and also says to them, "I've kept you in mind and I've planned this trip to be as interesting and easy for you to follow as possible. I care about you."

With your audience as your first consideration, you must also organize your message for yourself, the speaker. Read and try to make sense of the following:

INT HEV ERYC LARI TYO FTH EOR
GANI ZATI ONOF THES PEE CHT
HES PEAKE RISGR ANTEDAC ER TAIN
A MOU NTOFP OW ER!

The manner in which these letters are organized make the message almost impossible to understand. If, on the other hand, you *reorganize* the letters, the message comes through loud and clear: "In the very organization of the speech, the speaker is granted a certain amount of power!" This power, if used ethically and effectively, enables speakers to inform and persuade with great skill.

Organization also allows speakers to be perceived more credibly by the audience. It says to them, "You've kept us in mind and planned our stops according to our interests. You've made it easy for us to follow by telling us ahead of time and along the way what sights we were going to see. Finally, we knew we'd have a place to stay at the end of the day. Thanks for keeping us in mind." Audiences are very grateful for that, and see you as someone they like—or at least don't mind—listening to. Your credibility is also enhanced when your main ideas are clearly stated because it reflects your ability to think logically.

Finally, strong organization provides speakers with a vital delivery tool. It allows you to present a smoother, more focused delivery. You know where you are; you know where you've been; and you know where you still have to go. It also facilitates a more extemporaneous delivery in which you engage in a prepared, but seemingly spontaneous, conversation with your audience, the epitome of public speaking delivery.

## ■ Identify the Heart of Your Speech Creature— Your Thesis Statement

With an understanding that getting organized is important, effective speakers should then construct their thesis statement. This is also often referred to as the central idea. The thesis statement essentially reveals in one sentence what the speech will address. It also reflects your specific objective.

As we discussed in chapter 2, in order to create this thesis statement, you need to decide initially what your focus will be and what your specific objective is. Let's say you were interested in Pembroke Welsh Corgis and wanted to inform your audience about this particular breed of dogs. You could discuss the history of the breed, the fact that Queen Elizabeth has owned several Corgis, the breed's health problems, the characteristics of the herding breed in general, but you decide that your focus will be to inform your audience what makes it so fun to own one.

**Specific Objective:** To inform my audience about the highlights of owning a Welsh Corgi.

**Topic:** Pembroke Welsh Corgis

**General Goal:** To inform.

**Thesis Statement:** *Owning a Pembroke Welsh Corgi includes enjoying several aspects of this breed of dog.*

Or, even more specifically: *The highlights of owning a Pembroke Welsh Corgi include its sociability, its size, and its loyalty.*

When stated in the introduction of the speech, the thesis statement allows the audience to know that you will be discussing the pleasurable aspects of owning a Pembroke Welsh Corgi—its sociability, its size, and its loyalty. But taking the time to construct a good thesis statement has an additional benefit for the speaker. If done properly, the main points of the speech—the ones you think are most important to talk about—will just tumble out of your thesis statement. That is, these ideas will present themselves as obviously the main points of your speech. The main points then become skeleton of the body of your speech.

## Ethically Speaking

Speakers have an ethical responsibility to provide their audience members with accurate and reliable information. First and foremost, DON'T WASTE THEIR TIME by not being organized.

Now, can you enhance your opinion about these main points with supportive material from outside research? Just because you think your Corgi is loyal may not be all that exciting to an audience. Do others agree? Are there stories to be told? Are there examples to be shared? Do audience members have dogs of their own to which you can refer? Can comparisons be made with other breeds?

And finally, can an examination of these main ideas be thoroughly and equally covered in the amount of time allowed for your presentation? There must be a balance in addressing each of the main points you choose. In other words, each main point must be supported with about the same amount of material and must take about the same amount of time to develop. Further, the main points must be stated in a parallel structure or in a similar wording pattern.

I. Corgis are sociable with other animals as well as humans.

II. Corgis' low, long size make them a perfect house/lap dog.

III. Corgis are renowned for their loyalty to the owners.

or

I. Enjoyment comes from owning a dog that likes to play with other dogs as well as humans.

II. Enjoyment comes from being able to sit, your Corgi in your lap, in front of the fire on a winter's evening.

III. Enjoyment comes from knowing your Corgi will always be true to you.

## Get Your Body in the Proper Shape

Depending on the topic, the audience, and the specific purpose, speakers have several organizational options for the "shape of the body" of their speech creature. The first one is called the **chronological** pattern and refers to arranging the main points of the speech in a time sequence. This pattern is appropriate for a process, the recounting of a series of historical events, or providing a set of instructions.

### Interviewing for a Job

I. First, you must prepare for the interview.

II. Second, you must engage in the interview.

III. Third, you must follow up after the interview is over.

Each of these main ideas follows a first, second, and third sequence appropriate to the order in which things are done. (See figure 4.2.)

The **spatial pattern** is the second option for the speaker. As seen in figure 4.3, the main ideas are related to one another geographically or spatially.

### Settlement of the West

I. Settlement began in the Appalachian Mountains.

II. Settlement continued west into the settlement of the Ohio Valley.

III. Settlement spread further west along the Mississippi River.

IV. Settlement finally extended across the Rocky Mountains onto the Pacific Coast.

Spatial organization follows a directional pattern and is appropriate when explaining space or geographical relationships.

The third option for organizing the body of a speech is the **causal pattern**. This pattern is appropriate for informative and persuasive speeches in which you want to address the cause and effect of an issue. The pattern demands only two main points—one for the cause and one for the effect, and you can put them in either order.

### Excessive Teenage Drinking

I. There are three main *causes* for excessive teenage drinking.

II. The *effects* of excessive teenage drinking are widespread.

or

I. The *effects* of excessive teenage drinking are widespread.

II. There are three main *causes* for excessive teenage drinking.

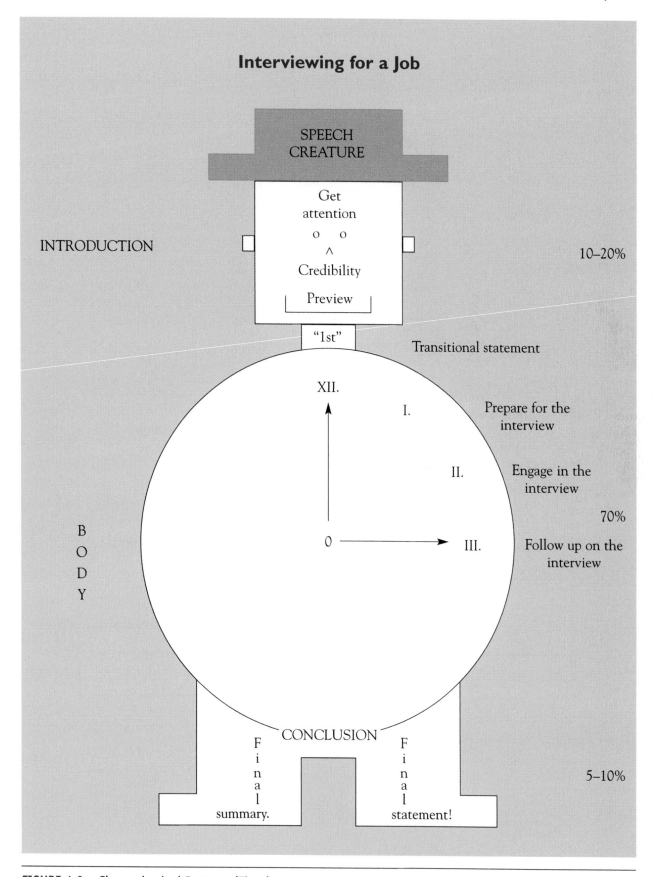

**FIGURE 4.2** Chronological Pattern (Time)

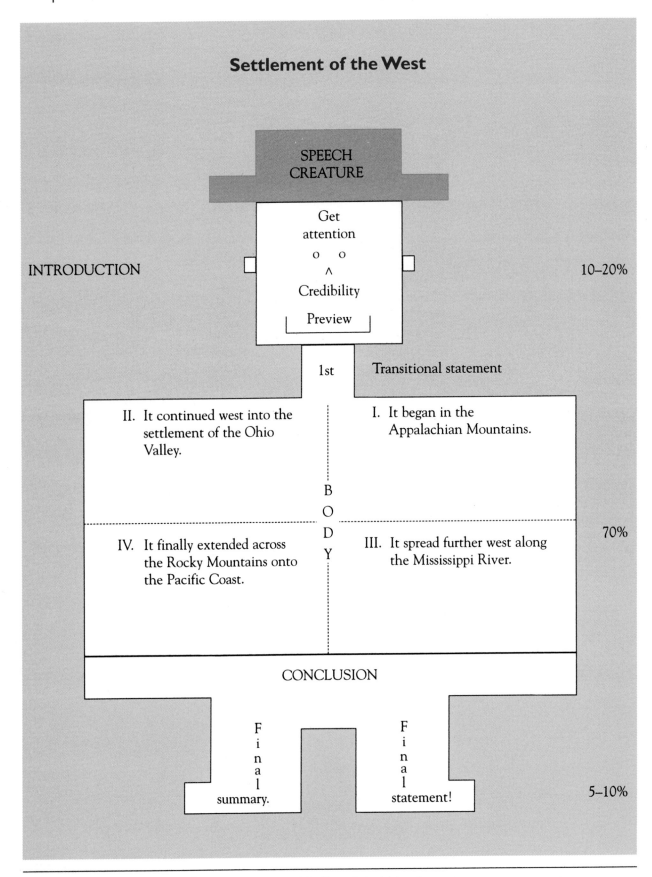

**FIGURE 4.3** Spatial Pattern (Space or geographically-related ideas)

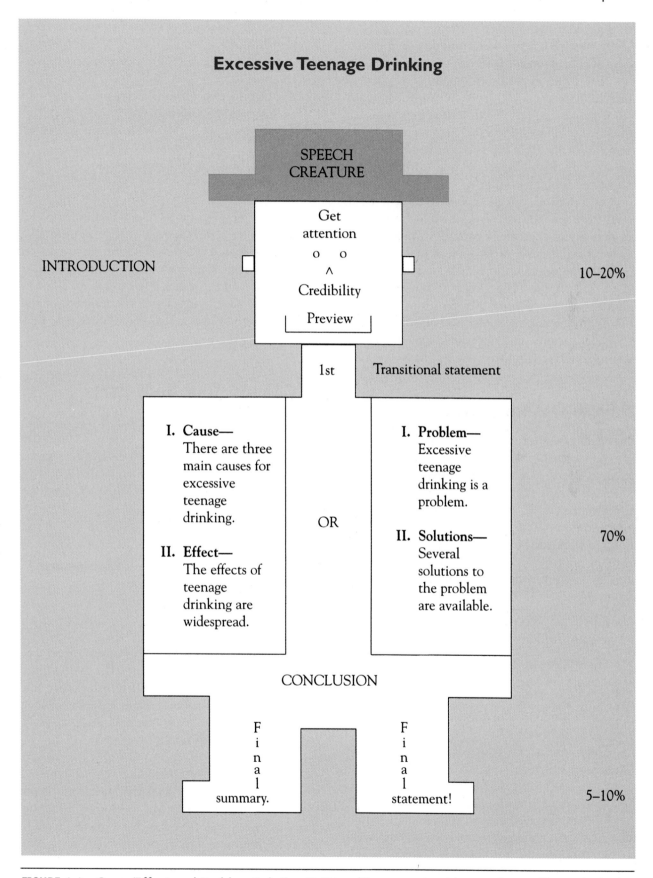

**FIGURE 4.4** Cause/Effect and Problem/Solution Pattern (One cause/problem and one effect/solution)

The final organizational pattern and the one that is most commonly used in informative speeches is called the **topical pattern**. You might consider this the "equal opportunity organization" because three to five aspects of a topic are discussed equally. For example, in a speech about the "Classical Influence on Public Speaking" (see figure 4.5), the speaker will discuss, with equal amounts of support, the sophists, Plato, Aristotle, and Cicero as they influenced public speaking.

Lest you think you are limited to those five patterns, there are alternatives. One such alternative is the **mnemonic or gimmick pattern**.[2] The use of this choice would depend on the topic as well as concern for the audience's retention of the material. In figure 4.6, a speech on "The Positive Communication Climate in Relationships" uses the letters C L I M A T E as the organizing device to help the listeners remember the different aspects involved in communicating positively in their relationships.

## Flesh Out Your Body

The main points or ideas of your speech are really just your opinions. What you must do now is bolster those opinions with the supportive material you have gathered in your research. You will need testimony, explanations, examples, statistics, narratives, comparisons, contrasts, etc. to support or give credibility to what you believe or claim. This supportive material must be accurate as well as appropriately and effectively arranged to flesh out your main ideas. For example:

I. There are three main *causes* for excessive teenage drinking.

II. There are widespread *effects* of excessive teenage drinking.

So let's support those main ideas.

I. There are three main *causes* for excessive teenage drinking.
   A. Alcohol regulations are not sufficiently enforced (statistics and examples).
   B. Parents have failed to control the behavior of their children (testimony and narratives).
   C. Peer pressure is responsible for teens behaving in abusive ways (examples, testimony, statistics, narratives).

II. There are widespread *effects* of excessive teenage drinking.
   A. Addiction can result (examples, narratives, statistics).
   B. Dysfunctional families can result (testimony, examples, statistics).
   C. Automobile accidents can result (statistics, examples).
   D. Deaths can result (personal narrative, statistics).

With some flesh on its "bony-main-idea-skeleton," the body of your speech is beginning to take shape. Your speech creature is beginning to take on a form of its own as it simultaneously makes sense to the audience and is reasonable to deliver. What is needed now are the ligaments, the muscles, or the connectives to hold it together and allow it to flow smoothly.

## Connect Your Body Parts

Just as ligaments connect the bones or organs of the body and muscles allow for movement, so must the speaker provide connectives to bind the various parts of the speech together and facilitate movement from one part to another. These connectives take the form of:

1. Transitional statements
2. Internal previews
3. Internal summaries
4. Signposts

Each in its own way serves to connect the introduction to the body's main points, the main points to the sub-points, the sub-points to each other and finally the body to the conclusion. Remember Plato's charge—*"extremities described proportionately to each other and to the whole."*

TRANSITIONAL STATEMENTS. These are statements that allow you to move smoothly from one main idea to another. Think of the transition as taking your audience's collective hand and gradually guiding them from one sight to another on your verbal adventure.

"Now that we've addressed the preparation for the interview, let's consider what you need to keep in mind during the interview itself."

"We've explored the hardships and accomplishments in the Appalachian Mountains, so now it's time to move westward with the settlers into the Ohio Valley."

"Let's first of all examine some causes for excessive teenage drinking."

**INTERNAL PREVIEWS.** More detailed than transitions, these are statements which forecast some of the main points that you will address next. Remember, the thesis statement previews all main points. The **internal preview,** previews only some of the upcoming points.

"In order to solve the problem of excessive teenage drinking, we must explore available solutions, which might include law enforcement, parental control, and designated driver programs. (Transition) Let's first examine increased law enforcement."

"The foundation of rhetoric originated with the classical philosophers. Today we will consider the sophists, Aristotle, Plato, and Cicero and their respective influences on public speaking."

"The remainder of the communication climate is composed of **A**–sserting yourself, **T**–aking criticism effectively and **E**–mpathizing with the other person. (Transition) As we continue, let me ask, "How assertive are you?""

**INTERNAL SUMMARIES.** These statements remind the audience of information they have already heard. Suitable for complex ideas that might need clarification, **internal summaries** also allow the speaker to reinforce previously stated ideas.

"Causes for excessive teenage drinking, then, are multiple. Inadequate law enforcement, lack of parental supervision, and the monumental impact of peer pressure each play a role in a teenager's potential abuse of alcohol." (Transition) "What effect, then, does this have on the individual, the family, and society as a whole? I'd like to talk first about the teenager."

"Now that we are halfway through with our Relationship Climate Control, let me remind you that thus far we've agree to **C** onfirm each other, **L** isten, use **"I"** language, and **M** inimize defensiveness."

**SIGNPOSTS.** Like highway signs on your verbal trip, **signposts** alert the audience to what is coming, what is important, what you want to emphasize, or what they should listen for.

"Never forget . . . "

"First, second, third"

"Be sure to keep this in mind; this is really important; above all you need to know . . . "

"Underline this in your mind."

"Always remember . . . "

## Exercise Your Muscles

A successful connection and transition must be thought out carefully and phrased appropriately with variety. You might experience a "pulled muscle" if you overuse phrases such as "next," "now," "moving on to my next point," or "the next thing I would like to discuss." Exercise your connectives with variety and good thinking, much as you would exercise your muscles in the gym.

## Prepare to Deliver Your Creature

As you consider delivering your speech, one very significant process is necessary—that is outlining the material, which until now has simply been organized primarily in your mind. Now you must translate your organization into outline form. "Organization is a strategy and outlining is a technique."[4] And this technique is important to both the audience and the speaker.

The audience benefits from an orderly, outlined presentation because it is much easier to follow than one that is randomly presented. Further, it communicates to the listeners that you are concerned for their ability to follow your message.

Even though it takes extra time initially, in the long run outlining is an efficient method of preparation for the speaker. It instills confidence because there is a prescribed order with a unity and coherence of supporting ideas with the main ideas. Further, and equally important, having an outline lessens the likelihood of the speaker's digression from the topic, while at the same time emphasizing certain points. Having a visible outline allows the

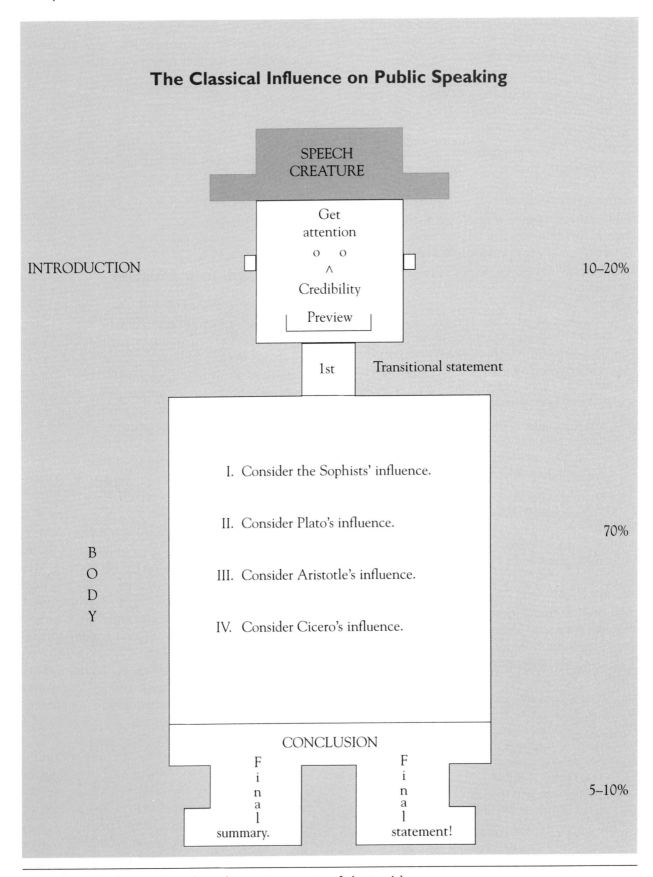

**FIGURE 4.5** Topical Pattern (Equal aspects or parts of the topic)

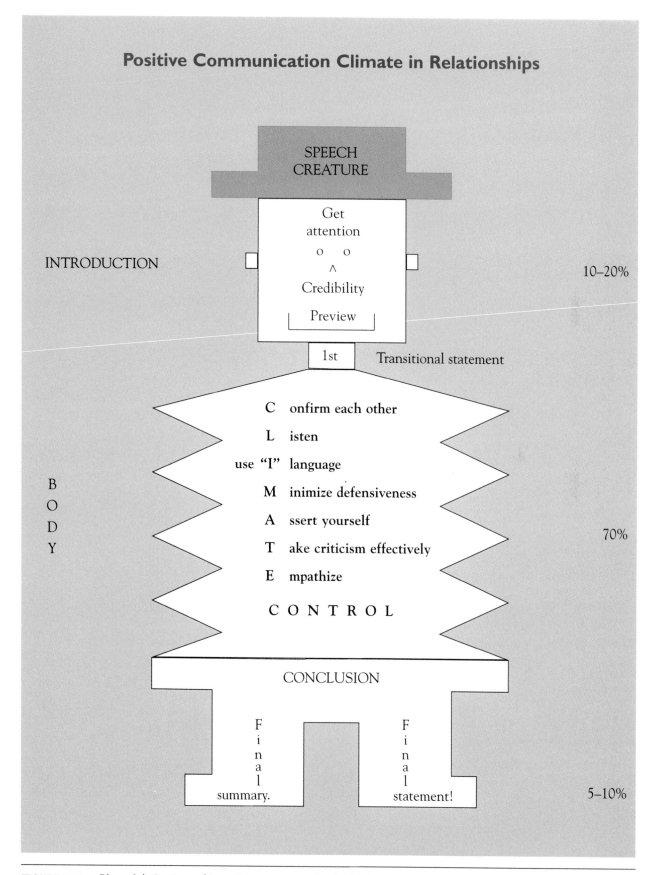

**FIGURE 4.6**    Gimmick Pattern (Creative, mnemonic device)

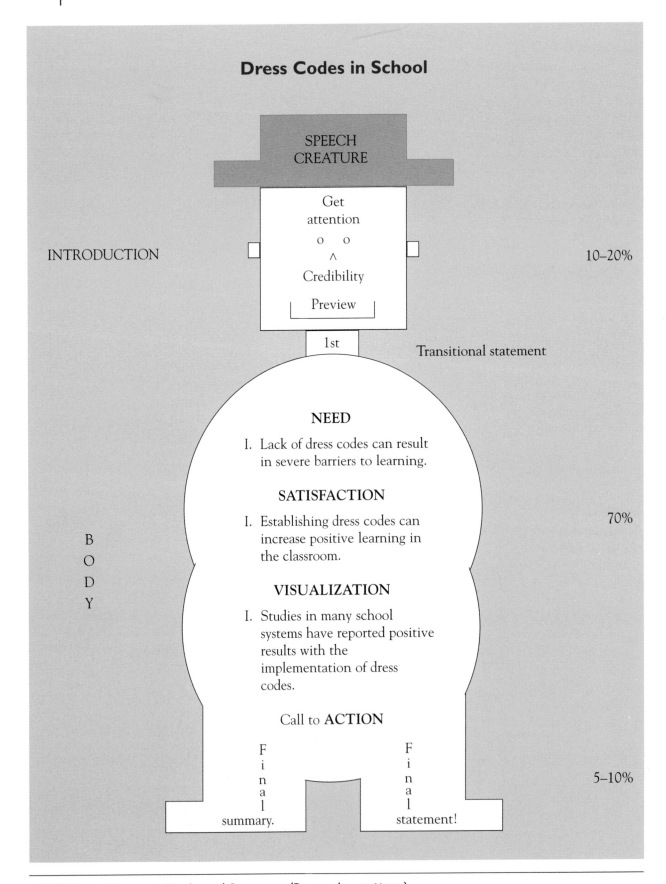

**FIGURE 4.7** Monroe's Motivated Sequence (Persuasive pattern)

speaker to actually "see" whether or not there is a balance among the main points, a logical relationship between main points and sub-points, and an appropriate amount and variety of supportive material for each main idea. It can also be "a creative and corrective" process.[5] It gives the speaker an opportunity to change and adapt order, enhance word choice, and select and order supportive material. Finally, there is a direct correlation between the effectiveness of the organization and the effectiveness of the speech. For all of these reasons, then, outlining is crucial for the speaker.

## Create Two Outlines

"Two outlines?!?! It's bad enough to have to create one outline and now you're suggesting I have to write TWO?!?!"

Only if you wish to be considered an effective speaker, for effective speakers create both *a preparation outline* and *a delivery outline.*

### Preparation Outline

The **preparation outline** is an organizing device that provides the preliminary organization of the speech. (See figure 4.8A and 4.8B.) It is a thorough, formal, and complete sentence document. Its focus should be "for an interested reader not having necessary prior knowledge of your topic."[6]. The preparation outline allows the speaker to follow the principles of coordination between main points, the subordination of sub-points with main ideas, and a balance among both. Its completeness can almost be measured by its potential to facilitate someone else's, albeit rough, delivery of your speech.

Appropriate outlining rules must be followed:

1. A consistent set of symbols should be used throughout the outline.

   ▌ Main ideas are identified with roman numerals.
   ▌ Sub-points, supportive material, are identified with arabic letters.
   ▌ Sub-sub points can be marked with numerals 1., 2., 3., etc.

   ▌ Roman numeral I. must have a II. and A. must have a B., etc.[7]

2. Each unit in the outline should contain one main idea written with parallel structure.

3. Main points should be limited to from three to five in number for the audience's ability to follow, assimilate, and retain the message.

4. Main points and sub-points should be written in **complete sentences.**

5. The first word in every unit should begin with a capital letter.

6. Less important ideas should be subordinate to more important ideas and shown by proper indentation.

The preparation outline is an invaluable tool throughout the development process of the speech creature. It is a formidable device as the speech progresses from the speaker's initial concept to its growth and development toward the eventual delivery. At that time, the speaker needs another device called the Delivery Outline.

### Delivery Outline

The **delivery outline,** less formal, but with the same order as the preparation outline, is used by speakers during the delivery of the presentation. "It accommodates you as a unique speaker."[8] This technique should enable you to employ an extemporaneous delivery, practiced, but with only keywords and

phrases guiding the flow of the presentation. This reduces your temptation to read or to memorize.

Here are some further tips for creating a useable delivery outline:

- Use key words or phrases.

  ▌ Exceptions for this are the thesis statement, transitions, and quotations.

- Use increased font size to enable easier reading.

- Indicate emphasis of words and with caps, colored markers, or underlining.

- Identify main ideas with arabic numerals 1., 2., 3., so they are easier to spot.

- Keep your outline simple.

- Use bullets instead of letters or numbers which tend to clutter the outline.

- Include source information to ensure you cite your research accurately.

- Identify delivery cues.

  ▌ Move
  ▌ Gesture
  ▌ Smile
  ▌ Slow down
  ▌ Pause . . . . . // . . . . . .

**TIPS**

"Remember, the more the speech is outlined in your head rather than paper, the better."[9]

Follow the format of the delivery outline in figure 4.9 (Model Delivery Outline). This model typically provides invaluable security for the speaker. As you "learn where to 'find' [your] information on the outline, [you] are less likely to lose [your] place. But if and when [you] do, [you] are more likely to locate [yourself] again with ease."[10]

With an appropriate organization, essential connectives and the creation of preparation and delivery outlines, you are ready for the delivery of your speech creature. You have considered your audience each step of the way, and are ready to inform, persuade, or entertain them using the most effective tools at your disposal. Plato would be proud of you!

**Heading:**
Name
Speech #: ____
Topic:
General Goal:
Specific Objective:
Thesis Statement and Preview of Main Points:
Organizational Pattern:

## Introduction

*(Tell 'em what you're going to tell 'em.)*

I. Get audience's attention; reveal topic/relate to the audience; establish credibility; reveal thesis statement; preview main points.

## Body

*(Tell 'em.)*

II. Main points are written in complete sentences with capital letters and periods.
   A. Sub-points are **written in complete sentences.**
      1. Sub-sub points are also written in complete sentences.
      2. Sub-sub points must begin with capital letters.
         a. Additional support are also written in complete sentences.
         b. Additional support is indented.
   B. Sub-points are written to support the main points.
      1. Examples
      2. Statistics
      3. Testimony
      4. Explanations
      5. Narratives

**Transition statement:** *Transitional statements connect main ideas.*

III. Main points are written with only one idea.
   A. Sub-points are written with parallel structure.
   B. Sub-points are written beginning with capital letters and periods.

**Transition statement:** *Transitional statements connect main ideas.*

IV. Main points are written in parallel structure.
   A. I. must have a II.
   B. A. must have a B.

## Conclusion

*(Tell 'em what you told 'em.)*

V. Review thesis statement; summarize main points; finalize speech with panache.

**FIGURE 4.8A**  Preparation Outline (Sample format)

**Heading**

**Name:** Pamela

**Speech #:** 3

**Topic:** Employee training

**General Goal:** To inform

**Specific Objective:** to inform the audience how to train new employees within an organization

**Thesis Statement:** When training new employees within an organization, the trainer should welcome them, give them a tour of the organization, describe their work environment, and train them on one task at a time.

**Organizational Pattern:** Chronological

**Documented Sources:**

Botero, Ingrid M. (2005). The secrets of effective employee training for New Employees. *Business Journal*, 210, 150-151.

Effingham, Alan K. (2004). Tying goals into employee training. *Personnel Psychology*, 84, 24-44.

Reader, Chris M. (2000). The importance of language in the workplace. *Personnel Psychology*, 44, 108-110.

Death With Dignity National Center (2005). You are not alone: Personal Stories. Retrieved April 14 2005 from http://www.deathwithdignity.org/

Tolson, Jay (2005, April 4). The spinal cord injury epidemic. *US News & World Report*, 94, 34-39.

Spinal Cord Injury Institute (2005). Spinal Cord Injury Statistics. Retrieved April 14, 2005 from http://www.ninds.nih.gov/disorders/sci/sci.htm.

### Introduction

I. I'm sure most of you plan to get a job after you graduate from college. So imagine yourself working diligently at your desk, when your boss comes into the room with someone you have never seen before.

II. A. He introduces you to the new employee and then informs you that you will be responsible for training her.

III. The example I just gave you happened to me at my current job. I was asked to train a new employee without any prior experience or training.

    A. Over a three year period, I have trained over one hundred new employees at Southeastern Book Company.

    B. After several training sessions, I realized that there was a distinct process in training new employees.

**Preview Statement:** When training new employees, the trainer should follow these steps: welcome them, take them on a tour of the facility, familiarize them with their work environment and train them on one specific task.

**Transition Statement:** First, let's look at welcoming the new employee.

### Body

IV. The first step in training new employees is welcoming them to your company.

    A. Introduce yourself with a smile, showing them they are important.

        1. You want them to feel comfortable.

        2. According to an article in *Business Journal* by Ingrid Murro Botero, "if the first day is not structured and if attention is not paid to new employees, then they are likely to feel unwanted."

    B. Do not leave them alone for extended periods of time.

**Transition Statement:** After establishing a positive training relationship, you should then focus on the organization.

V. The second step in training new employees is to take them on a tour of the facility.

    A. In this tour, the history of the organization should be discussed.

        1. Where or how it started.

**FIGURE 4.8B** Preparation Outline (Student example)

2. What is the purpose of the organization; why does it exist?

3. What are they wanting to achieve—goals?

4. What is important to this company?

5. An article in *Personnel Psychology* stated that "employees cannot embrace an organization's goals or values if they are not made aware of them."

B. You also want to go through the different departments, so they can grasp the whole process of the organization.

C. You want to introduce them to key people throughout these departments.

D. And last, you want to make sure they know where the bathrooms, water fountains and break areas are.

**Transition Statement:** Following the tour of the facility, new employees should be brought back to their department.

VI. The third step in training new employees is to familiarize them with their department.

A. Walk them through the entire department.

1. Introduce them to their co-workers along the way.

2. Familiarize them with how the department is set up.

B. Make sure they understand the language of the department.

1. According to an article from the Spring 2000 issue of *Personnel Psychology*, the language is "the technical language, acronyms, slang and jargon unique" to an organization, job, or profession.

2. One way to help them with unfamiliar terminology is to provide them with a handout of related terms and definitions.

C. Show them how the department is run.

1. Task involved.

2. Line of authority.

3. Who can be depended on for help.

4. Job responsibilities.

**Transition Statement:** Once employees have a good understanding of their department, you should then start them on a specific task.

VII. The fourth and final step in training new employees should be to start them on one specific task at a time.

A. You want to make sure they have a clear understanding of each task before they begin on the next.

B. One of the most important things for a trainer to do at this stage is to stay with the new employee.

1. Answer questions.

2. Correct mistakes.

3. Provide positive reinforcement.

C. And last, evaluate their progress and modify training to suit their individual needs.

## Conclusion

VIII. I have discussed five steps in training new employees: welcome them, take them on a tour of the facility, familiarize them with their department, and start them on one specific task at a time.

A. It is your responsibility to make sure new employees have a clear understanding of the organization and their responsibilities.

B. Remember, to these new employees, you represent the company; therefore, you should step up to the occasion and be the best trainer you can possibly be.

C. New employees benefit and so does the company!

---

**FIGURE 4.8B** Continued

I. **Getting the Attention**

On August 3, 2001 Brenda Sterling talked with her father. He had given no indication when she talked to him that he was thinking about taking his own life. Three days earlier he went for his doctor's appointment. For the next two days he lay in the bed, too sick and weak to get up except to go to the bathroom which was getting to be a chore for him. The next day she went to his home to fix his supper. She found him in his room with his head mostly blown off and blood and brain matter scattered all over his room and the hall to the bathroom. His 30/30 Winchester was sitting on the floor between his knees. It had been loaded with explosive tip shells, so the police investigator said. This story was taken from the Death With Dignity website on April 14, 2005.

II. **Showing the Need**

A. The problem is that in most places in the United States, when a person has a legitimate reason to want to end their life, they are denied the help of a qualified physician.

B. Sometimes people find themselves in the situation of having a disease that can't be treated, or with pain that can't be managed.

1. This pain can be the physical pain caused by cancer, advanced Multiple Sclerosis, or many other ailments that afflict the human body.

2. It can also be the mental suffering of having lost any trace of independence and self sufficiency.

3. This situation can also affect patients with irreversible brain damage even if they have made it known in writing that they don't want to be kept alive by artificial means.

4. In all states except Oregon, if a physician actually assists the patient in dying they can be charged with criminal offenses.

5. In all other states, the only assistance a physician can give a patient in ending his or her life is to sedate them into unconsciousness until they die of starvation or dehydration.

6. Because they know there is no help available, some terminally ill patients opt for violent suicide while they still have the capacity to act on their own behalf.

C. In the past 50 years medical technology has made great strides at keeping the body from dying. The problem is we have not yet figured out how to preserve the quality of life.

1. According to an article in U. S. News & World Report, written by Jay Tolson, and published April 4, 2005, there are as many as 35,000 people in the United States that can not respond to outside stimulation.

2. Numbers taken from the Spinal Cord Injury Institute website on April 14, 2005 state that there are about 117,000 people with spinal cord injury that has left the patient quadriplegic, and there are over 5000 more every year.

3. Don't make the mistake of thinking this couldn't happen to you.

III. **Satisfy the Need**

A. Because of these reasons, we need to allow the doctor patient relationship to remain between the doctor and the patient.

B. People that are diagnosed with a condition from which there is no hope of recovering could ask for the assistance of a physician in hastening their death.

1. The condition could be a terminal illness, untreatable physical pain, or mental suffering.

**FIGURE 4.8C** Preparation Outline (Student example)

2. The assistance could come in the form of an injection or a prescription, depending on the ability of the patient.

3. The patient would be required to initiate the discussion of assistance to prevent the physician from influencing the patient.

4. The patient would be required to make two requests separated by several weeks to give them time to think about their decision.

5. The physician would be required to advise the patient of other options including palliative care and pain management techniques.

6. Once the request has been made the patient would be required to submit to a psychological evaluation to establish that the patient is not simply suffering from depression or some other mental condition.

7. The patient would be allowed to withdraw their request at any time.

8. If the patient were severely brain damaged, and had made their wishes known in writing, the same humane death could be made available to them.

C. A law very similar to this was enacted in Oregon in 1997 and there has been neither a flood of people looking for medication to kill themselves nor doctors running around looking for people to kill.

D. Kill the Objections

1. Some people argue that legalizing doctor-assisted suicide will lead to euthanizing the mentally ill. The truth is that if a mentally ill person requested assistance in ending their life the psychological analysis would reveal the mental illness and they would get the help they need.

2. Others claim that doctor-assisted suicide would encourage the terminally ill to end their life prematurely and a cure may be found as soon as they do. The fact is that most of those that a choose suicide do it before it would otherwise be necessary because they fear becoming incapacitated and losing the ability to take their own life. If they were assured the assistance they required they would hold out as long as they could endure their condition.

3. Still others argue that life is sacred and only God should decide when to take it. There is more than one problem with this argument.

   a) First, one of the most fundamental components of our constitution is the separation of church and state. If this isn't a religious belief, I don't know what is. We must not force our religious convictions on other people. They have the right to choose for themselves.

   b) In addition, if you follow this argument through to its conclusion I would ask why we need doctors at all. If God wants us to die, we will. If it's not our time, we will go on living. There must be no need for doctors at all!

4. Another argument used to fight the legalization of assisted suicide is to conjure up images of Hitler and say that it's just the first step on the way to euthanizing anybody that society may see as undesirable. This is nothing more than an ill-conceived scare tactic. The circumstances under which a doctor could legally assist in a suicide could be clearly and carefully legislated. One situation has nothing to do with the other.

**FIGURE 4.8C** Continued

IV. **Visualize the Results**

A. If we continue to deny people the help of a qualified physician when they need it most we will continue to see violent suicides, and failed suicide attempts that leave people worse off than they were before.

B. If we are compassionate and allow people to control the course of their own disease, people will not need to suffer the indignity and pain associated with many of the conditions that often surround the final days of our lives, but they will still be free to do so if they wish to.

V. **Request the Action**

A. All I ask you to do is to stop and think about those you love. Would they want to be forced to endure unbearable pain, and would you want them to?

B. Don't just stand passively by and pretend this issue doesn't affect you. Politicians only do what they think the people that elect them want them to do. Let our elected officials know that it is time that we have options when life is coming to an end.

C. The medical profession has gotten very good at keeping us alive, but that doesn't guarantee we would want the life we may be left with. Some things simply can not be cured, and at times, conditions such as spinal cord injuries can leave us in uncontrollable pain. Some people opt for violent suicide because society tells them they have no choice, and they must suffer. Legalizing assisted suicide will not cause a flood of people wanting to kill themselves, or create blood thirsty doctors. If you have ever watched a loved one suffer in unbearable pain for weeks until death mercifully comes, you would know, it is clearly the compassionate thing to do.

D. I don't expect everyone to agree with me on this issue. For those that do, I urge you to let your elected officials know that it is time to give those that are suffering options in their final days. For those of you that don't, please don't be so cruel as to impose your beliefs on others and tell them they must suffer until they die.

**FIGURE 4.8C** Continued

## Delivery Outline

### (Sample Format)

(EYE CONTACT!  EYE CONTACT!  EYE CONTACT!)

(BREATHE!)

**INTRODUCTION**

    I. She was scared...

    II. Pets are the best when...

    III. I have had pets...

    IV. I'd like to share three reasons why pets...

**BODY**

    I. First....comforting

        A. Example of Susan

        B. According to TIME magazine in an article taken on June 10th 2004, over 16 million people have pets." (ONLY DIRECT QUOTATIONS MAY BE IN FULL SENTENCES!!)

        C. When I was sick...

*Transitional Statement* (connective):  Now that I've told you...

    II. Secondly....protection

        A. My grandfather was 75 when ........................burglars came in ............

        B. My friend Bob.................we ran down the street.................we ended up with two dogs......................

        C. There are agencies here in town that train.............

            1. Trainers are Us........concentrates on family protection

            2. Obedience USA........heavily involved in discipline....not expensive...

*Signpost* (connective):  This last point is very.................

    III. ............not difficult to maintain

        A. Groomers are available

        B. When I have to, I take Charlie.........    (SHOW PICTURE HERE!)

**CONCLUSION**

    I. Remember the three reasons....

    II. Having pets...

    III. .........please go right now and ..............you won't regret it.

(WAIT FOR APPLAUSE————DON'T WALK AWAY UNTIL LAST WORD)

**FIGURE 4.9**   Model Delivery Outline

Outline courtesy of Crystal Rae Coel Coleman.

## Notes

1. Beebe, S.A., & Beebe, S.J.,(1997). *Public Speaking—An Audience-Centered Approach.* (3rd ed.). Needham Heights, MA: Allyn and Bacon.

2. Grice, G.L., & Skinner, J.F. (2001). *Mastering Public Speaking.* (4th ed.) Needham Heights: Allyn and Bacon.

3. Beebe, S.A., & Beebe, S.J. (1997). *Public Speaking—An Audience Centered Approach.* (3rd ed.) Needham Heights, MA: Allyn and Bacon.

4. Daly, J.A., & Engleberg, I.N. (2001). *Presentations in Everyday Life.* Boston: Houghton Mifflin.

5. Osborn, M., & Osborn, S. (2002). *Public Speaking.* (5th ed.). Boston: Houghton Mifflin.

6. Grice, G.L., & Skinner, J.F. (2001). *Mastering Public Speaking.* (4th ed.) Needham Heights, MA: Allyn and Bacon.

7. Beebe, S.A., & Beebe, S.J. (1997). *Public Speaking—An Audience-Centered Approach.* (3rd ed.). Needham Heights, MA: Allyn and Bacon. "You can't logically divide anything into one part. Therefore, if you think you have enough material for an A., then include it into the main idea. Or if you think you only have enough material for 1., then include it into the sub-point."

8. Grice, G. L., & Skinner, J.F. (2001). *Mastering Public Speaking.* (4th ed.) Needham Heights, MA: Allyn and Bacon.

9. Osborn, M., & Osborn, S. (2000). *Public Speaking.* (5th ed.) Boston: Houghton Mifflin.

# 5 Beginning and Ending Your Speech

## CHAPTER PREVIEW

**1** Introductions and conclusions for different types of speeches

**2** The four functions of a speech introduction

**3** The four methods for grabbing an audience's attention

**4** The functions of a speech conclusion

> If impressions are lasting, what is said in your
> introduction and conclusion will either cause your
> speech to sizzle or fizzle.
>
> ⌒Stephon Gardner

## The Importance of Introductions and Conclusions

Delivering a speech is often a memorable experience. From the writing process to the actual presentation, there is nothing like the feeling one has when a well-crafted speech has been successfully delivered. Writing the speech, however, can be just as overwhelming as delivering it because main points and a speaker are only half the speech. Though the introductions and conclusions are the final components of a speech that are written, they leave the first and last impressions upon the mind of the listener.

Let's take a closer look at the importance of introductions and conclusions through a metaphor, which likens "introductions and conclusions to the foundation and roofs that provide both support and shelter to any well-crafted speech." In other words, without a solid foundation, a house will never stand. Perhaps there is foundation but with a weak roof above it. Obviously, four walls without a proper foundation or supporting roof is a sure sign of trouble, and so too is an uncrafted speech. A weak introduction to an otherwise well-worded speech weakens its main points, similar to four strong walls that rest atop an unstable foundation. An ill-worded, hurried conclusion is the flimsy roof that provides little or no shelter above the body it is designed to cover. An effective conclusion is one that is designed to prevent the external "storms" from ruining everything put into it.

## Analyzing Your Audience before Crafting the Beginning and Endings

Analyzing who your audience is before writing your speech is an important step in the speech-writing process. An **audience analysis** is simply different methods that are used for finding out about the differences in people, such as their age, gender, ethnicity, education, religion, and group membership. You should also know what their attitudes, beliefs, and values are toward yourself and the topic or issue.

If you are going to give a presentation to a group of civic leaders about whether or not you should vote for or against the commercial sale of alcohol in your community, an audience analysis is very important. For example, when introducing your ideas to church groups, it might be more appropriate to use *direct* or *rhetorical* questions concerning the moral or amoral implications of such a vote. This audience will consist of a difference in ages, gender, education, and group membership. Because of the ethical considerations that should be examined, such as morality issues, the presenter of the message should expect that most of the audience is likely to provide active feedback. Properly analyzing this audience will likely reveal that most members' sense of values are relatively the same.

However, this same issue presented at the local country club may have a similar mixture of ages, gender, and ethnicity, but the audiences' sense of values are likely to be more different than the church audience. The presenter of this issue would be wise to analyze the audience by using questionnaires or surveys to gather data that might help when addressing the country club.

## Four Goals of a Speech

The foundation and roof metaphor speaks volumes to those who have given speeches. The main points of a message will only be as effective as its introduction and conclusion. If not introduced correctly, people will become disinterested, and if a message isn't concluded properly, the audience will likely feel cheated of their time. So, like the foundation that gives a house support and a roof that gives it shelter, a well-written introduction and conclusion will have the same effect on the success and credibility of the speaker.

The introduction of a speech should accomplish these four goals:

- Grab the Audience's Attention
- Reveal the Topic of Your Speech
- Increase Speaker Credibility
- Preview the Main Points of Your Speech

Audiences are more likely to give the speaker their attention if these rules are followed. Failure to follow these fundamental rules will weaken the speaker's credibility before he or she even begins the body of his/her speech.

## Using Introductions

Where the body of the speech follows a more logical sequence of steps, the introduction and conclusion is generally a more creative process. Failure to grab the audience's attention will likely lead to a boring speech for the audience and decreased credibility for the speaker. Below are five common ways that an audience's attention can be captured:

- Dramatic Statements
- Stories
- Questions
- Quotations
- Humor

## Four Ways to Capture the Audience

**Dramatic statements** are effective in grabbing your attention in that they are designed to evoke a response from the listener. This will be the toughest thing you ever hear in your life. Technology is a double-edged sword; it entertains as it slices away our privacy. Everybody loves technology and the way it simplifies their life, but with this also comes disadvantages, such as invasion of privacy from numerous mediated sources." Most people haven't been cut or stabbed but can imagine the pain involved. Most people, however, can certainly relate to the advan-

tages and disadvantages of having technology in their lives. This introduction helps illustrate the point through a dramatic statement.

**Stories** are effective because most people like to be entertained; they like to hear stories whether they are real or created to prove a point. **Real-life stories** and **imaginative stories** are both effective in speech introductions. Let's first take a look at this personal, real-life story that was used in the introduction of Dana's persuasive speech about "Why everyone should support organ donation":

"Two years ago my family and I were faced with a decision that had never previously crossed our minds: organ donation. My younger sister was in a car accident that left her in a coma. Nearly a week passed as she lied in the hospital never speaking a word. As my family and I pondered the fate of my beloved sister, Rebecca, we gave much thought about what to do with her healthy organs. We knew that there were people in that very hospital who could benefit from Rebecca's organs if she didn't live. Before we would ever make that decision, my sister regained consciousness and began the long fight to stay alive. Today, she is alive and well, and what her accident taught me was that life is a precious thing. My family and I, including Rebecca, are all organ donors because of these events."

Real-life stories like Dana's are effective when they are directly linked to the speech topic. Dana gained credibility as she showed goodwill to her audience by relating the personal events of her life to the reasons behind her persuasive speech topic. She grabbed the audience's attention by sharing the personal story of her sister and creating a mood of sympathy, thus helping the body of the speech as the audience was more likely to hear what she had to say about organ donation.

Another effective way to use stories is the *imaginative story*, which puts the audience in the proper frame of mind according to the topic. Consider this imaginative story used by Amy in her speech about "The American Revolution: A Day in the Life of a Soldier," presented at a local history museum:

> "The year was 1763; the wind was cold and cruel as it spread like a disease across the war-scarred land. The once colorful autumn trees are now black skeletons left to die in winter's cold embrace. The soldier leaned his battered body against a lonely tree as he braved not only the weather, but the enemy who lurked somewhere closely in the wood. Despite all this, the soldier could only think of his wife and son who were far away, but close within his heart. Thoughts like these were short lived as he knew he must move on. The British were all around, and if caught he knew he'd never see his family again. The soldier summoned all his strength as headed toward a trail of smoke that he glimpsed through the withered trees. Soon he heard the voices of his companions, and a smile grew upon his face as he drew nearer. For weeks now, this became routine for the cold and lonely young man: just another day in the life a young soldier in the American Revolution."

Amy's speech used descriptive language, as it was designed to put the listener in a frame of mind that could more easily relate to these past events. An informative speech about a soldier's life in the American Revolution is hard for people today to relate to, so Amy wisely used creativity so that the audience could imagine what it would have been like to have actually been there.

**Questions** are another effective way to grab your audience's attention if done correctly. Questions have a unique way of capturing attention because they are audience-focused, which instantly tells the listener that the speaker desires a response from them. *Direct* and *Rhetorical* questions are two common types of questions used in speech introductions. These two types should be used if they are directly related to the speech topic. Let's take a look at examples of each type.

**Rhetorical questions** are those that are intended to encourage thought but not a direct response.

For instance, a student used this rhetorical question in his informative speech about the number of American lives lost in World War II:

> "Does anyone know how many American lives were lost during World War II? How many total human lives were laid waste of all the countries involved during this tremendous conflict? Can you even begin to imagine what it would feel like in today's society if a war happened to steal thousands of souls who are now close to us? What are the reasons for this many people losing their lives? Today, I will discuss these very issues. I've been interested in this topic for years, ever since my grandfather revealed his personal accounts to me about the war and the death it waged."

Students know about World War II from history class or even the movies. How many Americans died is a statistic many people would soon forget. Many students know how the war ended, but may not remember the detailed events that occurred in between. Jack decided the best way to get his audience thinking about his main ideas was to simply ask them through rhetorical questions.

**Direct questions** are designed to evoke a direct response from the listener, verbally or nonverbally, but usually a nonverbal response is given, such as a nod of the head that acknowledges the message. They are used to get the audience actively involved in the listening process. Here are a couple of direct questions in use: "Raise your hands if you agree that college textbook prices are getting out of hand." This next question seeks a little more participation: "For those students who did not raise your hands, quickly explain to the rest of us who buys your college textbooks." Obviously the speaker is more likely to get a direct response with the first direct question, but the second question is just as effective because the listener now becomes the center of focus. How about this direct question: "Are there any here today that pay their own tuition? How many of you feel a greater sense of accomplishment because you know that your hard-earned dollars are buying your future?"

**Rhetorical and direct questions** are effective when they are related to your speech topic and successful at generating audience feedback. The speaker must be specific with his or her language when using direct questions, or they will sound like rhetorical questions.

**Quotations** are frequently used when it comes to giving presentations. "My task, above all, is to make you see," said Joseph Conrad, literary author of such works as *Heart of Darkness* and *Lord Jim*. Abraham Lincoln once said, "If you would win a man to your cause, first convince him you are his friend." Language is a powerful tool when conveying important information, whether using it in a business meeting or in a speech at the local Chamber of Commerce. The deliverers of a presentation should ask themselves if the quotation is relevant to the topic or issue that will be addressed.

There are many sources that quotations can be drawn from, such as books of quotations, history books, academic texts and journals, as well as direct quotations from the person himself or herself. Three more common sources for quotations:

- *Bartlett's Familiar Quotations*
- *The Quotations Homepage*
- *Good Quotations from Famous People*

## The Humor Caution

*Humor* can be used to grab audience's attention because people like to laugh. However, a joke that is stale or not in good taste will have the opposite effect. When professionals give presentations in public settings, humor can be used to "lighten" the seriousness of the topic, but not altogether undermine the importance of the issue.

## Reveal the Topic of Your Speech

Audiences need to know early on what it is you will be presenting to them. If you have effectively grabbed their attention, it is likely that the topic or issue has already been revealed. Never confuse your listeners because it will affect your credibility as a speaker, and your audience will probably not pay attention to you.

Business and religious leaders, politicians, and teachers usually adhere to these rules when beginning a presentation. Often they will use stories, questions, or sometimes humor to motivate the audience to listen. Successful presenters are always those who are clear and unambiguous when letting their audience know what they will be speaking

about. Never disguise your topic with language that you cannot justify in your speech.

## Increase Speaker Credibility

Ethics is very important concerning the success or failure of a speaker. Speaker credibility or goodwill, or what Aristotle discussed as *ethos* concerns what one perceives as right or wrong, fair or unfair, moral or amoral, and just or unjust. Concerning introductions, establishing credibility as a speaker is crucial if that speaker desires to have an audience that will truly listen to what he or she has to say. For example, a small business owner once was delivering a speech to his local Chamber of Commerce about the "Abolition of Affirmative Action," and began the introduction by using a rhetorical question and statement which read: "Why are laws governing who American business owners should or should not hire? Government in a capitalist society should not decide how businesses conduct its hiring practices. Affirmative Action was created to help people be considered for jobs, but now it prevents even more people from getting interviews despite their qualifications. Once the facts have been read, you will get a better understanding of why affirmative action should be abolished."

Although you might not see it at first, this introduction faces several ethical considerations. The individual spoke on a topic that was sure to offend much of his audience, and used language that likely distanced himself from his listeners. Additionally, he mentioned "facts" that will supposedly prove that he is correct, but the critical listener will have inferred that "facts" of this nature sound more like "opinions." Does this speech sound fair? Is the speaker using this topic as a platform to change his business practices, or does he have another agenda?

## Preview the Main Points of Your Speech

An audience that has great listening skills will be able to hear a message one time and never forget it. Unfortunately, most people do not have great listening skills, which is why the presenter should always preview the topics or issues that will be discussed. Preachers usually use repetition in their sermons. An effective presenter, whether preacher, teacher, or corporate trainer, will not only reveal the topic but the main points as well.

## Three Goals of Effective Conclusions

Presentations have rules for their conclusions, as well as their introductions. Here are effective ways that a presenter should conclude his or her message:

- Signal the End of Your Speech
- Summarize the Speech and Re-emphasize the Thesis Statement
- Provide Closure: End with a Quotation or Dramatic Statement, Emotional Appeal, Question, Refer Back to Introduction

If the introduction of your presentation sparks first impressions from your audience, the conclusion is designed to create lasting impressions, something to remember or even respond to in some way. An effective conclusion also works similar to its introduction, because they are both designed to capture an audience's attention and interest.

These three rules for concluding speeches will provide the audience with a sense of completeness, which is necessary if the speaker expects a desired response from his or her audience. Let's take a look at the first rule for using conclusions:

## Signal the End of Your Speech

Always let your audience know that you are concluding the message of your presentation. Ways to signal that you are concluding are:

- "Remember the keys discussed . . ."
- "One last thought"
- "Never forget what I've told you . . ."

"In conclusion" and "To conclude" are commonly used, so be creative. Whatever the arrangement of words you choose to use, make sure this transition lets your audience know that you are moving out of the body of your speech. Importantly, however, these words alone do not constitute the end of your speech.

## Summarize the Speech and Re-emphasize the Thesis Statement

Once the main ideas of the speech have been delivered and the speaker has signaled the conclusion's arrival, a summary of the main ideas needs repeating. This may sound like more repetition, but it helps to drive the message home.

The more listeners of a message are exposed to it, the more likely they are to remember and respond to it. Summarizing the material presented in the conclusion of a presentation is using repetition that is found throughout the presentation. For example, the introduction reveals the topic to be discussed as well as the main points that will be covered, or "Tell the audience what you are going to tell them." In the body of the presentation, a speaker covers the main points and, if done so appropriately, will use internal previews and internal summaries to help reinforce these points. This is often referred to as "Telling the audience." Summarizing the points in the conclusion is called "Telling the audience what you've just told them."

Re-emphasis is not just a general summary, but used with the summary it probes deeper into the heart of the message. Re-emphasizing the main ideas of a speech is simply placing emphasis on these ideas in a way that sends the listener away with something important to remember and that is useful, and it is the last chance the speaker has to win the audience over. Consider this example of re-emphasis a company trainer used when concluding her training presentation to a small advertising firm:

"The importance of communication in organizations transcends all other functions. However, the effective adaptation and application of communication completes the organization. The goals set before you today are utilizing the knowledge and application of interpersonal, leadership, and organizational practices. Takes these concepts with you and use these to increase your company's productivity, commitment, and satisfaction. Don't be just another idle company who waits forever to turn itself around."

The speaker of this training presentation summarized her main points by clearly letting the audience know the importance of the message through re-emphasis. The difference between redundancy and repetition will be the difference between an effective and ineffective speaker; redundancy is information presented that is not useful, while the effective repetition of a message will make all the difference in the world.

## Five Ways to Provide Closure

**Quotations** are one of the more common ways to conclude a speech. As discussed with using quotations in speech introductions, make sure the quotation is related to the topic. Also, a speaker would be wise to use a quote from the same person they used in the introduction of their presentation, which helps provide a sense of closure to the overall message.

**Dramatic Statements** are smart ways to leave lasting impressions upon the mind of the listener. Saying something dramatic or startling usually gets a positive response; remember that the primary purpose of speaking is to get a desired response from your audience. Effective dramatic statements will evoke that desired response, so the presenter must use careful language and extemporaneous skills for it to be successful. **Emotional Appeals** are used to evoke emotional responses with your audience.

- "The life you save may be your own. So, if you don't want AIDS, please take action now by supporting these easy-to-follow guidelines that will help prevent the spread of the terrible disease."

- "This company should ACT NOW if it truly desires change. The inability to make a decision is often the difference between success or failure. Do you want to be a relic of the past or a product of the future?"

**Questions** are useful as well. Just as you began with a question, you can end with one. **Refer back** to the Introduction to also end your speech. Make use of the attention grabber used in your introduction.

Quotations and dramatic statements used effectively will provide a sense of closure to your speech. Your goal is to leave the listener with something to think about or respond to. Quotations are words taken "right from the horse's mouth," and dramatic statements are designed to evoke a desired response from the listener.

## The Finished Product

Thinking back to the foundation and roof metaphor at the beginning of this chapter, the reader will remember that the main ideas of a speaker's presentation will only be as effective as his or her introduction and conclusion. Four strong walls of a house are weak without the support and shelter that provides the backbone: the foundation and roof. A weak introduction or conclusion will inevitably weaken the presentation, despite the amount of logic and persuasive appeal found within the speaker. However, a well-crafted beginning and ending will allow a speaker to shine as he or she delivers an effective, polished presentation.

The finished product will be successful in giving the speaker the desired response he or she expected from their presentation. Remembering the rules for using introductions and conclusions is essential in the speech-writing process; but a speaker should always pay attention to other factors that can bring success or failure to a presentation, such as analyzing the audience and adhering to ethical considerations. Language that might captivate one audience may offend another; speakers may build credibility during one presentation while destroying it someplace else. Effective introductions and conclusions are those that can change from audience to audience, but should never change the meaning of the message.

# ACTIVITIES

# Beginning and Ending Your Speech

# Creating Introductions

1. Create Introductions for the following topics for both Informative and Persuasive speeches.
   - The Holocaust
   - Affirmative Action
   - Censorship

2. Watch a speech on television, or from another venue, and analyze the strengths and weaknesses of the speaker's Introduction and Conclusion. From television, you may want to watch CSPAN or any news related broadcast that will be giving presentations. Also, your local chamber of commerce, school-sponsored speaker, or local city council meeting are good locations to consider.

   Did the speaker adhere to the rules of Introductions and Conclusions, as discussed in the text? How would you have changed their use of language if given the opportunity?

3. Research presentations delivered by effective speakers like Abraham Lincoln, John F. Kennedy, Martin Luther King, Jr., or Mark Twain, etc. Did their Introduction support their main ideas? Did their Introduction contain descriptive language? After reading their speech, rewrite the Introduction according to the way you feel it would be more effective in today's audience (your classroom).

4. How would you adjust your speech Introduction when giving the same presentation to these different audiences? *Topic:* "In Support of Tax Increase for a Safer Community"; *Audiences:* local chamber of commerce, local churches, business owners, and property investors.

5. Compose Introductions and at least two main ideas for the following topic: "The Value of a College Education." Exchange with another classmate and critique their Introductions, and also add an effective Conclusion to the revised outline.

# Notes

# 6

# Speaking to Inform and Share Ideas

## CHAPTER PREVIEW

> At one point in your life, you will be called upon to share
> information to a group of people . . . an audience . . .
> this is the foundation of informative speaking.
>
> ⌐MJ Wagner

Now that you know how to gather and organize supporting materials for a presentation while keeping the audience in mind, you are ready to move on to the next step. We have laid the foundation for preparing to share ideas with an audience. In this chapter, we will consider types, purposes, designs, and guidelines for creating informative speeches.

## Eight Types of Informative Speeches

Based on the fact that you are in the educational process, we assume that you expect, one day, to be employed in a profession, such as business, education, law, or medicine. One of the most fundamental facts is that you will be required to speak well in order to be successful in your chosen career. There will be times when you will be expected to speak informatively about your profession and you may or may not be provided with a specific speech topic.

When you are asked to give an informative presentation, you will be expected to share your knowledge and understanding of a topic. There are many speech topics from which to choose, if that is your responsibility, whether you are presenting in this public speaking class, to the local school board, or at the Toastmasters' club. Therefore, you will need to narrow the topic to something specific. There are several types of informative speeches from which you may choose. The following categories are not the only ones available, but they provide several options for creating, analyzing, and organizing your informative presentation.

### Speaking about Concepts

When speaking about **concepts,** your topic will be about anything that is invisible, intangible, and unstable in form. This concept could be a belief, theory, idea, notion, or principle. Some examples might

include: love, democracy, evolution, attention deficit disorder, home schooling, or the Golden Rule.

### Speaking about an Event

You may be requested to speak about a specific **event,** which may have happened in the past, present, or be expected to happen in the future. You might consider a noteworthy occurrence, such as rock climbing, the Oscars, a basketball game, the Civil Rights movement, landing on the moon, or the Challenger accident. In addition to historical events, there are many current or future occurrences that might be applicable, such as balancing your checkbook or planning a wedding.

### Speaking about Issues or Problems

Perhaps you are employed by the local manufacturing plant and have been asked to address your fellow employees about the problems arising from the implementation of a new project on the assembly line. In this informative speech, you would not be required to persuade the audience to adopt the new project; rather, you would be expected to inform the employees about the **problems** or **issues** that may arise with the new procedure. This assignment provides a specific topic area for you as the speaker. However, there will be times when you are requested to address an audience when the topic is not quite so evident. You will be expected to come up with your own topic. Possible topics you might choose would be to provide an overview about a problem or a matter in dispute where people are seeking a conclusion, such as abortion, gun control, campus parking, or the problems that arise when you live with other people in a dormitory setting.

### Speaking about Objects

Perhaps the assignment you've been given is to present an **object,** such as a copy machine or a DVD player, to teach a group about the use of these types of technology. Each of these objects have specific qualities which are universal to any topic you might choose in this category. When speaking about an object, you will be choosing anything that is visible, tangible, and stable in form, but is not human.

### Speaking about People

When you are speaking about **people,** the topic usually focuses on historically-significant or compelling individuals or groups who have made either a positive or negative impact on society. For example, your history professor has assigned a presentation about a contemporary political figure, but you are having difficulty deciding who would be most interesting to you as the researcher and the audience as the listeners. You may choose such people as, Saddam Hussein, Tony Blair, Condoleezza Rice, or George W. Bush.

### Speaking about Places

As an aspiring travel agent, you may be required to address a civic organization to inform the audience about the destination of their upcoming trip. In the past, your group has traveled to such places as the Grand Canyon and Yosemite National Park, but this year they have decided to travel to Washington D.C. During this trip they will be visiting such sites as the Washington Monument, the Vietnam Memorial, and the Smithsonian Institute. You are responsible for sharing the highlights of the destination and informing the audience about the exciting trip on which they are about to embark. Other places they had considered for this year's annual trip included Disneyworld, the Bahamas, and Montreal.

### Speaking about Plans or Policies

There are many types of **plans** or **policies** that you might be required to give as an informative speech. For example, you might be requested to present an architectural plan to the local school board in preparation for building an addition to the local middle school, or you might be expected to explain the new health care plan to your company's employees. When presenting a plan or policy as an informative speech, you will need to be careful not to persuade the audience to take action or implement the plan or policy.

### Speaking about Processes or Giving a Demonstration

Speaking to inform an audience about a **process** or to give a **demonstration** would be to explain a systematic series of actions that leads to a specific result or product. You might inform the audience about the application, admission, and registration process into your college or university. To demonstrate how to change the oil in your car, how to create a web-page, or how to play the clarinet would also fulfill the assignment when you are required to speak about a process or give a demonstration. Professionally, you might be required to inform your co-workers about the process of filing a health care claim or the accepted method of presenting a sales pitch to a potential customer.

> The great seal of truth is simplicity.[1]
> —Herman Boerhaave

## Five Purposes of Informative Speaking

In informative speaking, you will define, describe, demonstrate, explain, or narrate.

### Defining

**Defining** is to identify the essential qualities and meaning of a word or term. You may use this approach in your informative presentation in order to create shared meaning and understanding between you as the speaker and your audience, the receiver. There are several methods of defining something, including:

- **By etymology.** When defining your terms by etymology, you are considering the origin of the word(s) being discussed. When you focus on the history of a word to illustrate the meaning of a word or term, such as Pro-Life vs Pro-Choice, you are able to create an understanding with the audience about the specific term. In this example, you might identify the differences and similarities between these two terms based on the origin of the words.

- **By example.** When defining by example, you explain the subject being discussed, i.e., demonstrating painting techniques, through the illustration or demonstration of the techniques. When defining by example something that is abstract, such as love, you might create a word-picture of the relationship between two specific individuals. The example helps the audience to understand your meaning.

- **By negation.** When defining a term by negation, you are describing what it is not. This technique might also be used when defining something abstract, such as courage. For example, the quotation, *"Courage is not the absence of fear"* (this is attributed to several authors, including Mark Twain, Robert Heinlein, and Ambrose Redmoon)[2], does not explain the concept in terms of what courage is; rather, it defines it by what it is not. This technique might also be used when defining objects, such as a beetle is not a mammal.

- **By synonym.** When we are talking with friends, we often use the technique of defining a term by comparing it with another similar or equivalent term. For example, you might talk about a movie such as *Daredevil* with your peers by comparing it to *Spiderman*. Both of these films are action-adventure tales, making them similar to each other, but they also have differences, which you might be able to explain through definition by synonym.

- **By operational definition.** When we conduct research, we often define the thing we are analyzing based on an operational definition. This definition identifies a term or word by what it does. For example, a DVD is the abbreviation for digital versatile disk or digital video disk, which is recorded using optical technology. This operational definition provides a shared understanding about the exact item being discussed.

## Demonstrating

You may choose to demonstrate your topic in order to effectively explain how it works or what it does. This method of informative presentation provides an opportunity for the audience to understand a process. For example, on his cooking show, Emiril demonstrates how to make chocolate chip cookies so that the audience is able to see the process. Other examples when a demonstration might be effective include *Trading Spaces, This Old House,* or *Surprise by Design.* Each of these television shows illustrates methods of redecorating your home by demonstrating the use of interior design or architectural techniques.

## Describing

When you design your informative speech, this purpose provides the audience with a mental image of something—either something abstract or concrete. For example, you could describe the experience of surviving a hurricane or the experience of getting married. Both of these examples are of something that is fairly concrete. In contrast, you could describe freedom of information in such a way that the audience is better able to understand the concept. This description is of something abstract or intangible.

## Explaining

When the purpose of your informative speech is to explain something to the audience, you will give the reason for or cause of something. Your explanation will help clarify and make the topic understandable

to the audience. Some examples of explanatory speech topics include: explaining your reasons for becoming president of your fraternity or sorority, explaining reasons for attending your college or university, explaining the cause of the increase in pricing of air travel to Paris, France, or explaining the reasons for the kiss between Madonna and Britney Spears at the MTV Video Music Awards ceremony. In each of these presentations, you as the speaker would logically develop the topic in order to help the audience understand the relationships that exist between the reason for an event and the event.

> Whatever words we utter should be chosen with care for people will hear them and be influenced by them for good or ill.[3]
>
> —Buddha

### Narrating/Storytelling

There are many times when telling a story, anecdote, or tale is the best method of providing an audience with an understanding of something. Whatever informative speech topic it is, there is usually a way of telling or providing spoken commentary that will help the audience better relate to you and your presentation. For example, when you want to tell about the Chinese practice of foot-binding, you might share the story of one woman's experiences getting her feet bound or your tale might focus on the political climate that has made foot-binding illegal in China after hundreds of years practicing this ritual. Or you might want to speak about preparing for the college experience, so you give a detailed anecdote of your own experiences: planning, packing, moving, and adjusting to college life. For each of these topics, narrating or storytelling causes the audience to be interested, captivated, and intrigued by the presentation.

## Designs of Informative Speeches

As discussed in chapter four, there are several organizational patterns you can use for designing your informative speech. This is not designed to provide in-depth background on how to design each pattern, but is a reminder of which arrangements are appropriate for the informative speech process. Your informative speech should not be persuasive—calling the audience to change an attitude, belief, or behavior. Rather, it should simply share information and create understanding for the audience. Those organizational patterns suitable for an informative speech include the following choices.

### Causal

A causal organizational pattern is appropriate when showing how some events bring about other events and may be used for speeches about events, issues, and processes. For example, rain brings about the use of an umbrella.

### Chronological

A chronological organizational pattern may be used when discussing anything that occurs through a sequence of time, including an historical event, such as the American Revolution or the Civil Rights movement, or a trend, such as the Hoola-Hoop or fashion trends. Chronology would also be effective when demonstrating a process, such as baking a cake or changing the oil in your car.

### Comparative Advantages (Compare and Contrast)

This organizational pattern may be effectively used for an informative speech, but you must be careful not to advocate one or the other of the items you are comparing and contrasting. The act of advocating or supporting one over the other may lend itself to a persuasive argument—calling the audience to action. You might use this organizational pattern informatively when discussing different breeds of horses or types of cars. Comparing and contrasting different types of cars may lead to suggesting that the audience prefer one over the other, and you want to avoid that in the informative presentation.

### Problem-Solution

A problem-solution organizational pattern is useful for the informative presentation when you are speaking about a process, concept, or issue. However, this pattern lends itself to persuading the

## Guidelines for Creating an Informative Speech

1. Analyze your audience. Relate your presentation directly to the audience's prior knowledge, but don't overestimate what they already know.

2. Approach your topic in a way that is fresh and interesting.

3. Be careful how much information you include in your presentation. It should not be either too much or too little. Strive for balance.

4. Create shared meaning and understanding by providing definitions for your terms.

5. Establish the relevance of your presentation for the audience in the introduction and reiterate it in the conclusion.

6. Include examples, analogies, and visual aids that enhance the presentation as well as help the audience retain the information presented.

7. Make sure your information is new, relevant, and interesting.

8. Personalize your ideas in order to reach and relate to the target audience.

9. Use repetition in your presentation to reinforce your message.

10. Use language appropriate for the audience's needs, fitting their age and education or comprehension level.

11. Use clear, concrete, and vivid language to clarify your audience's understanding—avoiding abstractions, technical language, jargon, euphemisms, and double-speak.

audience to enact a specific solution to the problem identified. The example provided in chapter four, *Excessive teenage drinking is a problem that has several solutions available*, may be used successfully as an informative speech. Be careful to inform the audience about the solution, not advocate a specific action for them to take.

### Spatial

This organizational pattern is appropriate for speeches about places, locations, or physical arrangements of objects. In addition, you could use this speech design when informing your audience about the location of items within a physical setting, such as giving directions to another location.

### Topical

This organizational pattern is appropriate for speeches that have main points that are of relatively equal importance and can be presented in any order relative to the main points without changing the message. This pattern has a natural design, for speeches such as the example provided in this chapter: *Dying to Be Thin: Anorexia Nervosa*. This sample identifies three specific areas about the disease and explains them using the topical pattern.

# Sample Informative Speech Preparation Outline

## (Topical Pattern)

This sample preparation outline provides an example of an informative speech utilizing a topical organizational pattern.

**Title:** Dying to Be Thin: Anorexia Nervosa[4]

**General Goal:** To inform

**Specific Objective:** To inform my audience of the warning signs of anorexia, medical and psychological problems of the eating disorder, and the road to recovery.

**Thesis Statement:** Anorexic patients develop ritualistic eating behaviors and a controlling, self-absorbed persona that leads to a strenuous recovery, which is not always permanent.

### Introduction

The introduction should gain the audience's attention.

I. In the original performance, the speaker displayed a picture of an anorexic female climbing rocks. Can you tell me what is wrong in it? I'll give you a hint; it has nothing to do with rock climbing.

A. If you answered "the girl," you are correct.

B. She is practically a skeleton.

This introduction establishes credibility both through peer testimony in II, but also through statistical evidence in III.

II. This picture is of one of my very close friends.

A. Through our sophomore and junior years of high school, I watched her waste away to a rack of bones. I laughed, cried, and prayed for her as she quickly disappeared.

B. I was there for her rocky recovery.

III. As reported by the Harvard Mental Health Letter, about one in 200 persons in the United States will develop anorexia at some point in their life.

In IV, the speaker relates the topic to both the male and female audience members.

IV. Don't think this applies only to women; at least ten percent of the anorexic patients are men.

V. This thesis statement indicates the speech structure and provides a sign-post for the audience.

V. Today I would like to share with you the warning signs of anorexia nervosa, how it affects the person and his or her family, and the endless road to recovery.

Each transition statement should bridge the sections. Here the transition links the introduction with the body.

(Transition: Let's first take an in-depth look at the behaviors associated with the eating disorder, anorexia nervosa.)

### Body

The main points (I, II, and III) are written to reflect those ideas identified in the thesis statement.

I. At some point in life, almost everyone is concerned about their weight. Because most people diet once in a while, it is hard to determine what behaviors constitute anorexia.

A. Perhaps the first warning sign occurs when a person develops ritualistic food and exercise habits.

This informative speech includes important sub-points in addition to the main points provided in the thesis statement.

1. Fat intake is drastically reduced and sometimes completely eradicated from the diet.

2. The person becomes disgusted with former favorite foods like meats, breads, and desserts.

3. She or he refuses to eat anything unless she or he has read and approved the food label.

4. The person exercises excessively and compulsively, keeping a harsh and strenuous regimen only through sheer willpower.

B. Socially, the anorectic becomes controlling and isolated.

1. The person tries to please everyone and withdraws when this task is impossible.

2. She or he tries to take care of and control others.

3. The person tries to control when, where, and what time the family eats.

4. He or she no longer spends time with friends, and does not partake in activities he or she used to love.

C. The anorectic develops distorted and obsessive views of his or her body image and begins to experience depression.

1. The person swears he or she is fat even though bones are becoming visible.

2. She or he detests certain parts of her or his body and believes she or he cannot be happy unless she or he is skinny.

3. The person becomes irrational and denies anything is wrong.

4. He or she argues when people try to help or disagree with him or her and becomes very competitive.

This transition statement creates a bridge between the main points of the body.

This second main point moves the discussion from identifying anorexic behaviors to the effects of the disease.

(Transition: Now that we are aware of anorexia warning signs, let's look at the medical and psychological problems anorectics face.)

II. If anorexia is not treated, starvation will lead to irreversible physical damage, lifetime psychological problems, and adversely affect family members.

    A. There are numerous medical problems involved with anorexia.

        1. When the body does not receive enough calories to provide the needed energy, it begins to eat away fat tissue, and when the fat supply runs out, it begins to digest vital organs.

            a. The body will first eat away at the body's muscle.

            b. It then moves on to destruction of the kidney, liver, and heart, among other organs.

        2. Growth is stunted due to malnutrition.

        3. Skin becomes dry, blotchy, and appears gray or yellow.

        4. Hair follicles die and hair begins to fall out.

    B. Psychological problems occur other than weight and food obsession.

        1. Anorectics often become severely depressed and feel hopeless, which can lead to suicide.

        2. They feel guilt and shame for giving in to food cravings.

        3. They become compulsive, and rituals dictate most of their activities.

    C. The family is always severely scarred.

        1. Family members struggle with guilt, worry, anxiety, and frustration. Nothing they do seems to help their child.

        2. Family members also find it hard to cope with anorexia because they cannot understand exactly how their child feels, and it hurts them beyond belief.

This transition connects the second and third main points of the presentation.

(Transition: With a disorder so physically and psychologically damaging, recovery is sometimes the most difficult part of the disease.)

III. Treatment for anorexia requires not only therapy and medication, but also constant support and understanding from the family as the anorectic copes with weight gain.

    A. Psychiatrists and physicians are required to make sure the anorexic patient gains weight.

        1. The aim is to restore her weight, change her eating habits, and prescribe medications to control anxiety and depression.

        2. Physicians ensure vital organs are no longer damaged and that the patient does not go into shock.

Once treatment has been sought for the disease, recovery from anorexia is discussed.

B. Psychologists treat the mental disorders of anxiety and depression. They use motivational enhancement techniques to change the patients thinking habits and calm his or her fears.

C. The family is essential for providing love and support to the anorexic patient.

This transition connects the body with the conclusion of the presentation.

(Transition: The warning signs of anorexia nervosa are not always evident to the person and his or her family, and there seems to be an endless road to recovery.)

## Conclusion

The conclusion, as stated in chapter 5, should summarize the main points of the speech, and provide the audience with something by which to remember the presentation.

I. Anorexia is an all-encompassing disease. It affects not only the person's attitude and behavior, but causes serious medical, psychological, and family problems.

II. Perhaps the most disturbing part of anorexia is that it is a chronic illness, ready to rear its ugly head at any weak point in a person's life.

III. Today, my friend from high school has recovered from anorexia. She hasn't won the battle by any means. She fights daily with thoughts of her weight and urges to relapse back to starvation.

IV. You might wonder how on earth I know so much about this disease. Well, this young lady in the picture is me.

## Bibliography

This sample bibliography follows the Publication Manual of the American Psychological Association (5th edition).

Anorexia nervosa. Part I (2003, February). *Harvard Mental Health Letter,* 19(8).

Anorexia nervosa: Part II (2003, March). *Harvard Mental Health Letter,* 19(9).

Anorexia Nervosa and Related Eating Disorders, Inc. (2002, April). *Eating disorders warning signs.* Retrieved May 17, 2003, from http://www.anred.com/warn.html.

Anorexia Nervosa and Related Eating Disorders, Inc. (2002, April). *Medical and psychological complications of eating disorders.* Retrieved May 17, 2003, from http://www.anred.com/medpsy.html.

Anorexia Nervosa and Related Eating Disorders, Inc. (2002, April). *Statistics.* Retrieved May 17, 2003, from http://www.anred.com/stats.html.

Anorexia Nervosa and Related Eating Disorders, Inc. (2002, April). *What causes eating disorders?* Retrieved May 17, 2003, from http://www.anred.com/causes.html.

Anorexia Nervosa and Related Eating Disorders, Inc. (2002, April). *Who is at risk for developing an eating disorder?* Retrieved May 17, 2003, from http://www.anred.com/who.html.

Miller, M. L. (1991). Understanding the eating-disorder patient: Engaging the concrete. *Bulletin of the Menninger Clinic,* 55.

# ACTIVITIES

# Speaking to Inform and Share Ideas

# Evaluating an Informative Speech

**Instructions:** Attend an informative presentation, such as a special lecture or workshop (preferably not a class), and outline the speaker's presentation. Answer the following questions regarding the speech.

1. What were the main points or ideas?

2. Which organizational pattern did this speaker use in this presentation? Provide evidence which illustrates this pattern.

3. Identify the supporting evidence the speaker used in this presentation. Was the evidence used effective and appropriate? Why or why not?

4. How did the speaker increase the audience's knowledge of the topic (provide examples)?

5. How did the speaker use vivid, clear language to enhance the presentation (provide examples)?

6. How did the speaker use defining, demonstrating, describing, explaining, or narrating/storytelling (provide examples)?

# Organizing a Speech to Inform

**Instructions:**

Assume you are preparing an informative speech on a topic provided by the instructor, such as the IDEAL MAN or IDEAL WOMAN (someone with whom you would like to be romantically involved). Your task is to generate a brief outline, including a specific purpose statement, thesis statement, three main points, and sub-points. (No research is necessary for this assignment. Be creative with your facts.)

Title:

Specific Purpose:

Thesis Statement:

Introduction:

       Attention Gaining Device:

       Establish Credibility:

       Preview Main Points, State Central Idea:

*Body*

I.    Main Point:

     A.    Sub-point

     B.    Sub-point

II.   Main Point:

     A.    Sub-point

     B.    Sub-point

III.  Main Point:

     A.    Sub-point

     B.    Sub-point

*Conclusion*

Summarize Main Points:

Memorable Final Statement:

## Notes

1. Retrieved September 28, 2003 from //www.cybernation.com/victory/quotations/subjects/

2. Retrieved September 4, 2003 from http://www.bartleby.com/quotations/.

3. Retrieved September 28, 2003 from http://www.quotablequotes.net/.

4. Author: Laura Lyons, written permission granted May 23, 2003.

5. Adapted from Buchanan, M. C. (2001). Public speaking icebreaker: Any old bag will do. *Selections from The Speech Communication Teacher 1996–1999: To accompany The Art of Public Speaking (7th ed.) by Stephen E. Lucas.* New York: McGraw Hill Companies Inc. (p. 86-87).

# 7 Giving Your Speech Visual Appeal

## CHAPTER PREVIEW

**1** The importance of visual aid use in speeches

**2** The purpose of visual aids in speeches

**3** Identifying the types of visual aids available for use in speeches

**4** Pitfalls of not practicing with visual aids

**5** Benefits and drawbacks of using each type of visual aid

**6** The importance of practicing with visual support

> The 'eyes' have it.—when you acknowledge this as a
> speaker, you can provide the visual appeal for your speech
> without weighing it down or detracting from it.
>
> ⌐Mary Kathryn Cash

You can see them on your favorite television shows, movies, and internet websites: pictures, graphs, charts, multimedia presentations, drawings, etc. Indeed, much of the way we receive information today is through visual channels. Visual images captivate the audience and enhance the verbal message being communicated. Speeches are no exception. Speeches can be enhanced using visual support aids that repeats, substitutes, or complements the verbal messages used by the speaker. Good speakers understand the value of visual support and recognize that visual support and verbal messages are equally important and mutually necessary.

## The Purpose of Visual Support

There are a variety of reasons for using visual support in an oral presentation. When thinking about how you might enhance an oral message with visual support, your first consideration should be: What do I want the visual support to do? What is its function?

And this leads to a second vital consideration. A visual "aid" is used to support a specific part of your speech—a specific main point, a particular piece of evidence, a specific process. It's not something attached to the complete speech after it's written; nor is it sort of an afterthought or requirement. Visual support should only be used when you can determine that it would add something of value to a point being spoken—an idea being communicated orally—at the time. So, visual support is used for specific purposes at specific times and places in your presentation. Indeed, I heard once that the thinking behind Microsoft's PowerPoint software is that it gives "power" to your "points." That is, it adds value to specific ideas in your presentation.

We have identified seven purposes—or ways of adding value to the spoken word. Keeping these purposes in mind before you create them will assist the audience in understanding both the oral message and the visual message and their connection

- to provide clarity
- to add emphasis
- to create connections between the audience and the speaker's ideas
- to make key points/ideas memorable
- to give your speech more concrete meaning
- to reduce speaker anxiety
- to minimize lengthy explanations in speeches

### Clarity

Visual aids can provide clarity to a speech when words alone cannot express the message in the exact way you want. For instance, if you were giving a speech on how to complete a voter registration card, you might want to have an enlarged sample voter registration card to assist your audience in following the steps.

### Emphasis

Visual aids can provide extra emphasis to your speech when the words you've chosen seem to fall short of the complete message you were trying to

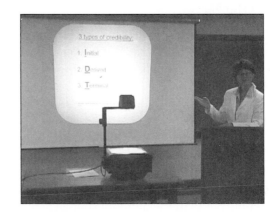

share. In another example, you might hit your fist on the podium to emphasize how strongly you feel about broken laws or criminal activity. Your simply saying that you feel strongly for or against a particular idea does not send as strong a message as those exact words coupled with a timely knock on the podium as you speak.

## Connections

Visual aids can provide the "links" between your spoken word and the audience's comprehension of your message. These connections can trigger common experiences in the minds of your audience members. For instance, placing a picture of a baby on an overhead projector, then asking the audience "What are the initial thoughts that come to mind when you see this picture?" Then transitioning into a moving persuasive speech about how appropriately used car seats can save the life of a baby. See how making those common connections can help draw in the interest of the audience at different points of your speech?

## Unforgettable

Visual aids can make your speech unforgettable. Since your audience will most likely forget a large portion of your speech, having visual aids that grab the audience's attention will aid in increasing the audience's retention of the material. If you were to use a computerized presentation software package to animate and automate your visual aids as opposed to using the same types of mediums (poster board, transparencies, handouts, etc.), your audience will remember the novelty of the visual aid as well as the message content you are presenting.

Keeping your visual aids novel and different will increase the likelihood that your audience will walk out and remember something more from your speech than simply the title. Remember, one of your key goals is to be remembered for your speech . . . be different!

## Concrete

Visual aids bring a certain level of concreteness to your speech. Your words are in many ways very abstract to your audience. Visual aids help to solidify your meanings in the minds of your audience and make your speech . . . memorable.

For many of you, you have built a comfort level in speaking abstractly rather than concretely. For instance, you might talk about the importance of dressing for success in a speech about interviewing well. Every audience member has a different set of experiences and perceives "dressing for success" differently. However, having models wearing the clothes you are describing or enlarged photographs of these clothes will increase the "common understanding" of your message.

## Reduce Speaker Anxiety

Practice and preparation are key in reducing your anxiety. However, visual aids can, for even brief moments, transfer the attention of the audience from you, the speaker, to the actual visual aid. This will provide an opportunity for you to gather yourself and mentally prepare for the next point as you are explaining the visual aid.

## Minimize Lengthy Explanations

Visual aids can minimize lengthy explanations in your speeches. At several different points in your speaking life, you will struggle for the exact words to use in your speech to convey a particular message. For instance, to show the impact of drinking and driving, a video tape of a drunken driver's car wrapped around a telephone pole might convey your message in a shorter time frame than spending an extra ten minutes of explanations.

In short, visual aids must serve a purpose in a speech. Visual aids cannot stand alone in a speech, nor should they detract the audience's attention from you for extended periods of time. You've reviewed the purposes for a visual aid; now, let's review the types of visual aids available for your speech.

## Types of Visual Aids

With so many types of visual aids . . . which one should you use? There are several types of visual aids that we can use in our speeches. Some visual aids are better than others. In any case, you will want to familiarize yourself with the following visual aid types:

- objects
- models
- photographs
- multimedia presentations and slideshows
- transparencies
- graphs
- charts
- audio, video, and handouts
- pictures
- speaker's own body

### Objects

**Objects** provide clarity for your message. You could give an informative speech about the adventure of rock climbing, but your bringing in the actual gear used to rock climb will help the audience understand the tools much better than just your simply speaking about the tool usage. Be very careful though; there are always some objects not suitable for the classroom. Be sure to get permission from your instructor before preparing your visual aids to bring to class.

### Models

**Models** are used as visual aids when the actual object is too small or too large to be used during the speech. For example, a student giving a speech about examining a car prior to leasing would want to use a model of a scaled-down car opposed to the life-sized version which is too large for use in a speech, especially in a classroom. You will want to note that models can be both costly and time consuming. You will want to keep this in mind as you plan your speech.

### Photographs

**Photographs** give you the flexibility to present your visual aid when you may not have access to the actual object or a model. With the advent of digital cameras and one-hour photo processing, you can have pictures at your fingertips within hours or minutes of taking the picture. You should note that pictures must be large enough to be seen from all sides of the room. Photos that you carry in your wallet or that sit on your desk at home are not appropriate. Enlargements would be necessary, and for many pictures, enlargements do not maximize the quality of the photo, but rather, the size of the photograph only. Keep this in mind as a limitation as you decide if a photograph is among the best ways to visually share the information with the audience.

### Speaker's Own Body

You may use your **own body** as a visual aid. If you were asked to give a speech about sign language, you would use your hands to demonstrate the different signs. You may even use your own body as you are giving a speech on CPR to demonstrate the exact placement of the hands. You will want to be careful to not turn your back on the audience as the speaker pictured below. You are blocking the line of sight for the audience to the speaker's right. Never turn your back on the audience.

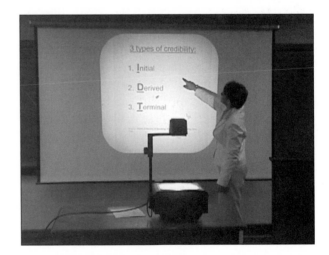

### Multimedia Presentations and Slideshows

**Multimedia presentations** animate and automate several visual aids for the audience. These can be used to integrate color, slides, videos, sound, graphs, and even charts into well coordinated visual aids.

These types of presentations can also be used to integrate Web page content into your speech. While this is a fantastic way to grab your audience's attention, this too can detract from your message. Multimedia presentations are usually easily converted into transparencies, charts, etc.

For today's fast-paced world, presentational software has replaced the more formerly used slide projectors to provide an inexpensive way of producing animated presentations. These types of presentations prepare you for those types of speeches you will give during your career-related work. For those of you who enjoy using presentational software, be wary that too many different fonts, pictures, animations, colors, etc. can be distracting. Understand that your audience will stop listening to you and choose to watch your visual aids only. The same holds true with videotapes. If you decide to use a brief selection from a video tape, you will want to preview for the audience what they are about to see and then debrief what was shown.

Slideshows are not as popular today as they once were. Today, slides are more expensive to produce, and the equipment to operate the slides is not as readily available. Multimedia presentations have quickly replaced these types of visual aids and provide pictures that are crisp and clear and that can be arranged and rearranged at your will. Multimedia presentations provide much more flexibility than its slide show predecessor.

## ▌ Transparencies

**Transparencies** are inexpensive ways to provide visual aids for the audience. A transparency is a thin, acetate film that when used with an overhead projector magnifies the image to three or five times the original size. Transparencies prevent you from spending countless hours creating a visual aid. To create a transparency, simply use your word processing software on your computer. Create the transparency using a large enough font size and type to be read; use graphics that are easily seen and reproduced in a black and white format. Note that transparencies can be reproduced in color, but the cost significantly rises in comparison to black and white reproductions.

As flexible as transparencies are, this flexibility can be a downfall. You will want to take care with your transparencies as the print may remove easily with scratches and bends to the film. Use a folder or notebook to keep the transparencies flat. Additionally, you will want to spell check your transparency before the

## Top 3 News Media Owners

1. **Disney**

2. **Dow Jones**

3. **General Electric**

Source: Riggins, A. (2004) News Media Owners in the Money. Media Publications: Chicago.

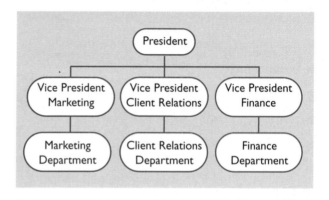

Organizational Chart
Pitney's Consulting, Inc.
Source: Pitney, A. (2005) Charting Our Leadership. Memphis: Pitney Printing.

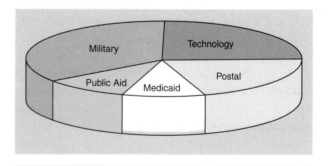

U.S. Budgetary Constraints
Source: Smith, J. (2004) The Strains of U.S. Money: A Look at Budgeting. Dallas: Coldwater Publishing Company.

day of the speech. If errors are found, you will need to create a new transparency.

## ▌ Charts and Graphs

Charts and graphs are great ways for you to display large amounts of information for the audience.

**Charts** are excellent for displaying categories or steps in a process. Audience members can easily follow the flow of the speech when charts are used to supplement your speech.

**Graphs** are good to help you clarify statistical information. For many students, statistical information is difficult to comprehend. For this reason, you will want to make any statistical portions of your speech as concrete as possible by using charts or graphs. This helps the audience avoid mental aerobics or a tug of war to comprehend your speech content. Graphs can also show comparisons or trends in your speech content. Many of your computer software packages make creating graphs an easy task.

### Handouts, Video, and Audio

All three of these visual aids require some practiced techniques to integrate into your speech smoothly and effectively. These visual aids will require your leading the audience into the visual aid you will use and debriefing the audience, once you have finished with the visual aid. For instance, a student preparing for a demonstration speech on the process of manufacturing homemade clay decides to use a handout to detail each step of the process. This speaker will want to hold the handout until the end of the speech to maintain the interest of the audience. Speakers using the handout in this way are providing information to aid in the retention of the information.

**Handouts** are wonderful retention tools for your audience. Many handouts that you will use should provide a summary of information for your audience to take with them following the speech. Handouts lose their effectiveness if given out during a speech or before the speech because they serve as a distraction for your audience. Usually, if there is information you'd like your audience to work with during your speech, transparencies or multimedia presentational software works best at meeting both your needs and the needs of the audience. You can prepare the audience for the visual aid by saying, "Now that we have walked through the process together, I have a handout for each of you to take with you that will enable you to repeat this process at home."

**Videotapes** are great tools in your visual aid "toolkit" as well; however, poorly edited videotapes can be your downfall during a speech. You will want to practice, practice, practice with the videotape each time to ensure your comfort level in its use. Always preview for the audience what they will see in the video clip and debrief them on what they've

seen once the clip has ended. This will assist the audience in following your message.

You may also do a speech that lends itself well to using sound in the introduction or during the first main point. You should preview the audience by saying, "Before we get into the essentials of meditation and relaxation, I would like you to sit in your seats and close your eyes. As you listen, pay close attention to what you hear and how you feel." Always have your **audio** and videotapes cued to the place you would like them to begin. Otherwise, you consume too much time searching for your video segments.

## Nine Guidelines for Preparing Your Visual Aids for Use in the Speech

As you prepare your visual aids, keep your audience in mind. You can think of being in the audience for a speech where you struggled to see or understand the visual aid being used. Likewise, you can also think of situations where you sat and listened to a speech without visual aids. When you craft your speech, you want your use of visual aids to fall between these two extremes to help you illustrate the key points of your speech. Effective speakers will use the following guidelines in preparing visual aids:

1. Establish **why** you want to use the visual aid. Think about the purposes of a visual aid.

2. **Keep it simple.** Visual aids should be simple and free from complications and clutter. Will the audience have an "Ah ha" moment or a "Huh?" moment?

3. **Use color and sizes effectively** . . . don't overdo it. Two or three colors is enough to maintain

emphasis and allow the audience to keep track of your point during your presentation. Using more than three colors or sizes will result in confusion for your audience. Choose softer colors for text and bolder colors for titles and words to be emphasized.

4. Use **font carefully** and effectively. Cute, elaborate or ornate fonts are great for invitations but horrible for visual aid use. Stick to fonts like Times New Roman and Arial. These are easy to see, regardless of font size.

5. Use **one font size** for the titles and another font size for the text. Most text should be at least 32 point font to be seen, and a 38 point font should be used for titles. Remember that your visual aids must be seen from any seat in the room. Using visual aids that are too small or difficult to read is a huge disappointment for your audience.

6. **Proofread** . . . proofread . . . proofread. Look for errors. Have a friend double check your visual aids for errors to avoid embarrassing situations.

7. Use no more than **six** lines of text down and six words across on any visual aid. You want to maintain a frame around your visual aid that can be seen clearly from any point in the room. Creating visual aids outside the guideline above increases the likelihood that the words will run off the surface of your visual aid (screen, poster board, etc.) or cause the audience to struggle to see the text. Text on your visual aids should be in key word format, not full sentences, to curb your tendency to read from the visual aid and minimize a cluttered appearance.

8. Pictures chosen must be **large enough** to be seen from the back of the room. Effective speakers keep their audience in mind at every stage of the speech creation process. So, you will want to consider how the room is arranged and how difficult it might be to see from any seat in the room. Start with pictures that are at least 8 1/2 x 11 in size. This is the smallest size you should use.

9. Make sure your visual aid **can be seen** from the back of the room.

## Seven Keys to Practicing with Your Visual Aids

Practice is key for effective use of your visual aids in your speech.

1. Practice with the visual aid in the same way you plan to use the visual aid during the speech.

2. Never display the visual aid until you are ready to use it. Allow the visual aid to remain concealed from the audience until you are ready to use it and remove the visual aid once you are finished. Otherwise this can be distracting.

3. Plan on what you will say while the video clip is being played, walking over to the visual aid, etc.

4. Always prepare to give the presentation without the visual aid, just in case the visual aid malfunctions, equipment failure, or is unavailable for use.

5. Always have a back-up plan.

6. Decide how you will best arrange the space where you will be delivering your speech. Make sure you, the podium, or other visual aids are not blocking each other.

7. Always visit the location where you will be giving the speech prior to the presentation to forecast any needs you will have and to assist in planning to give the effective speech.

### TIPS

- Preparing your visual aids early will provide an opportunity to check for grammatical errors.

- Practice with your visual aids to avoid choppy integration into your speech.

### Seven Tips for Using Visual Aids in Your Speech

1. Never block your visual aids with your body or another visual aid.

2. Always have a "lead-in statement" or preview statement in reference to a visual aid.

3. Always share the significance of the visual aid with the audience. Explain the visual aid . . . don't allow the audience to wonder why you are using it.

4. Place speaking cues in your speaking outline to remind you when to display the visual and when to remove it.

5. Make sure your visual aids are in the order you will use them to avoid experiencing confusion at the podium.

6. If you are using your body as a visual aid, make sure that what you are demonstrating can be easily seen throughout the room.

7. It is acceptable to point toward the screen, but avoid blocking your audience's view.

## Ethical Considerations

Using visual aids without citing the source is unethical and is equivalent to plagiarism.

# ACTIVITIES

# Giving Your Speech Visual Appeal

# Starting from Scratch: Creating Vibrant Visual Aids

**Student Textbook Instructions:** Of the speech opportunities listed below, describe three visual aids that could be used for each speech:

1. Process/Demonstration Speech—"The Three Basic CPR Techniques"

   Visual Aid 1:

   Visual Aid 2:

   Visual Aid 3:

2. Process/Demonstration Speech—"The Three Basic Steps in Applying for Graduate School"

   Visual Aid 1:

   Visual Aid 2:

   Visual Aid 3:

3. Process/Demonstration Speech—"The Basics of Creating a Resume"

   Visual Aid 1:

   Visual Aid 2:

   Visual Aid 3:

4. Informative Speech—"The Three Basic Parts of a Winning Essay"

   Visual Aid 1:

   Visual Aid 2:

   Visual Aid 3:

5. Informative Speech—"The Three Parts of a Crisis Plan for a Tornado"

   Visual Aid 1:

   Visual Aid 2:

   Visual Aid 3:

6. Informative Speech—"The Life of Ice Skater Michelle Kwan"

   Visual Aid 1:

   Visual Aid 2:

   Visual Aid 3:

7. Persuasive Speech—"Handwriting Should Be Taught in High School"

   Visual Aid 1:

   Visual Aid 2:

   Visual Aid 3:

8. Persuasive Speech—"Identity Theft Criminals Should Get Life Sentences"

   Visual Aid 1:

   Visual Aid 2:

   Visual Aid 3:

9. Persuasive Speech —"U.S. Citizens Earning Less Than $35,000 per Year Should Be Exempt from Paying Taxes"

   Visual Aid 1:

   Visual Aid 2:

   Visual Aid 3:

# Visual Aid Villains

Visual aid villains are those visual aids used inappropriately in a speech. Completing this activity will assist you in using visual aids effectively as well as giving constructive feedback to your classmates. Review the scenarios listed below and identify the visual aid villains and make suggestions for better visual aid use.

## Speech 1

Susan was all set to give her first speech on "creating origami animals." She began with a great introduction, gave a preview of her speech, and then proceeded to hand out a sheet of colorful paper to everyone in the audience. She explained that the audience could participate as she was giving her speech. Susan then returned to the podium and placed the piece of paper on the podium and began to fold the paper several times without pausing. Susan's audience seemed confused because they couldn't see the paper being folded. Once Susan was done she exclaimed, "Now, there! The steps are few and the process is quick, easy, and everyone can now do origami!" The class was then given an opportunity to give Susan feedback.

Visual Aid Villain: (What did Susan do wrong?)

Suggestion for better visual aid use:

Speech 2

Adam had just gotten a new suit and he wanted to make sure that he looked nice for his upcoming demonstration speech on "How to plaster a damaged wall." Adam chose a large bucket he had filled with plaster, a plastering tool, and a piece of plastered wall with a hole in it. Adam had done this several times when he worked for his dad, but he didn't practice his speech. As Adam was demonstrating how to apply the plaster, some of the plaster fell onto Adam's new suit and on his shoes. Adam ignored the accident and continued delivering the speech. After the speech concluded, the class was given an opportunity to give Adam feedback.

Visual Aid Villain: (What did Adam do wrong?)

Suggestion for better visual aid use:

# Visual Aid Buddy Check

For this activity, your instructor has asked you to bring in your speech and your visual aids. Choose a classmate and exchange speeches and visual aids. Now, using what you've learned in the textbook, evaluate your classmate's use of visual aids for their upcoming speech. Be tactful but honest in your appraisal of their "draft" version of this speech and the potential effectiveness of their visual aids.

Space has been provided under each checkpoint for your comments.

Buddy Name: _____

Topic Chosen: _____

❑ Font size is large enough to be seen from the back of the room


❑ Appropriate number of colors have been used to emphasize key points but minimize distractions


❑ Text on visual aid is in key word format


❑ Pictures are large enough to be seen


❑ Free from spelling or typographical errors


❑ No more than six lines of text down and six words across the visual aid


❑ Free from clutter


❑ Visual aid is appropriate for the topic chosen

Suggestions for improvement:

# Notes

# 8

# It's Not Only What You Say but How You Say It

## *The Power of Verbal and Visual Delivery*

### CHAPTER PREVIEW

| | |
|---|---|
| **1** | Four ways to deliver speeches |
| **2** | The importance of clear language |
| **3** | Devices for making the language of a speech more vivid |
| **4** | How words can be perceived differently |
| **5** | The use of rhythmic devices to enhance delivery |
| **6** | Seven vocal qualities that are necessary to vary for message impact |
| **7** | Key areas of nonverbal communication |
| **8** | A four-step method for practicing the delivery of speeches |
| **9** | Tips for delivery in mediated communication settings |

Dr. Martin Luther King, Jr., Adolph Hitler, Elizabeth Dole, Barbara Jordan, Ghandi, Saddam Hussein: their messages were different—The emotional impact on their listeners was just as strong.

It is about *what* you say; but it's also about *how* you say it. It's not nice to call a friend *stupid*, but it's unlikely he/she will be upset if you're laughing as you say it. However, if you call that friend *stupid*, while raising the volume of your voice and while creating an angry expression on your face, it's very possible that an altercation will take place. The words we choose to use and the way we choose to use them will impact the listener's perception of us as speakers. The words we use and how we use them will make or break friendships, romances, and business relationships.

When it comes to public speaking, the content and coherency of a message is necessary if you want to make a lasting impression. However, absent a dynamic delivery, the effect will be minimal. Think about school. All of the classes are important, but usually, the classes that have the most impact on us are the ones in which instructors had interesting, unique, or dynamic delivery styles. Therefore, all speeches should be written and delivered for maximum impact or what's the use of doing them? IF YOU DON'T HAVE ANYTHING TO SAY, AND YOU DON'T KNOW HOW TO SAY ANYTHING WELL—WHY SAY ANYTHING?

This chapter focuses on four key areas: the four ways to deliver a speech, verbal delivery, visual delivery and a four-step process for any public presentation in or out of the classroom. There are also some tips for techniques in mediated communication settings. The written text in this chapter is minimal because the verbal and nonverbal exercises should be heavily implemented after a basic understanding of each principle is explored.

READ, LISTEN, LEARN, WRITE,
AND DELIVER!

## Four Ways to Deliver Your Speech

### *Reading Your Manuscript*

Anyone can write something and read it word for word. Reading your speech is ONLY necessary when complicated material is being presented. Financial reports, reports on healthcare, press conferences (where the attorney has approved information) are examples of presentations that warrant reading. If you have complicated statistics or scientific data, reading that information is acceptable so that you won't misquote something or present incorrect data. However, you still should not have to read the entire speech from start to finish; you should only have to read the sections with the complicated information.

### *Memorizing Your Manuscript*

Memorizing a speech looks impressive if done properly. However, novice speakers should avoid this style of delivery because nervousness and inexperience can cause memory loss, and long pauses will make you look unprepared. This would be a detrimental error, especially if you really were prepared. You must have your speaking outline to allow for possible stumbles and lost thoughts.

### Impromptu Speaking

Impromptu speaking is probably used more often than most of us wish it were used. You may be called to "say a few words" at a fraternity function, company banquet, wedding, church gathering, etc. You will learn to give impromptu speeches in Chapter 10.

### Extemporaneous Speaking

Preparing an entire speech, condensing it to a one-two typed page *delivery outline*, and then presenting your thoughts to your audience is the most recommended way to deliver any speech. You need to know more than the main points of your speech. You should write an entire speech so your thoughts are visible. When you see your thoughts on paper, you may realize that they won't make sense to an audience of strangers. If you write down your thoughts instead of just "keeping them in your head," you will be able to make more coherent statements and you won't appear as if you threw your speech together.

After you write your speech in a preparation outline and condense it to a delivery outline, you will be ready to follow the four-step process in this chapter. The use of this four-step process will help you to improve your verbal and visual delivery.

## Verbal Delivery

Verbal delivery includes the language we create and the vocal qualities we use. It could include the tone in our voices, the pitch of our voices, our choice of language and even our volume.

### Language

The key to language is: keep it simple and make it memorable!

Language should be used clearly, correctly, and vividly, with a sense of gender and culture differences and with an awareness of the connotative and denotative meanings of words.

### Language Should Be Clear

Everyone is unique, so the words we use could be perceived differently by different people. Therefore, words that can be interpreted the same way by the

majority of people are the best words to use. Words like *a lot, many,* and *always*, are dangerous because they can have multiple meanings. These words are abstract and have ethical considerations because their usage categorize, information that may not be statistically true. **A lot** could mean 20 or 2,000 depending on who hears the message. You don't want your message to be confusing if your listeners discuss your speech afterwards. Using *specific* names and numerical references are better than generic titles.

*Some tennis players are outstanding role models* does not present as clear a meaning as *Venus and Serena Williams are outstanding role models in the field of professional tennis.*

### Language Should Be Used Correctly or Not at All

There is nothing worse than mispronouncing a word or mispronouncing someone's name during a speech. When in doubt, look it up or ask! Make sure all names of people you don't know are double-checked for correct pronunciation. People are often offended when their names are pronounced wrong because it gives the perception that you didn't care enough to make sure they were identified correctly.

All non-standard words should also be used in the correct context. Speaker credibility is extremely affected when a word is used incorrectly in a sentence. Some words often misused are: *amiable, compel, ascertain, ramification, rectify, implore, patronize,* etc.

### Vivid Language Will Enhance a Message

Metaphors, similes, personification and hyperbole can create imagery. You don't want to be over-dramatic, but you do want to create mental pictures of your message so that the audience has a more clear understanding of your main points. People are often visual, so showing something or creating images in our minds will make a lasting impression.

The following devices should be used but sparingly. Too many imagery techniques can make you appear insincere. Make sure you have some of these in all of your speeches but don't use them in excess.

**Metaphor:** A metaphor is text that creates an image that shows the similarity between two things that are different.

*The forgiveness of God is an ocean of love.*

**Simile:** A simile is text that creates an image that shows the similarity between two things that are different and the words *like* or *as* are always used.

> *The forgiveness of God is **like** an ocean of love.*

**Personification:** Personification is attributing human qualities to inanimate objects.

> *Forgiveness is an ocean.*

**Hyperbole:** Hyperbole's are extreme exaggerations.

> *I've forgiven my friends a million times.*
>
> *Ronald has received tons of standing ovations.*

## Language Can Reflect One's Gender/Culture without Being Offensive to Others

There's nothing wrong with being happy with yourself as a person, but be aware of gender differences. The simplest word can be perceived as sexist or exclusive to your audience.

- Don't use words that are masculine when referring to both men and women: *he, chairman*

- Don't label genders based on professions that are traditionally male or female because there are men and women in all job categories. *I'm sure **he** was a nice policeman. I think the nurse will be here soon. I hope **she's** nice.*

- Be sensitive to other cultures and subcultures. Investigate the usage of words that you know could be offensive. Stay away from regional and local slang. *Anyways* is not a word, and *ya'll* is not proper English. Know your audience and adjust your language.

- Be careful of profanity. If a speech contained profanity and you were in the audience, would it bother you? Perhaps it would depend on what the profanity was or how it was used and by whom. Nevertheless, it's best not to use it unless you are positive that it has some important significance for your message and you're sure your audience will embrace it. REMEMBER: Professionalism and credibility!

## Be Aware of the Denotative and Connotative Meanings of Words

An awareness of denotative and connotative meanings can help a speaker to choose words that the masses will understand and embrace.

The **denotative** meaning of a word is the dictionary definition of a word. The words *American flag* will have the same dictionary definition meaning for the majority of people. The American flag is a symbol. It's cloth. It has red and white stripes. It has stars.

The **connotative** meaning of a word is figurative, variable and emotional. So, the American flag also has a connotative meaning for those who listen to a speech about it. You have to be aware of the uniqueness of life experiences. Some words will create strong emotions in some and no emotion in others. The American flag will trigger thoughts of freedom, war, peace, etc., depending on who is listening.

## Rhythm Enhances Message Retention

Beginning and advanced speakers should use methods for creating rhythm from language that produces emotion and memorable words. Using alliteration, antithesis, repetition, and parallelism, and onomatopoeia can enhance the rhythm of a speech.

**Alliteration:** Alliteration is the repeating of the initial consonant sound in a sentence.

> *Final exams cause some students to c̲ram, c̲ringe, c̲ry, and c̲all home for support.*

**Antithesis:** The use of antithesis is excellent to show opposite ideas in the same sentence.

> *It's not about how we can get the most out of this world; it's really about how this world can get the most out of us.*

**Repetition:** Repetition is the repeating of words, sounds or phrases. The most famous speech that exemplifies repetition is Martin Luther King's "I Have a Dream" Speech. The following is an example of repetition.

> *I'm not going to talk about war, I'm going to tell you about peace. I'm going to speak about the things that will inspire and motivate you to be more productive. I'm not going to talk about war. There are enough negative and destructive speeches heard in the classrooms and in the boardrooms. I'm not going to talk about war. We need to concentrate on what will enhance our lives and not cripple our minds. Today, I refuse to talk about war.*

**Parallelism:** The construction of parallel wording helps your listeners to remember your ideas. Putting your sentences and phrases in a similar pattern will create memorable rhythms.

> *College students are often overlooked during presidential campaigns; and they are perceived as immature.*
>
> *But let's talk about whom the real college students are.*
>
> *These students are intelligent.*
>
> *These students are aware.*
>
> *These students are involved.*
>
> *These students are informed.*
>
> *And these students are concerned.*
>
> *These are the real college students.*

**Onomatopoeia:** This device involves using words that sound just like the objects they are signifying.

> *The train whistle blew Woo Woo! and we jumped off the tracks and ran away as fast as we could.*

## Effective Delivery Requires Seven Vocal Qualities

1. The **volume** is the loudness of your voice. It must be varied throughout the speech. Increase and decrease your volume when you want to emphasize certain points. Different emotions can be conveyed with a loud or soft voice depending on what message you wish to convey. Practice the different levels on a tape recorder and practice in front of a mirror.

2. The **rate** of your voice refers to how fast or slow you speak. The rate of a speaker's voice needs to vary according to the emotional level of the speech.

3. The **pitch** is the highness or lowness of your voice. Raising and lowering the pitch of the voice will impact the final impression a speaker leaves with an audience.

4. The **pronunciation** of words should be clear and correct! Pronunciation is the accepted sound of words.

5. **Articulation** has to do with the clarity of speech sounds. Consonants are often left off words and cause articulation problems. The use of *axe* instead of *asked* is a major mistake. Articulation during a speech is important for speaker credibility. The end of each word should be clear. The speech sounds you make will affect whether you appear intelligent or lazy. When a speaker says I fell on the *flow* instead of *floor,* an otherwise intelligent person will be perceived as unintelligent. This may be unfair but unfortunately it's true.

   In addition, **dialects** need to be controlled. If you grew up in a region of the country where people say I'm going to *warsh a load of clothes* instead of I'm going to *wash a load of clothes,* you must be aware of the sub-cultural bias that could affect the perception of your message in a traditional corporate workplace.

6. **Enunciation** *is the preciseness of speech sounds.* You must be able to *speak* distinctly and not blend your sounds together. *Howya doin* is a clear error of enunciation. *How are you doing?* is appropriate.

7. **Effective pauses** are essential for signaling the important main points or subpoints. Pauses are planned and free from fillers like **"um," "ah," "you know," and throat clearing** Pausing is especially effective during the last sentence of any conclusion. The slight pause in the middle of that last sentence, followed by a full glance at the entire audience, will help signal the end of your speech. At other times, pauses are great when you want to get an audience's full atten-

tion for a point you are making. When the room is quiet, people will focus directly on you.

## Visual Delivery

Visual delivery includes the speaker's appearance, body movements and facial expressions. It will impact whether an audience sees you as a credible speaker or as a nervous presenter.

### *Appearance*

A speaker's appearance should reflect competence, character, and credibility. If you look sloppy, chances are your mood and delivery will be sloppy. Unless you intentionally dress to emphasize a point like the tragedy of homelessness, an unkempt appearance will likely affect the strength of your message. You should be neat for classroom speeches and professional business presentations.

### *Eye Contact and Facial Expressions*

A speaker must have *constant* eye contact with his or her audience and use facial expressions that reflect the emotion of the language. If you read your speech or ignore looking at certain areas of a room, the people you don't connect with will be the people who don't listen to what you have to say.

If you want to emphasize certain points within your speech, your expressions need to reflect the exact emotions you are trying to convey. Using a monotone voice for a sales presentation will not convince us to buy a product from you. An absence of a smile when you are speaking about a loved one

will not convince us that you truly love that person. Let your face reflect your words.

### *Body Language and Gestures*

Body movement should be poised and controlled, and planned gestures are necessary for making a speaker appear vibrant and not rigid. (There should be an absence of swaying, touching hair, throat clearing, hands banging on the podium, hands constantly moving, etc.)

Although your body movement should be controlled, planned gestures to emphasize points or to create a visual image in the minds of audience members are strongly encouraged. When saying: **I live in a big house,** stretching your arms out wide to your sides is a good way to gesture and show that your house is large. This would be planned and noted in the margin of your speaking outline so you remember when to gesture.

## Delivery in Mediated Communication Settings

Delivering speeches in mediated communication settings can be different. Microphones, cameras, and constant audience feedback can make a speaking situation more stressful. There is more uncertainty about your audience, and more delivery techniques are required to be successful when speaking in a mass communication setting.

### *Microphones*

Speaking with a microphone requires an awareness of sound. Too often, people speak too closely or too

far away from a microphone. If you are not accustomed to using a microphone and one is provided, you must test the sound before beginning your speech. You should arrive early and practice using the microphone. Ask someone to stand in the back of the room while you talk. They should provide feedback as to whether they can hear you clearly or not. If the microphone squeaks, hold it further down from your mouth or stand farther away from the podium. If you can't be heard, speak louder and more clearly. You must know how to handle a microphone or your message can be disturbing to your audience, despite its worthwhile content.

## Cameras

It's been said by the television industry that cameras add 10 pounds. Be aware that your appearance on camera may look different. In addition to the extra weight, camera lighting may distort your appearance. White shirts without any color are often discouraged, and absent the proper lighting, all black could make you look washed out. Avoid colors that are too dramatic, and stripes are not the best for camera appearances. Neutral colors and conservative clothing are best. Hair, jewelry, and make-up should look neat and not distracting.

## Public Forums

Question and answer sessions can be stressful due to the uncertainty of audience questions. You must be poised and prepared for these forums. Be ready to tell short stories for some of your answers and be ready to just answer with a "yes" or "no." Stand still and don't fidget or you will look nervous and possibly dishonest. Try to use people's names as much as possible. Make direct eye contact. If possible, try to move away from the podium and stand closer to the audience. You want to appear friendly and willing to answer their questions. If you don't know an answer, don't try to fake it. Just tell the person that you will find out and get back to him or her later.

### REMEMBER

- You get one chance to present your message!
- Use the four-step process for verbal and visual delivery!
- Practice with a tape recorder and listen for vocal flaws!
- Practice in front of a mirror and correct nervous movements!
- Know the setting!!!
- Know the audience size!!!
- Know if you have a microphone!!!
- Know if you have a podium!!!
- Know yourself and practice, practice, practice!!!

### Ethics

You must make sure that your delivery and language are ethically sound. The tone of your voice and the words that you use should be emotionally charged but they should not incite reckless or dangerous behaviors from your listeners. You should not promote violence, destruction or intentional emotional distress. Your role as a speaker is to inform, persuade or entertain. The information doesn't always have to be serious but *you* should be serious about your role as a positive communicator. Don't be abusive, biased or offensive. Watch *what* you say and *how* you say it!

# ACTIVITIES

# It's Not Only What You Say but How You Say It

## The Power of Verbal and Visual Delivery

# Fixing Language Laziness

Read the following list of words in pairs. Do you notice the difference between the sound of the first word and the second word in each set? If not, keep practicing until your *pronunciation and articulation* are clear and accurate. For more impact, practice with a friend or speech coach.

a<u>s</u>k------------------------axe

pi<u>c</u>ture ---------------pitcher

house ------------------how

get ------------------------git

he's---------------------heez

for sure-----------foe show

Too often, due to "language laziness" we speak quickly and we don't *enunciate* our words.

Can you decipher the following sentences? Write the correct sentence, use the correct spelling and practice your enunciation so your words sound clear and comprehensible.

Ged outta ere.

Tha sound good ta me.

Heze oundin presidential.

Wahaddayawan?

The dogz bing noddy.

I waz up inda how.

# I've Got Rhythm

Read one of the famous speeches by Martin Luther King, Jr. (Ask your instructor for titles). Write down as many words or sentences that reflect repetition, alliteration, antithesis, onomatopoeia, parallelism, metaphors, and similes. Share your results with the class. This can be done individually or in groups.

# Poetry in Motion

Read the following poem with emotion. Raise and lower your volume and pitch. Speak slowly and then speak quickly. Notice what sounds good and what doesn't. Make a point to vary your voice as much as possible. Practice it over and over out loud and do it differently each time. This will help you to get comfortable with vocal variety and facial expressions. **This exercise is most effective if done in front of a mirror and with a tape recorder.**

*I am my poem.*

*Wrapped around a rhythm and a rhyme and a reason.*

*Full of meaning, and life and energy and anger and joy and love.*

*I am my poem.*

*Read the lines, read between the lines, the lines are lined with me.*

*It's all about me and how it's never about me but about you.*

*I am my poem.*

*For those who wish to read it, I'll never stop writing.*

*Will you stop reading . . . did you ever start?*

*Stop.*

Poem courtesy of Crystal Rae Coleman.

# Nonverbally Speaking

Get into groups of 3-6 people and create a 30 second television commercial using an object in your room. You cannot speak. You must get your message across without talking. Use body language and facial expressions to relay your group's message. Each person in the group must participate in some way. Take 20 minutes to prepare. Perform the commercials for your classmates and discuss the various **visual delivery** techniques that were used.

# Notes

# The Delicate Art of Persuasion

## CHAPTER PREVIEW

Eleanor awoke at 7:30 a.m. and realized she had a meeting with her professor in half an hour. Eleanor's roommate, Sue, was also just getting up to begin her day. Eleanor requested to use the bathroom first so that she could get ready in time to make her meeting since Sue's class didn't begin until 8:30. Sue agreed as long as Eleanor hurried. During the meeting with her professor, Eleanor requested a one-day extension on her paper because her diskette was damaged when it fell out of her purse and her friend accidentally stepped on it. She took the diskette as well as a copy of the most recent draft of her paper. She was granted the extension. After her morning classes, Eleanor called her mother to ask for a loan. Eleanor's timecard had been misplaced and she didn't get paid this week. She would repay her mom the following week when she received the check with the pay for both weeks. Her mom agreed and offered to meet her for dinner that evening and bring the money. Eleanor then called a coworker to ask her to trade shifts so that she would be able to complete her paper. Eleanor offered to take any shift in place of the one this afternoon. The coworker wanted off Friday night and agreed if Eleanor would take that shift. Later in the afternoon, Eleanor asked a friend if she could borrow his scanner to scan to a new diskette the draft of her paper so that she wouldn't have to type it all back in. Eleanor reminded her friend, George, of the time her printer saved the day when his printer ran out of ink. He allowed her to use his scanner. Eleanor completed her paper at 9:00 p.m. She asked Sue if she would like to go get an ice cream cone. Sue was hesitant because of the time. "I'm buying," said Eleanor. Although Eleanor may not have realized it at the time, she spent much of her day seeking to persuade others.

## The Challenging Psychology of Persuasion

Persuasion is a psychological proposition. The process of persuasion is necessary when there are two differing viewpoints or understandings about an event, idea, or concept. When these different view-points exist, the speaker feels it necessary to offer an argument for his or her viewpoint. Perhaps a speaker feels that city council members should be paid, but many in the audience do not. Or, perhaps a speaker feels that city council members should be paid a salary to include health benefits, and many in the audience believe the council members should be paid but not receive health benefits. Different points of view do not have to be completely opposed for there to be a disagreement calling for some form of persuasion. Sometimes it is simply a matter of degree. But whether differences are extreme or minute, persuasion is a challenging matter.

## Essential Elements of Persuasion

Defining persuasion is difficult because when we define a concept, we, in effect, limit that concept. However, there are certain elements of persuasion that many definitions have in common. The communicator uses these elements together to seek to influence the other party. Aristotle suggested that persuasion is effected through three primary means: ethos (the character or credibility of the speaker), pathos (the emotion stirred in the hearers), and logos (the arguments). Many recent definitions of persuasion include these elements. For instance, Makay states that "persuasion is communication intended to influence choice through appeals to the audience's sense of ethics, reasoning, and emotion."[1] Beebe and Beebe define persuasion as "the process of changing or reinforcing attitudes, beliefs, values, or behavior."[2] Whether the emphasis is on process or effect, persuasion is one of the most difficult types of speaking. O'Keefe reminds us that it is important to remember that a feature of persuasion is that it includes "some measure of freedom (free will, free choice, voluntary action) on the persuadee's part."[3] Even though you have offered a sound argument, the audience (persuadee) still has the freedom to agree or disagree, whether you think they are being logical or not. Thus, the process of persuasion does not guarantee success in terms of gaining the desired outcome from your audience. For the purposes of this chapter, then, we will adopt Woodward and Denton's definition of persuasion as "the process of preparing and presenting verbal and nonverbal messages to autonomous individuals in order to alter or strengthen their attitudes, beliefs, or behaviors."[4]

Persuasion ties together all that you have been learning thus far. Persuasion is pervasive in all that we do. We seek to influence family members to see our point of view concerning activities and ideas. We try to influence our friends to do certain things or go particular places. In the organizational setting, we attempt to influence coworkers to change procedures or trade shifts; or we ask our supervisors for a raise or a change in working conditions. And in the community we share our ideas with the PTO to provide a better learning environment for our children, or we plead with the city council to uphold a zoning ordinance or build sidewalks in our neighborhood. As a persuasive speaker, you are seeking to change the minds of others and hopefully get them to act on those changes. Persuasion is a challenging and necessary part of daily living. In the next few pages, we will discuss some of the basics of being a good persuasive speaker. However, this is a skill that you should refine and develop for the rest of your life.

## Understanding Your Audience

Each day we wake to face hundreds of persuasive messages. A host of these messages are directed at us. Advertisers seek to convince us to purchase their product. A government official wants our vote. A family member or friend requests our help. But in addition to all of these pleas for our attention and attempts to influence us are the myriad opportunities we have to influence others, as Eleanor did with her day. Because persuasion occurs in the midst of

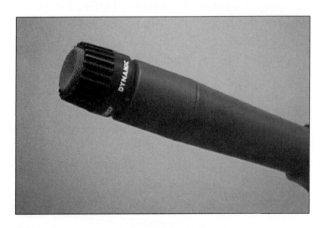

disagreement, we must remember to think in terms of dialogue. We are at least in *mental* dialogue with the audience as we seek to influence the audience's thought process or attitude. Thus, we are looking for ways to "connect" with our audience as we step to speak at the microphone.

Aristotle spoke of the enthymeme. Cooper explains that in rhetoric, "to conclude from certain assumptions (something distinct from them, yet dependent upon their existing) either universally or as a rule"[5] is an enthymeme. Thus, Aristotle thought persuasion more effective when based on common ground. According to Larson:

> This common ground permits persuaders to make certain assumptions about the audience and its beliefs. Knowing these beliefs, the persuader can use the *enthymeme*, a form of argument in which the first or major premise in the proof remains unstated by the persuader and, instead, is supplied by the audience. The task of the persuader, then, is to identify common ground, those major premises held by the audience, and to use them in enthymematic arguments.[6]

Literary critic Kenneth Burke believes that common ground or "identification" is important in persuasion. For instance:

> A is not identical with his colleague, B. But insofar as their interests are joined, A is *identified with B*. Or he may identify himself with B even when their interests are not joined, if he assumes that they are, or is persuaded to believe so.[7]

Thus, as you prepare for a persuasive event, you must pay close attention to your audience.

Earlier in this book, you learned about audience analysis and its importance in your preparation. This is especially true for a persuasive presentation. Whether you are seeking to influence a family member, friend, coworker, or customer, you must understand what is important to them to be able to address adequately the issues and questions that must be answered if you are to have the potential to influence their thoughts and motives. Who is your audience? What are their social status, age, and religious belief? What makes them tick, motivates them, interests them? What do you have in common with them that will enable you to relate to them? What can you do or say to help your audience identify with you and/or your message so that their minds may be open to your evidence and reasoning?

These questions should all be answered *before* you complete your presentation preparations because what you say and how you say it will be based on your analysis of the audience as you seek to find common ground that will allow you to make that all-important connection with them.

## Creating Audience Analysis Surveys

If you do have the opportunity to develop and administer a written survey of your audience's demographic and attitudinal data, there are three types of questions you can use to gather information: (1) closed-ended questions, (2) scale questions, and (3) open-ended questions. First, closed-ended (or fixed-alternative) questions provide respondents with options from which they can select the appropriate answer. Examples of closed-ended questions include true/false, agree/disagree, or multiple-choice questions (e.g., Circle one: Male or Female or Check one: Democrat____, Republican____, Independent____). Second, scale questions measure the respondents' impressions or reactions to a question or statement. If you wanted to measure the audience's feelings about current economic conditions, you could propose a statement (e.g., "The economy will be stronger one year from today") and have respondents rate their reactions (strongly disagree—1—2—3—4—5—strongly agree). Finally, open-ended questions do not provide options from which respondents select answers. Open-ended questions allow respondents to freely answer questions in their own words. Open-ended questions can provide great insight into the dispositions, beliefs, and actions of the audience (e.g., "If you did vote in the last presidential election, explain the most important factors influencing your voting decision." "What qualities are you looking for in our next U.S. President?" "If you did not vote in the last presidential election, please explain why you did not.").

Clearly, these three types of questions produce different types of useful data. The key is to select the best combination of these questions to reveal important information about your audience's demographic and attitudinal traits. Here are some helpful guidelines to keep in mind when creating an audience analysis survey.

1. *Keep them brief.* The survey should be brief enough that an audience member can complete it in 5-10 minutes. Remember that closed-ended questions take the least amount of time

and open-ended questions take the most time to answer.

2. *Ask clear, unambiguous questions.* Vague questions produce vague answers. Specific questions will provide more helpful information. For example, "How should society punish criminals?" is too vague. Providing questions about specific crimes will elicit clearer insight into respondents' beliefs about "appropriate punishments for criminals."

3. *Carefully plan and pretest to ensure your survey will elicit the desired information.* It is a great idea to ask a few friends to complete the survey before you distribute it to audience members. Based on their feedback, you can determine if questions need to be revised, added, or deleted, and if the survey questionnaire is an appropriate length.

## Defining Your Goals: Changing Attitudes or Actions

Having clearly defined goals is critical to success for much of life. Persuasive speaking is no exception. You must know what it is you want to accomplish if you expect to have a chance to influence your audience. If you don't know what you desire from them, how will they? This sounds simple and obvious, but people often jump into persuasive situations without a plan or a clear goal. Sometimes people actually get what they ask for, but not what they really desired.

*Charlie checked his schedule at work and realized he was scheduled to work every Thursday and Friday evening for the next two months. Up until now, he had always worked Monday, Tuesday, and Wednesday. The additional hours were much needed and he would be pleased with his paychecks, but this Thursday there was an important party at school that he had helped plan. In fact, he was in charge of the evening. He had not told his supervisor, Tom, because he never worked Thursdays, so he did not anticipate it being a problem. Although he wasn't sure what he would say, Charlie immediately went to see Tom. Charlie indicated he had never worked Thursdays before and didn't know why he had to now. Tom seemed a bit agitated with Charlie, but he indicated he would take care of it. When Charlie checked the schedule later that afternoon, he found that he was no longer scheduled for any Thursdays or Fridays. In fact, there were some Mondays now that he was not scheduled for. Instead, Carol, the newest employee, had the additional hours. Charlie went to see Tom again and found out that Tom had been angered that Charlie would*

*indicate earlier in the week that he desired more hours and then complain as soon as he received them. Charlie had failed to have a clearly defined goal when he went to see Tom the first time. Indeed, he did desire that one Thursday off, but he was happy with the other hours. However, because he hadn't planned properly or had clearly defined goals, he failed to communicate what he meant to Tom. Charlie was persuasive, and he influenced Tom to do exactly what he asked for, but not what he expected or desired.*

Clearly defining your goals is essential in a persuasive presentation. What do you expect to accomplish? Some speeches focus on changing attitudes. In this case, you seek to convince your audience to share the views that you have. Sometimes you are seeking to completely change their attitude, and other times it may simply be a matter of degree. If your audience shares your point of view, you are simply attempting to reinforce or strengthen their attitudes. If, however, your audience disagrees with you, your job is more difficult as you try to move them in their understanding so that they share your perspective.

Some speeches demand action. In this case, you are seeking to actually bring about change. Change requires your listeners to act—register to vote, sign a petition, stop using a product, try a new product, learn a new skill, etc. The effectiveness of your presentation depends upon what actions members of your audience take. Motivating your audience to take action is probably one of the hardest goals you will face as a speaker. Making sure your goals are clearly defined, then, is essential if you expect any level of compliance.

What is it, then, that you expect from your audience? Are they already doing what you desire? If so, then your goal is for your audience to *continue* with

that course of action or attitude. "You all are doing a fantastic job with the neighborhood watch program; let's keep it up." Perhaps you want your audience to begin doing or believing something new. "Crime has decreased 75 percent since Springknob implemented their neighborhood watch program; I urge you all to consider beginning such a program as well." If so, then your goal is for your audience to *adopt* this new idea or plan of action. Sometimes, what you desire is for your audience to **stop** doing something. "Since we began parking on the street in this neighborhood, there have been three accidents already; let's make sure everyone parks in his or her driveway instead of on the street." In this case, your goal is for your audience to *discontinue* some attitude or action. It is also possible that what you really desire is for your audience to avoid doing something. "You all know that Mary was injured by a drunk driver yesterday; I urge you to please find a designated driver if you drink away from home, and don't drive when you have been drinking." In this case, your goal is *deterrence*.

## Persuasive Methods

Earlier in the chapter, we indicated that Aristotle suggested persuasion is effected through three primary means: *ethos* (the character or credibility of the speaker), *logos* (the arguments), and *pathos* (the emotion stirred in the hearers). We also mentioned that these three elements continue to be focal points in understanding persuasion. It is important for you, the speaker, to consider each of these elements before deciding on your topic, while doing your research, and during your presentation. You would also be wise to keep these elements in mind as you review your results after you have made the presentation.

## Credibility and Public Speaking

As discussed in Chapter 3, credibility is key, especially in persuasive speaking. You must establish your credibility as an audience centered speaker. As a review, there are three types of credibility: **initial, derived,** and **terminal.** Initial credibility involves anything you do from researching up to your introduction for your speech. Derived involves anything you do during the speech (vidual aids, delivery, content, etc.). Terminal involves your conclusion and how you handle questions from the audience as well as heading to your seat. Can you imagine the impact of falling on your way back to your seat? How persuasive might you be after that?

## Using Your Ethos, Logos, and Pathos

Understand that your audience is the "consumer" of your ideas. Not all speakers are equally effective at getting audiences to consume presentations because some fail to adapt their message to meet the needs of audience members. You will want to adapt the three elements—**Ethos, Logos,** and **Pathos**—to fit the needs of your audience:

- Ethos: The character and credibility of the speaker.

- Logos: The logical appeals in the presentation (e.g., evidence, facts, or reasoning).

- Pathos: The emotional appeals in the presentation (e.g., appeals to love, pride, or power).

You will conduct research to enhance the ethos (credibility), logos (logic), and pathos (emotion) of your presentation. Let's first look at why ethos, or credibility, is so important.

## Addressing the Audience's Skepticism, Confusion, and Apathy

Avoid assuming that our audience is highly motivated and interested in listening to our presentation. Unfortunately, every audience can be tempered if you understand the three categories:

- The **Skeptics**—people who don't believe your message.

- The **Confused**—people who don't understand your message.

- The **Apathetic**—people who don't care about your message.

*How do we overcome these problems? How do we get everyone to believe, understand, and care?*

By conducting an audience analysis, you can custom build your presentation to fit your audience's unique characteristics. Audience analysis allows you to strategically select the best combination of credible fact, logical arguments, and engaging ideas. The

*Skeptics* doubt because they don't believe you or your ideas are credible (i.e., poor ethos). The *Confused* don't understand because your facts or ideas are unclear (i.e., poor logos). The *Apathetic* don't care because you have not stirred their interest by relating your content to their lives (i.e., poor pathos). By analyzing your audience and discovering appropriate research, you will have the tools to build a solid presentation that is credible, clear, and interesting to your audience.

## The Strength of Evidence

Just because something is clear to you does not mean it is clear to your audience. You need to make sure your audience understands your viewpoint by supporting your thoughts and ideas with evidence. In an earlier chapter, we discussed research tools and procedures. It is important for you to review that information because good research skills are necessary to develop strong evidence. Good evidence can help to build your credibility, especially when you are not the authority on the topic you are presenting. Specific examples, statistics, and anecdotes can help to build your case and support your proposal.

The type of evidence you use will depend greatly on your topic, the audience, the occasion, and your relationship to the topic. A presentation to a group of business executives about why they should adopt your inventory software is going to require significant facts and statistics to convince them that your system is better than the system they are currently using. A presentation to a group of young adults about joining a health club may require some facts and statistics, but will probably require more anecdotes and examples to be convincing. Again, audience analysis is vital. You need to understand who your audience is and what is likely to be of importance to them.

## The Importance of Sound Reasoning

Aristotle's idea of *logos,* however, goes beyond the evidence. Logos emphasizes reasoning. It is important that your appeals and evidence be linked. Your claims and arguments need to be connected in an understandable and logical manner. This requires critical thinking, a skill that is much sought after by employers. As a persuasive speaker, you will reason inductively (moving from the specific to the general) or deductively (moving from the general to the specific). As we consider the process of reasoning, it is important to note the difference between fact and inference. Fact is what is true. Inference is what is derived from evidence. This *may* be true, but is not necessarily true. Often our inferences are inaccurate because we do not have all the evidence that we need. For example, you notice a fellow student falling asleep in class. You know that this student was at a party the night before because you saw him or her there at 8 p.m. Thus, you infer that the student stayed out too late and did not get enough sleep. This could be true, but there are other possibilities as well. Perhaps the student went home at 8:30 p.m. and got 9 hours of sleep. If this were the case, your inference would not be fact. Perhaps the student has narcolepsy or is on a prescribed medication with drowsiness as a side effect. It is easy to see how we infer from the evidence what might not be fact. Thus, as a persuasive speaker, you must provide enough evidence using appropriate reasoning to help your audience ethically arrive at an appropriate conclusion.

## Inductive Reasoning

If you use inductive reasoning in your speech, you seek to move the audience from specific examples to a more general principle. When you argue this way, you are asking the audience to infer that since certain specific examples are true, a more general principle must also be true. For example, you might follow a pattern of logic such as the following:

- Sammy took Organizational Communication and said the class was easy.

- Julie took Organizational Communication and said the class was easy.

- Michelle took Organizational Communication and said the class was easy.

- Alberto took Organizational Communication and said the class was easy.

- Therefore, the Organizational Communication class must be easy.

As you can tell from this example, inductive reasoning is not foolproof. It is quite possible that these individual experiences do not add up to a correct conclusion. It is possible that all of the students were in the same class, and other classes taught by different professors are not as easy. Even if they were

in different classes with different professors, it is possible that these four students are straight A students who think all of their classes are easy. Perhaps the semester was unique, or the class isn't quite over yet. In this case, your sample is likely not large enough, and you will be jumping to a conclusion based on information that is not complete.

In cases of inductive reasoning, you cannot be absolutely sure of the accuracy of your conclusions because you are only looking at a sample. Thus, as a persuasive speaker, you must convince your audience that the conclusion(s) you are making from your data are reasonable and probably true. At times, you may want to decrease the certainty of your conclusion in order to actually strengthen your argument. In the case of the example above, your argument would be stronger by decreasing your claim: "Therefore, the Organizational Communication class is probably easy," or "Therefore, the Organizational Communication class might be easy."

As we mentioned in an earlier chapter, word choice and language are essential tools in the speaker's craft. It is important in inductive reasoning that you choose your words carefully to indicate the degree of probability in which you are developing your proposal. Making exaggerated claims that are too certain will weaken your argument and cause your audience to question your logic—and possibly your integrity. For instance, suppose you and several of your coworkers have talked to your supervisor about your schedules. She won't consider changing the schedule, so you claim that she does not care about her employees. The limited number of examples (and in this case unclear number) coupled with your strong claim may cause some questions in the minds of your audience. How many employees went to the supervisor? What kind of scheduling problems

were there? What were the experiences of other employees? However, if you claim that the supervisor doesn't seem to care about you or doesn't seem to care about some employees, your argument would be stronger. Of course, offering more specific examples—number of employees with concerns, exactly what the scheduling problem was, specifically what the supervisor did or didn't do or say—would also strengthen your inductive argument.

There are, of course, claims we can be certain about that do not need a weaker probability claim. For instance, we have observed the sunset in the West every evening since we can remember. We do not need to claim that the sun *might* set in the west. We have seen it get dark every night after the sun sets. We do not need to claim that it is *possible* it will get dark tonight. We can safely say these things will happen. But in many cases, you must supplement your reasoning with substantial and coherent support in order to convince your audience of your claim. Consider this portion of an argument related to bicycle injuries in children:

> Unintentional injuries related to bicycle collisions have received a great deal of attention because of the protective effect of safety helmets. Bicycle injuries account for 10% of all pediatric traumatic deaths. In the United States in 1998, 203 children ages 14 years and under died in bicycle-related crashes (National Safe Kids Campaign, 2002). Although boys in the 5- to 14-year-old age group have the highest incidence of bicycle related injuries, young children are also commonly injured (Powell & Tanz, 2000). U.S. statistics on bicycle injuries have shown that 76% of head injuries and 41% of deaths from head injury occurred among children younger than 15 years of age (Sacks, Holmgreen, Smith, & Sosin, 1991). Bicycle crashes are the most common cause of serious head injury in children (Weiss, 1994).[8]

Including strong support will strengthen your inductive argument. Strong support helps your audience more fully understand and analyze your argument.

## Cause—Effect Reasoning

People begin organizing their experiences in terms of causality as early as infancy.[9] We like to think in terms of cause and effect because it simplifies things for us. It also allows us to place blame. Politicians do

this all the time. For instance, Democrats argue that because the economy was better under President Bill Clinton, the economic policies of President George W. Bush have caused the economic decline we are experiencing in 2003. This allows the Democrats to blame the Republicans for the economic problems of the times.

There is, however, a difference between correlation and cause. A correlation indicates a relationship, but not necessarily a cause and effect. For example, you might argue that ice cream sales at your local Dairy Queen increase in the summer; therefore, the summer heat causes better sales. That sounds plausible, but there are other factors that could also affect the sales. Children are out of school and thus have more free time to go to Dairy Queen. It is also possible that Dairy Queen (and grocery stores for that matter) have more ice cream products available in the summer. In fact, the Dairy Queen in Murray, Kentucky is not open from November to March. Obviously, they won't have any sales during those months. Yes, the heat of the summer is a contributing factor, but it is not likely the sole cause. Pure cause and effects are rare. Make sure that you recognize contributing factors and base your claims on reasonable criteria. If what you have is a correlation, recognize the extent of the claim you can make. If you feel you have a cause and effect claim, support your claim with sufficient evidence.

Referring back to the economic condition in the United States mentioned above, we can see that Bush's policies must be a factor; however, there are other circumstances to consider as well. The bursting of the dot.com bubble in the stock market and the subsequent decrease in the value of technology stocks has had a far-reaching impact. The terrorist attacks of September 11th also impacted our nation in a variety of ways. The travel industry is still suffering as a result. Placing blame on Bush and his policies, then, is only partially accurate. In fact, the economy is also impacted by policies begun by the previous democratic administration. There is a correlation to Bush's policies, but not necessarily a cause and effect.

When used effectively, cause and effect reasoning can be an excellent persuasive tool; however, if the cause and effect relationship is not sound enough, you will undermine your credibility with your audience. Be sure to ask yourself the following questions:

- Are there other factors I should consider?

- Is something else really the cause of this effect?

- Is there a strong enough relationship or is the relationship irrelevant?

- Are there a series of causes that lead to this event?

Sound reasoning depends on your ability to use critical thinking and identify clear connections between events.

## Analogy

Analogical reasoning depends upon your ability to establish connections between similar—and sometimes not-so-similar—events and concepts. This is an effective persuasive tool when you are able to convince your audience that one event or concept is similar enough to another event or concept to merit comparison that will demonstrate that since something is true in one situation, it is likely to be true in another situation as well. For instance, the curbside recycling program worked well in Boulder City, Nevada, a town with a population of about 15,000; therefore, a curbside recycling program should work equally well in Murray, Kentucky, which also has a population of about 15,000. In order for this analogy to be acceptable to the audience, they must be convinced that the two towns are similar enough. Population alone may not be adequate to make that connection. There may be differences in the cities that would affect the establishment of such a program in Murray. Thus, analogies, too, must be supported with relevant facts, statistics, testimonies, examples, etc.

Analogies are good tools because they help your audience get a mental picture of your claim. They also help your audience by showing your plan (or a similar plan) in action in another situation, thus helping them see the validity of your claim. No analogy is going to be exact. There will be some differences. Your job is to make sure that the differences in what you are comparing are not significant enough to undermine your argument. You do need to ask yourself some crucial questions to ensure strong analogies:

- Are the cases similar enough to merit the comparison?

- Are there other cases that reinforce or disprove your analogy?

- Are the similarities of the cases of significance in terms of the argument you are making?

- Are the differences minor enough so as not to undermine your comparison?

## Deductive Reasoning

In deductive reasoning, you make connections between statements that serve as premises—something assumed or taken for granted—and move from those general observations to a more specific claim. For example:

- Premise: All dogs bark.

- Premise: Shep is a dog.

- Therefore, Shep barks.

Thus, if your audience accepts your premises, it is likely they will accept your claim. It is often not necessary to explicitly state the entire argument, as your audience will fill in the blanks. (This is the enthymeme referred to earlier in the chapter.) In circumstances when you have such agreement with your audience, it allows you to establish a sense of common ground with them. As they complete your argument, it becomes theirs as well. For instance, suppose you claim that if Shirley becomes district manager, some of us may lose our jobs. If the coworkers you are speaking to know that Shirley has always run over budget in her position as store manager, and her solution has been to lay off workers to cut costs, they will complete the argument for you. This will also make the argument, at least in part, their argument as well as yours.

You must be aware of the extent of your premises, though. If you are not 100 percent sure of your premise, your argument will take a slightly different form. As an example, consider the following:

- Wearing helmets is likely to decrease incidents of serious head injuries in children bicyclists.

- More children are wearing bicycle helmets.

- Therefore, it is likely that serious head injuries in children bicyclists will decline.

Deductive reasoning, too, can be a powerful persuasive tool, but it also is strengthened with good, strong, supporting evidence of facts, statistics, testimonies, and examples.

Sound reasoning is vital if you are to be an effective persuasive speaker.

## Using Emotional Appeals

The use of **emotion** (*pathos*) is another important element of persuasion. We will consider two aspects of your use of emotion as speaker. First, it is necessary to consider your emotional involvement in your topic. If you seem to care and be emotionally involved in what you are presenting, it is more likely that your audience will find you more credible. Therefore, one aspect of emotion ties back to the idea of *ethos*—your credibility and believability as a sincere and caring presenter. An ethical consideration, however, is the extent to which your emotional involvement is sincere and not simply an acting ploy. Ethical speakers exhibit genuine concern for the well being of their audience.

The other aspect of the use of emotion is your appeal to the emotion of your audience. You can influence your audience by encouraging emotional involvement and arousing feelings that create a sense of imbalance in your listener that begs for correction. In other words, if your audience becomes emotionally involved in the problem, they will develop a feeling that something must be done to correct the situation. For example, consider the following excerpt from an article on drunk driving legislation:

> Suddenly, in her rearview mirror, Driscoll saw a speeding dark blue GMC utility van. "I'd never seen anything like it," she recalls. "I thought he was going about a hundred. I don't know if he even saw us." Behind the wheel of that stolen vehicle was Wayne Winslow, a 49-year-old Providence man with a long rap sheet,

which included a previous drunk-driving charge.

> What happened next was a blur. "I don't remember the sound," Driscoll says. "I do remember the impact. I remember we spun, and spun, and spun. I remember my children screaming. I can still hear my daughter's voice, 'Oh, my God! Oh, my God!' My son was yelling 'Mommy!'" Driscoll's vehicle catapulted across the median. When it finally stopped, she looked in the backseat to find her son unconscious and her daughter crying in terror. What Driscoll didn't know was that, in its terrifying lurch across the highway, her minivan had crossed in front of Brigid Kelly's car and was struck by it. Miraculously, Driscoll and her children, though injured, survived. Brigid died instantly of head trauma.[10]

Certainly, the author could tell you that Winslow's utility van hit Driscoll's minivan, shoving it into the path of Kelly's car. Kelly was killed and the Driscoll family was injured. Technically that would be correct, but the added detail not only makes the scene more concrete and understandable for the audience, but it also appeals to the audience's emotion, drawing them into the terrible nature of the situation so that they feel a need for legislation to end this kind of tragedy. Throughout the article you find out much more about the life of Brigid Kelly and the history of the drunk and drugged driver that killed her. The author relies on more than the facts; the author appeals to the emotions of the audience. Persuasive speakers are more influential if they include emotional appeals in the mix of their persuasive tools.

## Ethical Considerations

This is a good place to briefly discuss ethics in persuasive speaking. You have power in speaking situations when you have a captive audience. Persuasive presentations have a unique aspect to that power in that the speaker is seeking to influence the audience to some action or change in thinking. There is the potential for harm associated with action; therefore,

## Ethical Consideration

Is it ever OK to lie in a persuasive presentation?

the persuasive speaker must be especially sure to have as a goal what is best for the audience. Even when the speaker has the audience's best interest in mind, there is the potential for the audience to take the action too far or not far enough. For example, if you are seeking to persuade your audience to lose weight, someone in your audience could take your plea too far and become anorexic. This would likely be worse than being mildly overweight. You cannot, of course, control the response of your audience, nor should you take full responsibility for their actions. You should, though, prepare your persuasive presentations with the awareness that your goal is to influence them to act. Those actions have ethical implications. Be careful, then, what you ask your audience to do or think.

## Identifying the Organizational Structure of Your Persuasive Speech

Part of determining your goals and developing a plan for your persuasive presentation is to decide the type of persuasive presentation you will offer. Will you be dealing with a question of fact, value, or policy? Each requires a little different approach. To determine which type of presentation you will make, look at your thesis statement. What are you trying to accomplish with your presentation? What are you proposing? What do you expect your audience to do as a result of hearing your presentation?

### Questions of Fact

What is a **fact**? One definition of fact is "reality" or "truth."[11] We all know that reality and truth are subjective. In other words, our interpretations of events or situations or concepts often differ. A persuasive presentation dealing with a question of fact involves the attempt to get the audience to understand an event, situation, or concept in the same way that we do. For instance, we might propose that exercise builds confidence and self-esteem. Some of our audience might disagree with that fact. Our job as the speaker, then, is to provide the necessary proof to change the minds of those in the audience who do not believe that statement to be true. Or you might propose that America has become a leisure society. It is likely you will have members in your audience who do not see it that way. You, then, must provide sufficient proof for them to see your point of view and, hopefully, accept your point of view as the correct one.

These same topics could easily be informative topics as well. For instance, your specific objective could be "to inform my audience of the effects of exercise on confidence and self-esteem." Or your specific objective could be "to inform my audience of the effects of technology on the leisure time of Americans." It is a fine line that separates an informative speech based on a question of fact from a persuasive speech based on a question of fact. In the persuasive speech, you must demonstrate to your audience that your viewpoint is correct. Thus, your speech must provide proof based on some accepted standard that your audience could accept. Remember the importance of audience analysis.

### Questions of Value

What is **value**? Value has to do with the usefulness, worth, or goodness of an event, concept, or situation. Thus, values are related to morality—what is proper or satisfying. Value is often determined, at least in part, by our religious beliefs. Again, an understanding of your audience is very important. Your goal as a speaker in this situation is to prove the worth or goodness of a statement. While a question of fact might be "there are not enough parking spaces for students," a question of value would be "our campus parking situation is worse than other campuses" or "the parking situation damages the image of the school." In these instances, you are basing your arguments on beliefs in the value of parking and the effect that parking has on the university. In the case of the examples above, you would be seeking to get your audience to see the parking situation as a bad thing for the school. As another example,

consider the topic of volunteering for the Big Brother/Big Sister program. A question of fact might deal with the fact that the program keeps kids out of trouble. A question of value could suggest that volunteering in the program is worthwhile.

## Question of Policy

The speaker presenting a topic that deals with a question of fact or a question of value asks for *belief* from the audience. The speaker presenting a topic dealing with a question of policy asks for *action* from the audience. Key words that make these questions fairly easy to spot are "should," "ought to," "have to," or "must." Although those words are not always present, they are implied. Questions of policy deal with course of conduct—how we should act. Returning to the parking example, we might propose that "the parking situation must be improved," or, more specifically, "the university should build a parking garage." The Big Brothers/Big Sisters example could be presented as a question of policy as well: "Everyone should volunteer as a big brother or big sister."

To be convincing, presentations on policy need to include several things. First, the speaker must establish that there is a need for change. Remember to relate the need to your audience. In order for the audience to be convinced to take some course of action, they must first be convinced that the present situation is unacceptable and requires change. Thus, in the beginning stages of your preparation, you should ask yourself if the status quo really is unacceptable. You must be convinced that change is necessary before you can begin to persuade your audience. Your argument will be more convincing the more specific your needs statement is. If you

present your need too abstractly, you will leave it open to differing interpretations by your audience. Even a concrete statement is open to differing interpretations. Don't make it harder on yourself by being too abstract.

Second, you need to offer some solution for the problem/need you have established. Your audience wants to hear about some practical way this problem you have presented could be fixed. If you expect your audience to act, they must have some solution presented to them that they could conceivably do.

## Using Monroe's Motivated Sequence to Organize Your Speech

Communication is a process that connects the speaker and the audience. Thus, it is especially important in persuasive contexts to remember that the process is transactional. You must take into account the mental dialogue of your listeners and the stages they pass through as they consider your message. One way to organize your persuasive speech is by a method known as the motivated sequence. Alan H. Monroe, a communication professor, developed this method in the 1930s.[12] He focused on five steps to motivating your audience to act: attention, need, satisfaction, visualization, and action. If you remember that you are in a mental dialogue with your audience, you can use these steps to address the things that will be important to your audience as each individual in the audience considers your message. Many organizations teach a version of the motivated sequence to their sales forces to help them close deals by taking customers through the mental process.

### Attention

The first step in the motivated sequence is to gain the attention of your audience. There are many ways you can do this, and several ways were addressed in an earlier chapter. Sometimes telling a joke is appropriate. However, not everyone is good at telling jokes. If humor is not your strength, do not feel obligated to begin with a joke. A joke that flops can undermine your confidence, and recovery can be challenging. For example, you can ask your audience a rhetorical question, offer an anecdote, or present a shocking fact. Whatever you decide to do, make sure that it is appropriate for your topic and your audience. You cannot persuade your audience, though, if you do not first get their attention.

## Need

The next step is to establish a sense of need. Remember, your audience is egocentric. The members of the audience are all wondering what you have to say has to do with them. You must establish that there is indeed a problem—something that needs to be fixed—that relates to them. You want to make sure your audience understands what the problem is and how it affects them personally. Give this step adequate emphasis. If you move too quickly to the satisfaction step without clearly defining the need, your audience may not be interested in your solution. Why would your audience need satisfaction for an issue they do not perceive as a problem?

## Satisfaction

The satisfaction step is where you offer a solution for the problem you established in the need step. What is it you desire from your audience? What belief, attitude, or action do you expect from them? You should, of course, base your solution on your research. Offer evidence, statistics, facts, testimony, and examples to support your plan. Be specific. Make sure your audience understands your plan, as well as the costs and benefits that go along with it. Again, remember that you are in a mental dialogue with your audience, so make sure to answer any objections and concerns that you anticipate might be on their minds. This is the point where a visual or audio aid might be especially helpful. Explain how your plan is worth the price or commitment involved. This would also be a good time to show how this or a similar proposal had worked in a comparable situation. This is also when you will want to address any opposition to your plan. Remember that you are in a mental dialogue with your audience and you need to anticipate questions they might have. Your goal is to get your audience to agree that the proposal you are offering is the correct solution for the problem/need you established earlier in your presentation.

## Visualization

The visualization step is your opportunity to explain to your audience how acceptance of your plan would benefit them. What would your audience gain or profit by accepting and putting into action your proposal? This is also the time you might indicate what would happen if they did not take the action you have suggested? Explain the benefits in concrete and specific terms. Help your audience see themselves benefiting from the proposal you have offered them. Help them mentally experience the joy or excitement they would receive from accepting your plan. Also, help them mentally experience the discomfort they would experience if they did not accept and act on your plan. Prepare them, then, for the call to action you are about to make.

## Action

Your final step is to call your audience to a specific action. Be specific about what you want your audience to do. If you are not calling for a particular action, be specific about what you expect them to believe or value—what point of view they should now have. Besides the specifics of the action, you may also need to address the timing of the action you expect. This is an important step that students often leave out or fail to make explicit. This is the point in the presentation when the sales executive will ask for the sale or the politician will ask for the audience's vote. If you want to complete the process of persuasion, it is important for you to make clear to your audience what you want them to do, and then ask them to do it!

Because speeches to persuade have behavioral or psychological change as a goal, it is important to follow the motivational process that listeners often follow. Giving an effective persuasive presentation is challenging. Following are two examples of actual student persuasive presentations that used the motivated sequence. While they have some strong points, they also have some weaknesses. Some of those are highlighted in the commentary accompanying the presentations.

# Go Greek[13]

## Jennifer

(Used with permission.)

**Specific Purpose:** To persuade students to take part in Greek events or organizations on campus.

### Attention

Attention Step: The speaker opens with some interesting statistics to arouse the audience's interest. The audience may be curious as to the validity of this these facts, however, and it might be helpful for the speaker to give the sources of this information.

What else could the speaker have said or done at this point to make the introduction stronger?

I. How does 2% equal 80%? It is impossible mathematically, but this ratio is a startling statistic of our nation's leaders.

II. Only 2% of the male population of America are members of a Greek fraternity; however, approximately 80% of the executives of Fortune 500 companies belonged to Greek organizations.

III. Much of the same statistics hold true for females too. Sorority graduation rates and placement rates mimic that of fraternities.

IV. According to *The Positive Experience*, the graduation rate of Greek men to non-Greek men is 59%-47%. This is a startling 12% difference.

**Transitional Statement:** Today I want to encourage all of you to join a Greek organization.

### Need

Need Step: The speaker decides to emphasize that students need to gain leadership experience as well as achieve academic success in order to impress potential employers. But is Greek life the only way to gain this experience?

The speaker needs to connect the second point more clearly to Greek organizations. How are Greek organizations needed in this environment?

The third point is confusing here because it does not fit with the need step. These are questions the audience may be asking, but would fit much better in the Satisfaction step (point IV). However, to be effective, these misconceptions need to be addressed. The audience needs to know why they are misconceptions and what the truth really is.

I. High achievement in both academic and extracurricular activities is needed to have a successful future after college. Leadership potential and experience are the highest assessors of success rate after college.

   A. Employers look for leadership potential when selecting the person for the job.

   B. Most employers also look for involvement on campus and activities in all aspects of college life.

   C. Most leadership skills are learned in situations outside of the classroom, through experience.

II. People want to make good grades and graduate with high achievement.

   A. Graduation rates are steadily declining.

   B. Grades are also going down, leading to a lowering of expectations by both colleges and employers.

   C. Extracurricular activities and involvement are becoming staples for good career placement.

III. Many common misconceptions are shared about the Greek community.

A. Greek organizations are too expensive.

B. The only point is to "party."

C. "The people are all the same."

D. "I don't have enough time to join one."

**Transitional Statement:** By seeing these needs and examining these misconceptions, Greek organizations stand out as great opportunities for future success.

## Satisfaction

I. Students who join Greek organizations learn leadership skills and develop higher levels of social interaction with other students and members of the community.

II. Joining Greek organizations helps to actualize leadership potential and develop leadership skills.

A. Greek organizations offer a variety of offices within each system to manage situations on campus or within the organization itself.

B. Such skills as how to set and meet goals, how to inspire, how to delegate responsibility, and how to set an example are all learned.

C. Greek life resembles that of a business situation, including certain aspects such as order, responsibility, and room for growth.

III. Graduation rates and career placement are higher among those who were involved in Greek organizations.

A. According to Tau Kappa Epsilon "Rush Statistics," over 70% of fraternity and sorority members graduate, compared to less than 50% of non-Greek students.

B. 76% of senators, 80% of Fortune 500 executives, 71% of those listed in *Who's Who in America,* and 19 Presidents were members of Greek organizations.

C. Greek organizations also, according to The Murray State Web Page "Greek Grade Report," have higher GPAs than does the independent population of students.

D. Greek organizations are an excellent way to get involved on campus:

1. Within the Greek organization itself,

2. Through community service provided by the Greek organization,

3. In committees or associations on campus where Greek organizations flourish.

---

Has the speaker already accomplished what this transitional statement suggests has been accomplished so far in this speech?

Satisfaction Step: Here the speaker is offering a solution to the need for academic achievement and leadership experience.

The Tau Kappa Epsilon statistic indicates quite a bit larger range than the statistic offered in point IV of the attention step. Do you see this as a problem?

The audience might want to know a bit more about the source of information concerning senators and executives.

The audience might also wonder about national statistics concerning GPAs of those involved in Greek organizations. Here the speaker cites only one specific university.

The speaker should be more specific about the campus involvement of Greek organizations. What is offered here is very general.

In point IV, the speaker attempts to address some of the questions the audience may have. However, the audience is again left wondering about specifics.

Transition statements are important. However, the speaker has not spoken about any other organizations in this speech, so claiming that joining a Greek organization is incomparable to any other campus organization is sure to raise some questions in the minds of the audience, especially those who have good grades and hold leadership positions in other organizations.

Visualization Step: This is the place in the speech where the speaker needs to help the audience see the benefits of following the proposed plan. Has the speaker done that to your satisfaction? What does "numerous percentages on the success rate of Greek graduates" mean? What exactly does the Intrafraternity Council and five Panhellenic sororities mean to a non-Greek, and how does that point help the audience visualize themselves as successful Greek participants? The speaker could do much to strengthen this step.

Action Step: This is a very important part of a persuasive speech, the place where you actually ask your audience to take some action.

Who is Casey Jenkins? Is one person enough evidence to base such a sweeping generalization on?

Step II is a continuation of the visualization step.

IV. Misconceptions held by some outside the Greek community are blatantly false and obviously biased.

   A. Financial obligations to Greek organizations make up around 2% of a college student's expenses throughout his or her time as an undergraduate.

   B. Parties are a small part of the Greek experience. Yes, they are a way to have fun, and are usually made public to the college, but they are rarely considered to be anything other than a fundraiser or way to unwind.

   C. The variety of Greek organizations is also a large part of the Greek experience. There is an organization for every type of personality or background.

   D. Fraternities and Sororities do not take up all of your time, but help you to budget your time effectively.

**Transitional Statement:** If people examine the facts and statistics, the benefits of joining a Greek organization are incomparable to any other organization on campus when it comes to involvement and achievement.

### *Visualization*

I. All indications are that Greek organizations promote higher leadership potential and a higher success rate for those involved.

II. The Greek grade report on the Murray State web page reported that higher job placement opportunities and higher graduate school acceptance rates are given to those involved in Greek organizations.

III. Tau Kappa Epsilon "Rush Statistics" reported numerous percentages on the success rate of Greek graduates.

IV. There are eight members of the Intrafraternity Council along with five Panhellenic sororities at Murray State University, each offering a different and unique Greek experience.

### *Action*

I. Casey Jenkins (Personal Communication, April 21, 2000), past president of Alpha Gamma Delta, said that she has never talked to anyone who has been disappointed with their Greek experience; in fact, she said that most everyone thought it was one of the best opportunities of their lives.

II. Weigh the facts: Greek life promotes higher graduation rates, higher success rates after college, developing leadership skills, ways to get involved on campus, and experiences that you will not regret.

It is clear what the speaker wants the audience to do, but for the call to action to be more effective, the speaker needs to give some specifics in how to become Greek.

III. The main objective of college is to prepare you, the student, for the real world. However, there are some things that cannot be taught in a classroom, only learned through experiences. The best learning experience of your college career would be to GO GREEK!

## Bibliography

Murray State University. *Greek Grade Reports*. Retrieved May 22, 2003 from http://www.murraystate.edu.

Alpha Tau Omega (1985). *The positive experience*, (4th ed.). Champaign, IL: Alpha Tau Omega.

University of Wisconsin Milwaukee. *Rush Statistics*. Retrieved May 22, 2003 from http://www.uwm.edu/StudentOrg/tke/rush/stats.html.

Muse, W. V. & Terry D. R. (1966). *The teke guide: Tau Kappa Epsilon*. The Fraternity

# Becoming a Big Brother or Big Sister[14]

# Julie

(Used with permission.)

**Specific Purpose:** To persuade my audience to get involved in the Big Brother/Big Sister Organization.

**Central Idea:** At-risk children benefit from the Big Brother/Big Sister organization.

## *Introduction*

Attention Step: The speaker opens by trying to draw you in through your fond childhood memories.

She then addresses the need and satisfaction as she gives you a clear idea of what she will address.

**Attention:**

I. Most of us have many wonderful childhood memories.

  A. One memory might be having special friendships with someone to always turn to.

  B. We also might have a memory of celebrating holidays with the sweet taste of eggnog and the comfort and warmth of a loving family.

  C. Amusement Parks, messy ice cream cones, and the challenge of roller-skating are all part of our childhood memories.

II. Not every child is as fortunate as you or I might have been.

  A. Many children, for a variety of reasons, will miss important parts of childhood that make memories so special.

  B. These children are looking for a special friend.

III. Big Brother/Big Sister is a program that can help children feel "in place" and helps at-risk students.

A. This program gives children that need the special attention an opportunity to make friends and have a role model with someone to look up to.

B. I will discuss the characteristics of the children involved in the program, how they are endangered in being an at-risk student, how you can prevent these children from being at-risk, and how to get involved today!

III. B serves as a brief transition statement and overview of what she will do in her presentation.

What else could the speaker have said or done at this point to make the introduction stronger?

### Body

**Need:**

Need Step: The speaker emphasizes the special needs of children who do not come from stable home environments.

I. The children involved with the program come from many different families and backgrounds.

A. Little Brothers and Sisters range in age from eight to high school.

B. Some of the children live with a single parent because of divorce or the death of a parent.

C. Other children live with both parents but because of illness or family hardship they do not receive adequate attention and nurturing.

Citing sources is important, but simply rattling off the website is probably not effective. It is difficult for the audience to follow, and they are left wondering about the credibility of the source. It would be more effective to cite the organization that sponsors the site.

II. Children who do not come from a stable family are endangered of becoming at-risk students.

A. The definition I found at http://www.ericfacility.net/ericdigests/ed3166117.htm stated that an at-risk student is a child that is endangered of not giving their full potential at school due to poverty, family composition, and inadequate or inappropriate educational experiences in the school or community.

B. These circumstances could cause the student to drop out, attempt suicide, rebel against their parents, skip school, make poor grades, or experiment with drugs or alcohol.

The author does give some good specific information outlining the specific need for the program.

III. You may be wondering how often any of these factors could happen.

A. http://www.canada.compassion.net/sharingcompassion/childrenatrisk.asp#1 showed statistics on poverty. This website showed that 1.2 billion people, or one fifth of the world's population, live in poverty; more than 600 million are children.

A transition statement would be helpful here.

B. On that same website I found statistics showing that for young people 15-24 years old, suicide is the third leading cause of death, behind unintentional injury and homicide. In 2001, more teenagers and young adults died from suicide than from cancer, heart disease, AIDS, birth defects, stroke, and chronic lung disease combined.

The author does a good job of identifying the source of her information here. However, as stated earlier (IIA), the first line of IVA1 is unnecessary in the oral presentation, but the website does belong in the sources/bibliography at the end of the paper.

**Satisfaction:**

IV. The program to help these at-risk children is Big Brother/Big Sister.

    A. Maybe you're wondering if this program actually helps.

        1. http://www.teaching.com/EarthDay97/center/text/web-stock21.htm. According to a recent study by a policy research organization called Public/Private Ventures, it absolutely does. The study found that the addition of a Big Brother or Big Sister to a young person's life for one year dramatically reduced first-time drug use, school absenteeism, and violent behavior by 30 to 50%.

        2. One of the greatest indicators of a child's success is having a positive relationship with a stable adult role model, other than a parent, in his or her life.

        3. Research shows that this supportive one-to-one mentoring is proven to aid a child's development in areas including self confidence, academic achievement, peer and family relationships, ability to make decisions, and interest in learning new things.

Visualization Step: This author seeks to show the audience the benefits of following the proposed plan by explaining her own personal experience.

She does raise a question here, however, as her Little Sister was seven years old. She stated earlier that the program began with children eight years of age. One wonders why the exception here. Has the speaker explained that to your satisfaction?

**Visualization:**

V. I personally know this program helps because I was a Big Sister for one year to Jessica.

    A. Jessica was 7 years old and came from a low-income, single-parent family.

    B. I would drive to Clarksville twice a week after school and take her to the park, help her on her homework, and just talk to her and be a friend.

    C. Coming into the program Jessica was doing poorly in school and didn't want to participate in class.

    D. After a few months talking to her about pretty much anything from school to family to boys, she started to open up and her teachers noticed a change in her schoolwork and just her overall attitude to everything.

Action Step: This is a very important part of a persuasive speech, the place where you actually ask your audience to take some action.

The author does an excellent job of encouraging the audience to get involved and giving the specifics of how to take action.

### Conclusion

**Action:**

I. Now it's time to get involved and make a difference.

    A. Now that you know the characteristics of an at-risk student, how they are endangered, and how you can prevent these children from being at-risk, it's time to get involved!

B. Volunteer in a Big Brother/Big Sister program in your area. Look in your phone book for the number of your local Big Brother/Big Sister office. If you live here in Calloway county you can:

1. Visit BBBS of Calloway County at 808 Chestnut Street,

2. Call BBBS at (270) 759-2221

3. Visit online at www.bbbsa.org

C. Approximately 30,000 children are currently on the waiting list of the Big Brother/ Big Sister program.

II. In conclusion, no child can choose how or where he or she is born.

A. They can only live through the memories that they make.

B. I urge you to help these children in need; make memories like you have made that they too will never forget.

Make sure websites you use are from reputable organizations. It would be helpful if the author had pulled some information from some other sources as well, such as peer reviewed journals, newspapers, magazines, etc. Make sure your sources are legitimate and credible.

## Sources

*http://www.canada.compassion.net/sharingcompassion/childrenatrisk.asp#1*
*www.bbbsa.org*
*http://www.teaching.com/EarthDay97/center/text/webstodk21.htm*
*http://www.ericfacility.net/ericdigests/ed316617.html.*

---

Persuasive Speech
Debbie Faraone
Public Speaking

# Preparation Outline

I. GETTING THE ATTENTION

He has big brown eyes and a bright, beautiful smile. He is an amazing little boy. To see him today you might not suspect his difficult beginning in life. His birth mother, for reasons known only to herself, decided she couldn't keep her baby boy. So, at four weeks of age she left him with a Guatemalan lawyer and disappeared forever. The little boy was sent to live in an orphanage. Sadly, this is the case for many children around the world.

II. SHOWING THE NEED

A. The problem of orphaned children throughout the world has reached epidemic proportions.

B. According to Richard Stearns, President of World Vision, taken from the World Vision website on June 10, 2004, "millions of children are living in crisis...children who've been abandoned, abused, malnourished, neglected, and orphaned.

1. The World Vision website also stated that, "...by 2005, there will be more than 20 million AIDS orphans around the world, 16 million of those in Africa alone.

2. The U.S. State Department website, taken on June 10, 2004 states that the number of immigrant visas issued to orphans coming to the U.S. for adoption increased from about 7,000 in 1990 to

nearly 18,000 in the year 2000. Of course these numbers only reflect orphans able to be adopted because they are from countries that have adoption procedures. Many countries have no established procedures for international adoption or simple don't allow it.

3. Holt International, an intercountry adoption agency based in Oregon states on their website, taken June 10, 2004 that in 2002 over 6,000 children were placed from China alone, mostly in part as a result of China's one child policy. This policy states that Chinese families are allowed to have only one child. A boy is most desirable, leaving many Chinese baby girls orphaned.

C. Every child deserves a family. The problem of orphaned children affects all of us because a society that cannot or will not care for it's most helpless, children, is a society in grave danger.

III. SATISFY THE NEED

A. While the issues that create the situations that cause children to be in crisis are complex and hold to simple answers, there is one solution that works in many cases, adoption.

B. International adoption is a complex process that requires persistence on the part of adoptive families but, in the end, produce a wonderful result.

1. Allow me to briefly describe the process of international adoption.

2. The first step is to locate a reputable adoption agency. The internet is a good place to begin, however, be sure to check out the agency thoroughly before making any commitment.

3. After choosing an agency, the next step is to begin the laborious paperwork process. The most important aspects of this process include the home study, completed by a licensed social worker and the compilation of documents for your dossier.

4. Typically, once these documents are complete, you are then referred a child. Upon acceptance of the referral the final stage is initiated, approval of the adoption in the child's country of origin.

5. The entire process can take anywhere from 10-22 months.

C. While this may seem like a difficult process, it can be done.

1. According to the June 1, 2000 Time Magazine article, over 200 families adopted children from other countries last year and that number is likely to rise this year.

2. Also, in the aforementioned U.S. Department website, families with these children have expressed mostly satisfaction from these adoptions.

D. Now I know what some of you are thinking.

1. You might be thinking, "But, I have heard that families who have adopted children are having lots of problems with those children."

a. According to research, as stated in Holt's adoption guidebook, the vast majority of adopted children adjust well and grow into well-rounded, productive adults.

b. Developmental delays due to institutionalization are usually overcome, especially when early interventions are used by the adoptive families.

2. However, you might also argue that adoption is way too expensive.

a. The average cost of childbirth in America is $8,000, according to Dr. Jon Wynstra, OB/GYN of Jackson Purchase Women's Healthcare.

b. The average cost of international adoption ranges from $10,000 to $15,000; however, in the case of adoption, those fees are broken up and spread out over a 10-22 month time period. Also many agencies offer scholarships to families willing to adopt.

c. Finally, the IRS gives families who adopt a $10,000 tax credit.

IV. VISUALIZE THE RESULTS

    A. If more families would be willing to consider the option of building their families through adoption the world would be a much better place. I know because I've been there and done it! My husband and I have three beautiful biological daughters. We reached a point in our lives, though, where we felt our family wasn't complete and we had room for one more. After praying about it, we felt God was telling us to add to our family by adopting. Why bring another child into the world when there were already so many children out there who needed loving families of their own.

    B. How do I know adoption works? Let me show you how I know...

        1. I'd like to introduce you to my son...Brandon.

        2. Remember the little boy in the story? This is him!

        3. Our family is now complete, thanks to adoption.

V. REQUEST THE ACTION

    A. Most of you are not at a point in your lives where you could consider adopting a child, yet one day you might be. Keep international adoption in your heart. It was a desire in my heart for more than 20 years before I actually adopted.

    B. There are, however, two things you can do right now.

        1. First, stay informed about the issues affecting orphaned children throughout the world. Issues like AIDS, hunger, civil wars, etc. Get involved in some way. Be a part of the solution.

        2. Secondly, consider child sponsorship through a credible agency of ministry.

            a. I have composed a list of sponsorship organizations that I know to be excellent and that I recommend wholeheartedly.

            b. Presently, for the millions of children in Africa orphaned due to the AIDS epidemic, child sponsorship is the most direct way to impact their lives.

    C. While the issue of orphaned children throughout the world is a complex one, I hope I've been able to show you the reality of one possible solution, adoption.

    D. Likewise, the next time you see a TV commercial about hungry children, or see a family at Wal-Mart who has obviously adopted a child PLEASE don't just think "How neat" or "I wish I could do something for those poor children." You CAN do something!

Preparation Outline courtesy of Debbie Farone.

---

"After I finish typing my speech and print it out, I read it aloud several times, trying to get the whole speech in my head. Then I go through and highlight the main points with a highlighter and read it aloud one more time. Finally, I write my speaking outline on note cards and try speaking from that."

        —Matt[15]

## ■ Barriers to Effective Persuasive Speaking

Persuasive speaking is a part of your life and work every day. It is challenging to do it well, but a necessary skill for success in business and personal relationships. Perhaps one of the biggest barriers to doing so is failing to plan your communication in persuasive situations. It is important to remember the motivated sequence and apply those steps to your presentation, keeping your audience in mind throughout the process. Another barrier to effective persuasive speaking is in all-or-nothing thinking. If you consider yourself a failure if you have not fully convinced your audience to see things exactly the way you do, you are practicing this kind of thinking. Remember that sometimes persuasion is a matter of degree. Perhaps you have moved your audience along the continuum slightly closer to your viewpoint. Next time you may be able to move them even a little further. Perhaps one of the most common barriers, however, is the closed mind. You need to have an open mind just as the audience does. If you keep your mind open to new ideas, you may discover new ways to influence and connect with your audience. You might also discover, occasionally, that you were wrong and you need to adjust your own viewpoint. Having an open mind is necessary to be a good critical thinker, a vital skill for effective persuasive speaking.

# ACTIVITIES

# The Delicate Art
# of Persuasion

## References

1. Makay, J.J. (1995). *Public speaking: Theory into practice* (2nd ed.). Fort Worth, Texas: Harcourt Brace College Publishers, p. 372.

2. Beebe, S. A. & Beebe, S. J. (2000). *Public Speaking: An audience centered approach* (4th ed.). Boston: Allyn and Bacon. P. 357.

3. O'Keefe, D. J. (2002). *Persuasion: Theory and research* (2nd ed). Thousand Oaks: Sage Publications, p. 3.

4. Woodward, G. C. & Denton, R. E., Jr. (2000). *Persuasion & influence in American life* (4th ed.). Prospect Heights, IL: Waveland Press, Inc., p. 5.

5. Cooper, L. (1960). The rhetoric of Aristotle. Englewood Cliffs, New Jersey: Prentice-Hall, Inc., p. 10.

6. Larson, C. U. (2001). Persuasion: Reception and responsibility (9th ed.). Belmont CA: Wadsworth, p.8.

7. Burke, K. (1969). Rhetoric of motives. Berkeley, California: University of California Press, p. 20.

8. Coffman, S. (2003, January/February). Bicycle injuries and safety helmets in children: Review of research. *Orthopaedic Nursing*, 22(1), p. 9.

9. Schlottmann, A. (2001, August). Perception verses knowledge of cause and effect in children: When seeing is believing. *Current Directions in Psychological Science*, 10(4), p. 111.

10. Drexler, M. (2003, July). Under the influence. *Good Housekeeping* 237(1), p. 143.

11. *The pocket Webster school & office dictionary* (1990). New York: Pocket Books, p. 263.

12. Gronbeck, B. E., German, K., Ehninger, D., & Monroe, A. H. (1995). *Principles of speech communication* (12th ed.). New York: HarperCollins College Publishers.

13. Student speech presented at Murray State University in May 2003.

14. Student speech presented at Murray State University in May 2003.

15. Murray State University student in May 2003.

16. Student speech presented at Murray State University in May 2003.

# 10 Preparing Speeches for Everyday Life

## CHAPTER PREVIEW

**1** Purposes of special occasion and impromptu speeches

**2** Types of special occasion and impromptu speeches

**3** Guidelines for creating special occasions speeches

There are many occasions in your everyday life when you will be required to prepare and give a speech of some sort. You might be asked to give a eulogy at your grandfather's funeral or a toast at your best friend's wedding. You might be asked to present an award to a coworker or accept such an award from the organization for which you work. These rituals or ceremonies punctuate our everyday experiences and help make them memorable. In this chapter we will consider purposes, types, and guidelines for creating special occasion and impromptu presentations.

## Five Purposes of Special Occasion and Impromptu Speeches

- Agenda Setting
- To Celebrate
- To Commemorate
- To Entertain
- To Inspire

There are several purposes or functions that a special occasion speech can fulfill in your everyday life. A special occasion speech can be defined as any presentation that is prepared for a special occasion and for the purpose of that specific event. Speeches for special occasions are different from the informative and persuasive presentations we have discussed earlier in this text. Although they may have many of the same elements, their primary purpose is not so much to inform or persuade, as it is to set the agenda, introduce the topic or speaker, celebrate, commemorate, entertain, or inspire.

> Speech is power: speech is to persuade, to convert, to compel. It is to bring another out of his bad sense into your good sense.[1]
>
> ⁓Ralph Waldo Emerson

### To Set the Agenda

One purpose for a special occasion speech might be to set a social agenda for a group, by establishing or reinforcing the goals, values, beliefs, and rituals of the organization sponsoring the event. Occasions that might call for agenda-setting speeches include gatherings of issue- or cause-oriented organizations such as the local battered women's shelter, fund-raisers such as the sorority or fraternity philanthropy committee, campaign banquets such as the mayoral candidate's announcement banquet, conferences such as the United Nations Conference on Trade and Development, and conventions such as the National Communication Association Annual Convention. For each of the groups, a speaker may be invited to describe the organization's activities and outline its plans, or agenda, for the future. A speaker might be asked to deliver a keynote address at a conference or convention focusing on the theme of the meeting.

### To Celebrate

A second purpose for a special occasion speech might be to celebrate a person(s), a place, or an event. These types of events might include weddings, anniversaries, retirement parties, and awards banquets, which call for the speaker to recognize the person(s), place, or event being celebrated. When giving a special occasion speech to accomplish this purpose, the speaker is expected to praise the subject of the celebration and to observe the rituals and norms of the occasion and organization.

### To Commemorate

The third purpose for a special occasion speech might be to **commemorate** a person, place, or event. Commemorative events can be held for many different occasions, including anniversaries, dedications, memorials, or commencements. When giving a commemorative presentation, the speaker is expected to honor the person, place, or event. For example, a commemorative event might be the anniversary of the September 11, 2001 terrorist attack on America at the World Trade Center Towers in New York City and the Pentagon. In general, a commemorative address is delivered using formal language and serious attitude.

### To Entertain

In comparison to the commemorative address, the fourth purpose for special occasion speech may not use formal language or serious attitude. A presentation designed to **entertain** the audience is usually lighthearted and amusing. Depending on the event, the speaker may be expected to provide information about the topic at hand. A speech to entertain may be given at a banquet, awards dinner, roast, or toast. For example, when speaking at the Homecoming Banquet, a special speaker will be expected to entertain the audience after the dinner has occurred. Many of the different types of special occasion presentations may require the speaker to entertain the audience, including the after-dinner, commencement, dedication, and introductory speeches.

### To Inspire

The fifth purpose for a special occasion speech is to **inspire**. In a presentation designed to inspire the audience, the speaker will inspire the audience about a person, place or event. For example, inaugural addresses, keynote speeches at conventions, commencement speeches, and the annual State of the Union Address are each designed to inspire the audience. The speaker may also pay homage to the person or event being commemorated, such as the anniversary of the Martin Luther King, Jr. "I Have a Dream" speech.

## Building an Impromptu Speech

If called to do so, the following steps, if implemented, should help you to create a speech quickly and with little apprehension.

**Step 1.** *Create an introduction.*

> The easiest way to begin is by acknowledging what you were asked to do.
>
> *I was asked to say a few words about Sara.*
>
> You could also use one of the types of introductions discussed in chapter 5. Quotation introductions are a great resource if you memorize a few quotations that could be used in many situations, and for many types of speeches. When you're asked to speak, one will immediately come to mind. This can trigger your creativity and give you time to think of your main points.
>
> My father always said that you can't change anyone but yourself. The wonderful thing about Sara is that she never tries to change anyone but herself. She's the person in this company who constantly strives to not only be a better co-worker but also a better citizen. She deserves this company award.

**Step: 2.** *Think of two to three main points.*

> Since you don't have a lot of time to think, and an impromptu speech is meant to be short, two to three main points are all you need to get your message across to your audience.
>
> Two things that exemplify her dedication to humankind inside and outside of the office are her involvement in our new daycare center and her work in the city at the local Needline.

**Step 3.** *Support your main points with examples, statistics and testimony.*

> It's hard to walk around with accurate statistics in your head, but if you remember some that would aid your speech, then use them. Otherwise, examples to support your main points are more likely to be used. If you have a personal testimony or know of someone's true thoughts about your subject, feel free to share that information.
>
> Be careful of quoting other people unless you are positive your quote is accurate or you may have problems later.

About ten years ago, this company resisted the idea of a daycare center fearing rejection from clients. Sara fought our former CEO and the forces that be. She almost lost her job, but, thankfully, we got a new boss, a new vision and a new daycare center. Only a few have the fortitude to fight for mothers and all family members who benefit from these centers. But Sara is not only passionate about work, she also supports all of humankind through the giving of her time at the Need line. So many need our help but only a few take the time to dedicate hours to helping someone we may never know.

**Step 4.** *Summarize and conclude creatively.*

Summarize the two to three main points and try to conclude with a creative statement.

So as we can see, Sara supports men, women, and children. She's a champion of human rights. So when dad stated: "Be a part of the solution and not a part of the problem," he may not have been speaking of our Sara Douglass at that time, but he certainly, unknowingly, was speaking of Sara's contributions to the betterment of all of our lives. At our company and even in society, she has always been a great part of the solution.

## Types of Special Occasion and Impromptu Speeches

The special occasion can include many types of events, each with a different set of expectations. Some special occasion speeches focus on an event, such as the after-dinner or commencement speech, a dedication, eulogy, or the farewell speech. Some of these events focus on a person, such as the eulogy, farewell, introductory, or nomination speech, a roast and toast, or a tribute. For each of the types of special occasion and impromptu speeches presented, we will discuss the corresponding expectations.

### Acceptance Speech

An **acceptance** speech is an opportunity for the speaker to give thanks for a gift, award, or some other form of public recognition.

On March 10, 2002 at the 8th annual Screen Actors Guild awards, Ben Kingsley received the award for "outstanding performance by a male author in a television movie or miniseries." His acceptance speech was only 122 words. Kingsley

first recognized Hannah Taylor Gordon, who played Anne Frank, and claimed he was only reacting to her performance. He then acknowledged Otto Frank, Anne Frank's father. He accepted the award on behalf of his own children, and then thanked the Screen Actors Guild.

This speech, although short, has many elements of a good acceptance speech. Kingsley is modest and gracious. He sincerely recognizes the contributions of others in helping him to achieve the recognition he received. He is grateful and expresses his desire to live up to the recognition in the coming years. It is very effective and appropriate for the award received.[2]

Certainly, there are other things you can include in a speech of acceptance—recognition of others (other actors, family members, friends, etc.) who have helped you achieve this success, a description of how you arrived at your present level of accomplishment, describing fully what the award means to you. The key point to keep in mind in giving an acceptance speech is that your theme should center on a gracious thank you. Brevity is usually expected, but generally a good acceptance speech goes beyond a simple "thank you to all who have helped me along the way." A personal anecdote about someone who helped you along the way or the meaning of the award is an excellent way to tie it all together.

### After-Dinner Speech (Banquet)

The **after-dinner speech** is frequently used at luncheons, dinners, and banquets and is a common speech for organizational or convention banquets. Middle management officers and their superiors in an organization are expected to be capable of delivering a short humorous speech for an audience of professionals. The after-dinner speech should provide an entertaining or compelling message on a theme. There are some general guidelines you should follow in accomplishing these goals:

- **Be acceptable.** In general, speakers should strive for humor that either produces relief on the part of the audience or that demonstrates an incongruity. Humor may also violate an audience's expectations or display the superiority of either the speaker, the audience, or both.

- **Be appropriate.** Your gestures should either reinforce the humorous content of the speech or appear natural and un-motivated.

- **Be brief.** Use the allotted time wisely. Do not exceed the time limit.

- **Be clear.** Poor enunciation or incorrect grammar can alter the meaning and clarity of the humor.

- **Be creative.** The sources for the after dinner speech are too often exaggerated for humor. That is, the speaker may take legitimate sources that give legitimate information about the subject and apply the sources in the speech, clearly indicating to the audience that the source statement is taken out of context or otherwise used or exaggerated in a way that was not intended. This technique is used for humorous effect.

- **Be extemporaneous.** The speaker should refrain from announcing his or her jokes by stating, "I heard a funny story last week . . . ." In addition, the jokes should be told extemporaneously, not read.

- **Be tasteful.** Humor should be in good taste and relevant to the topic at hand. The speaker should keep his or her audience in mind when devising jokes, puns, and one-liners. Relate your humor to the audience if possible, perhaps using "inside" jokes about their industry.

- **Be thoughtful.** The speaker should avoid humor that stigmatizes, vilifies or disparages particular individuals or groups.

- **Be timely.** When using humor, timing is important! The speech should be free of lapses in memory or breaks in fluency in order to be humorous. Deliver the punch-line effectively to enhance the humorous nature of the jokes. Avoid long, rambling stories. Speakers should strive for a varied vocal delivery style that accentuates the humorous content of the speech.

## Commencement Speech

Graduation or **commencement** day celebrates the transition in life when a student graduates from an educational institution and moves on to another step in life, perhaps into the job market or on to another level of education. During the commencement speech, the speaker praises, congratulates, and inspires those graduating because they have formally completed a prescribed set of educational requirements. The person chosen to deliver the commencement speech may be the class valedictorian or other outstanding student. The school principal; the college or university president, dean, faculty; notable people from the community; or distinguished alumni may also deliver this address.

During the commencement address, the speaker will not only congratulate the individuals being honored, but is also expected to offer the graduates some kernels of wisdom to sustain them over the course of their future journeys, calling them to look ahead and carefully consider their future role in society. In addition, because commencement audiences consist primarily of parents, relatives, and friends of those graduating, the speech will be complimentary of the students' accomplishments.

The commencement speech is expected to be relatively brief because audience members are anxious to see their graduates perform the ritual of receiving the diploma or certificate. The ritual should be much more time consuming than the actual commencement address.

## Dedications

A **dedication** speech celebrates a special occasion when something new begins, such as the dedication of a new building, road, bridge, ship, plane, or some other new commodity is presented. This speech commits the new "beginning" to an ideal or value, like improved community relations, community development, or community service. This type of speech is usually rather short and acknowledges the contributions of those involved in the creation of the new structure. The speaker will also describe how the future of the item symbolizes an ideal or value.

On July 24, 2003, Tommy G. Thompson, U.S. Secretary of Health and Human Services, dedicated the new AHRQ (Agency for Healthcare Research and Quality, http://www.ahrq.gov/) Building in Rockville, Maryland.[3]

## On AHRQ Building Dedication

Thank you, Carolyn, for that warm introduction. Carolyn, you are a great leader of AHRQ, an excellent advisor on health quality, and a worthy successor to Dr. John Eisenberg.

Under your leadership, AHRQ has worked to improve patient safety by encouraging health care leaders to implement new consensus standards that will help prevent medical errors. You are also helping rural hospitals invest in information technology so that patients' records can be computerized and up to date.

Thank you for your service.

Henry Wadsworth Longfellow wrote,

"Lives of great men all remind us
We can make our lives sublime,
And departing, leave behind us
Footprints on the sands of time."

Throughout his career, our friend John Eisenberg dedicated himself to ensuring that patients have the highest quality, safest health care possible. And his commitment and enthusiasm for this goal inspired colleagues within the Department of Health and Human Services and across the federal government. He left deep footsteps on the sands of time.

When John got sick, he not only showed great courage in battling his illness; he even wanted to continue working and continue to improve American health care for others.

Since the day he joined AHRQ in 1997, John was an exceptional leader who built a motivated and dedicated team. He coordinated and led government efforts to reduce medical errors and improve patient safety. Largely through his efforts, improving patient safety and health care quality are top national priorities.

I knew from the first time I met John that he was passionate about excellence in research and improving the quality of health care. He knew that the quality of our health care affects not only our health, but also our quality of life.

Part of John's legacy was to ensure that our system translates scientific evidence into better health for everyone. And this building represents the culmination of that legacy.

This building not only bears John's name, it also fulfills one of his priorities: allowing all AHRQ staff to work together under one roof. He appreciated the idea that a single building for all of AHRQ meant improved efficiency and better teamwork within the Agency and for its customers.

But John's greatest legacy is the excellent staff of AHRQ, who work every day to help ensure that American health care remains the best in the world. If he were here today, I know he would be as proud of you as I am.

At the funeral of President Grant, President McKinley said, "A great life never dies. Great deeds are imperishable; great names immortal."

Although it was shorter than we would have liked, John led a great life. His great deeds are imperishable, and continue through your work. And his great name, on this building and in our hearts, is immortal.

We were privileged to work with John as a colleague, but we were even more proud to call him a friend. And as one friend to another, it is my honor and privilege to dedicate the new AHRQ building to our friend Dr. John Eisenberg.

### ▌ *Eulogy (Funeral)*

A **eulogy** is a formal commendatory presentation at a funeral. Your objective is usually to remember and honor the individual who has died. How long your presentation is or what style it takes will depend upon the expectations of the family. You have, no doubt, been to funerals that are very somber and serious. Perhaps you have also been to funerals that were full of laughter and fond memories. Both are appropriate, depending upon the expectations of the family. There are a number of websites where you can purchase ready-made eulogies for specific occasions (brother/sister, parent/grandparent, child, friend/neighbor, etc.). Perhaps you could get some general ideas that way, but you could not give an effective eulogy from such a purchase. Eulogies must be tailored to the person, situation surrounding that person's death, family expectations, and your relationship to the deceased. No canned eulogy can do that. The length of the eulogy also depends upon the expectations surrounding the individual situation. Some funerals or memorial services call for brevity, while others call for more lengthy presentations. As we have indicated throughout this text, audience analysis is vital. In addition to understanding the person, you must know and understand your audience and their expectations to give an effective eulogy. You do not necessarily need to have known the person to do this. If, however, you did not know the deceased, you have some research to do. You must, in those situations, interview others who did know the person in order to formulate your remarks in an acceptable and meaningful manner.

## Farewell Speech

Properly saying good-bye is a widely practiced tradition across the globe. **Bidding farewell** is usually done by a short, formal presentation. Farewell speeches may be given when a person retires, relocates to another city, changes employers, or takes a leave of absence. The speech may be given in two ways, either by the person leaving or by those remaining. For example, when Jane Hall was leaving her position as faculty advisor for Springer-Franklin Residential Hall to take another position, she may have given a farewell speech as a means of saying "good-bye." Or when Hall was leaving, Sara Bailey, the Residential Director, may have given a short speech saying "good-bye." In either presentation, the primary purpose is to celebrate the relationship between the person who is leaving and those who will remain. The special occasion may be a sad or emotionally powerful event—when saying "good-bye" to a friend—and the presentation commemorating that event should focus on the person, their merits as a friend or member of the organization, encourage the person to maintain contact with those remaining, and highlight the future of the person leaving. This speech should maintain goodwill between the person leaving and those remaining through positive communication. This is not an opportunity to speak negatively of the departing person. A formal farewell speech is appropriate in every context: socially, professionally, politically, and religiously.

## Inspiration (Political or Religious Events)

Many of the speech types discussed thus far **inspire** audiences. However, there are other special occasions which call for a presentation that is meant solely to inspire as its main goal. For example, ministers, rabbis, priests, and other religious leaders deliver inspirational speeches in the form of sermons. "Pep talks" at sales meetings and nomination speeches at political rallies and conventions are inspirational. When we think about the business world, there are many inspirational speakers who earn their living making presentations. For example, the Nashville Speakers Bureau (NSB) represents more than 550 speakers, including Ambassador Alan Keyes, Mark Victor Hansen, Sue Thomas, Orel Hershiser, Oksana Baiul, Derek Parra, Pat Williams, Cal Thomas, Jack Canfield, and Ken Davis; its roster continues to grow.[4] There are actors, authors, celebrities, comedians, Christian speakers, editors, Olympians, athletes, sports figures, political leaders, journalists, youth speakers, storytellers, commentators, anchors, and pastors who are registered with this speakers bureau. These presenters are for hire to speak for fundraising events, assemblies, women's events, civic and college groups, personal appearances, conferences, churches, town hall meetings, and corporate events. Some "in-demand" topics for these speakers include abstinence, comedy, sales, pro-life, motivation, and ethics.

Regardless of the special occasion, when the goal of the speech is to inspire, the speaker should motivate the audience to positively consider, reflect on, and sometimes even act upon their request. Therefore, the inspirational presentation should entertain and persuade the audience. This speech should be uplifting, encouraging, and help the audience to see things in a positive light. Effective inspirational speakers use pathos—appealing to the audience's emotions—to motivate people to change an attitude, belief, value, or behavior.

When a speaker uses an emotional appeal to reach the audience, it is wise to use several delivery techniques. For example, the use of vivid description and emotionally-charged language are effective uses of pathos. Other language techniques motivational speakers often use include repetition, alliteration, parallelism, and rhythm. When appealing to the audience's emotions, a speaker should avoid using sexist or racist language, which would be offensive. There are some general guidelines you should follow in accomplishing the goal of inspiring the audience:

- **Be audience-centered.** Focus on ways to uplift the audience using language and nonverbal delivery techniques. Seek to help the audience see things positively.

- **Be clear.** Clearly establish your speech goals. Inspirational speeches run the risk of being vague, which may leave the audience unsure about what the message was. Make sure the audience clearly understands what you are trying to motivate them to do: change an attitude, belief, value, or behavior.

- **Be dramatic.** Use a dramatic ending to inspire the audience to remember the theme of the speech and to take action. This technique might include the use of a startling statement, quote, story, or rhetorical question.

- **Be dynamic.** Use a dynamic speaking style to inspire not only through the content but through the delivery as well. Using both an energetic style and a powerful message will motivate the audience.

- **Be organized.** Consider using verbal devices such as an acronym, pneumonic device, or specific steps to organize the speech. This helps the audience understand and remember the message. For example, chapter 4 discusses the acronym CLIMATE, which helps the speaker create a constructive, positive communication climate. Another pneumonic device you might use would be Roy G. Biv (red, orange, yellow, green, blue, indigo, and violet) for remembering the color wheel. Each of these linguistic devices will help you, as the speaker, be organized and help the audience remember what you have told them.

- **Be relevant.** Use examples and stories the audience can relate to easily. The more realistic the example or story, the more likely the audience will find the presentation relevant to them.

## Introductory Speech

A speech of introduction is a presentation that introduces another speaker—the main speaker—to the audience. When you are making this type of presentation, it is important to remember that you are the channel through which the audience comes to know something about the speaker. It is your responsibility to prepare the audience for the speaker and his or her presentation. Your goals are to build up the audience's anticipation of and interest in the speaker and topic. There are some general guidelines you should follow in accomplishing these goals:

- **Be personal.** Generalizing about the speaker is not likely to build audience interest. Adapt your remarks to the occasion and help the audience to connect with the speaker they are about to hear.

- **Be accurate.** Personalization is great, but make sure you have your facts straight. You don't want to embarrass the speaker by overstating or understating accomplishments or statistics. Don't put the speaker in the awkward position of being forced to decide whether or not to correct your inaccuracies before beginning his or her speech. And make sure you pronounce the speaker's name correctly.

- **Be consistent.** It is important that you understand the approach of the speaker. You do not want to set a humorous tone if what the speaker has to say is somber and serious. You also don't want to set too serious of a tone if the speaker's remarks will be humorous. If you do not know, ask the speaker ahead of time about his or her intentions.

- **Be thoughtful.** Be careful not to shift the attention from the speaker to yourself. If you are too funny or focus on yourself, you might steal the show. You are supposed to be building up the speaker. Don't summarize what the speaker is planning to say. Your job is to prepare the audience to listen to the speaker. Don't build the speaker up beyond what he or she can live up to. Create realistic expectations.

- **Be brief.** It is your responsibility to prepare the audience for the main speaker, not be the main speaker yourself. Therefore, your remarks should be brief. Share pertinent information about the speaker, but you do not need to give their entire resume. Don't throw the audience into information overload. It is better to be too brief than too long-winded.

- **Be a catalyst.** End your remarks by calling the audience into action. "Join me now in welcoming . . ." and then guide your audience in that welcome by leading the applause.

- **Be attentive.** Your job is not over after your remarks. After you have introduced the speaker, you need to remain attentive as an example to the rest of the audience. Be prepared to respond appropriately (with a head nod, smile, etc.) should the speaker refer to you or something you said in his or her speech. This is especially important if you are sitting up front with the speaker facing the audience.

## Nomination Speech

There are many times in life when a person might be nominated for an office, honor, or award. On such special occasions, the nomination may be made in a traditional fashion—with a long-winded speech. However, the typical nomination speech should be fairly brief and succinct. A formal nomination consists of a persuasive speech in which an individual is publicly put forward as a candidate. As the nominator, your speech should explain why the candidate is the most qualified and credible person for the office, honor, or award. In your explanation, you should include: a description of the qualities necessary for the office, honor, or award; a list of the candidate's qualifications that meet these criteria; and feature the candidate by name. Reinforcing the candidate's name to the audience will help them remember to vote for that person for the office, honor, or award.

## Presentation Speech

Each year we participate in a number of presentational situations. High school or college ceremonies honor us or our children and grandchildren with diplomas, awards, and various recognitions. Organizations honor our fellow employees or us for accomplishments. Communities honor those who have contributed in unique ways to the betterment of life for the area. Professional sports honor athletes for their achievements. Television and movie stars are recognized for stellar performances. Whether as presenter, recipient, or audience member, we have all experienced these presentations.

In each of these situations, the presenter has the same objectives—to explain the significance of the award and to explain why that particular person is receiving the recognition. The type of award will

dictate exactly how you should accomplish this. Sometimes the award is given in honor or the name of some individual. In this case, it would be appropriate to explain the reason the award was developed and describe the achievements of the person or people for whom it is named. In any case, your presentation should address both the audience and the recipient of the award itself. Brevity is key. Personalize the presentation through anecdotes about the person—humorous or serious—but choose your words wisely. Take the time you need to explain the award and introduce the recipient, but stick to the necessary details.

## Roast and Toast (Wedding or Retirement)

There are special occasions, *roasts*, which call for a humorous tribute to a person, one in which a series of speakers jokingly poke fun at him or her. On the other hand, there are special occasions, *toasts*, which call for a short tribute celebrating someone's achievement or accomplishment. In both of these award presentations, the primary goal is to celebrate the person and his or her achievements. You may be called upon to participate in a roast or make a toast at many important social events, including weddings and retirement parties. There are some general guidelines you should follow in accomplishing these goals:

- **Be brief.** Roast and toasts are usually fairly short tributes to the honoree. One reason for brevity is that many speakers will be involved in the celebration; therefore, it is important to refrain from taking up too much time.

- **Be complimentary.** Try to restrict your remarks to one or two of the most unique or recognizable attributes of the honoree. Focusing on the positive will help set him or her apart and highlight reasons for the celebration.

- **Be positive.** Even when you are giving a roast, poking fun at someone, being positive will help you maintain goodwill. The overall purpose of the roast is to pay tribute to the honoree, so be kind. Avoid embarrassing the person being honored. This could turn a festive event into an awkward situation.

- **Be prepared.** The roast or toast sets the tone and expresses the purpose of a special occasion. When you are asked to make this type of presentation it is best to be prepared in order to avoid errors and anxieties that occur as a result of being caught off guard. It might help to rehearse your presentation in front of a trusted friend or family member. Practice helps you know how long your presentation may be and allows you time to alter the speech.

### Tribute

Publicly honoring and acknowledging the major or long-term accomplishments of an individual or a group is known as a speech of tribute. This type of presentation tribute is similar to a toast in that it may honor a person, but it might also honor a group or organization. A tribute might be given on a special holiday that celebrates the accomplishments of an individual or group, such as Veterans Day, which honors all U.S. military personnel for their service. Also, a tribute might be given when a person retires or to a community group when it raises large amounts of money for special causes, such as when the local Relay for Life event raises $100,000 for the American Cancer Society.

The content of a tribute may be similar to that of an award speech, but it does not involve giving a physical award to the honoree (such as a plaque). When planning for the tribute, you should show respect for the honoree by expressing strong appreciation for the accomplishments of the individual or group. In addition, the presentation should arouse a sense of admiration and gratitude from the audience. Other tributes might be given as a eulogy or a toast.

## Seven Guidelines for Creating Special Occasion Speeches

Whether you are introducing the keynote speaker at a business meeting, presenting or accepting an award, delivering a eulogy, toasting the new bride and groom, addressing the city council, giving an after-dinner speech, or dedicating a building, there are some general guidelines you should keep in mind.

- **Adapt your presentation to the speaker and/or occasion.** Just because audiences have expectations about the types of things they expect to hear for a particular situation does not mean that you must deliver a standardized or canned speech. For instance, suppose you are called upon to introduce the same person as speaker at the community arts festival and as keynote speaker at the annual meeting of your organization. The basic elements may be the same, but you will need to approach the introductions differently in order to effectively connect with the different types of audiences you will be addressing.

- **Avoid trite language.** Although we have indicated that audiences have certain expectations about what types of things you might express at specific situations, they do not want to hear a string of clichés. Find fresh ways to express expected sentiments.

- **Honor time expectations.** Generally, speeches of introduction, toasts, award presentations, and acceptance speeches are brief. After-dinner speeches and keynote addresses are longer. Eulogies, dedications, and tributes fall somewhere in the middle. Whatever presentation you are making, be aware of the time expectations. For instance, if you are giving the keynote address at a Kiwanis club lunch meeting, know what expectations the audience has of you. If the meeting generally begins at noon and usually lasts until 12:45 pm and you begin speaking at 12:20, know that you probably have only 15-20 minutes to speak so that they can wrap up the meeting by 12:45 and return to their respective jobs. If you are introducing a speaker who is to talk for 20 minutes, your introduction should probably be two minutes or less. You are not to be the focal point. Therefore, if you take six or seven minutes to introduce the speaker, you have begun to shift the focus from him or her to you. Present within your time limits and expectations.

- **Know the facts.** Make sure your presentation is accurate. If you are going to share personal information about an individual or recite a chronology of events, for instance, make sure that you have them correct. You don't want to embarrass yourself or the person you are introducing or honoring by failing to do your homework. Make sure you have all of your facts and numbers correct.

- **Know whom you represent.** Whether you are giving the toast at the kickoff of a new product at your organizational staff meeting or presenting an award to the salesman of the year, remember that you represent the others in the organization as well. You have been chosen to speak and have the responsibility of choosing the words to use, but do not forget that you represent the others as well.

■ **Meet expectations.** Be sure that you prepare your presentation to the expectations of the organization and situation surrounding the event. Audiences expect to hear certain words in particular ways. Whether you are delivering a eulogy or introducing a speaker, make sure you understand the expectations surrounding the occasion. Don't disappoint your audience. Do your homework and know what is expected of you.

■ **Sincerity is the key.** Audiences can tell when you do not mean what you say. Don't try to fake it. False sincerity will offend your audience, as will bragging. Be sincere and humble in your presentation. For instance, if you do not know the person you are introducing or honoring personally, find people that do. Thus, instead of faking your intimacy, share what others have said about the person. If you are accepting an award, be gracious, but do not brag. No one wants to know how highly you think of yourself. The award you are receiving is because of what others think of you. Let that speak for itself.

## TIP

### Audience Analysis

Throughout this text, we have addressed audience analysis. At this point it should only be necessary to review its importance. It is vital that you analyze your audience if you expect your special occasion speeches to be effective. You must understand who your audience is and what their expectations are within the set of circumstances and social context within which you find yourself. Not all award ceremonies are the same. Funerals are different. Speakers are unique. You must adapt. In addition, remember the importance of your own personal attributes. Don't try to be someone you are not. Understand what your strengths are and capitalize on them within the expectations of the specific presentation opportunity. Prepare, adapt, and be yourself.

# ACTIVITIES

# Preparing Speeches for Everyday Life

# Discussion Questions

1. Why do you suppose it is difficult for people to accept an award? What public speaking advice might you give someone who is about to accept an award?

2. As a society, we seem to be predisposed to give a speech to celebrate a lot of different occasions. Why? How do you think this type of specialized speaking emerged and became a tradition?

3. What are the primary differences between an after-dinner speech and a speech to inform or to persuade? What is the role of humor in an after-dinner speech?

4. What is the fundamental purpose of a commemorative speech? Why does a successful commemorative speech depend so much on the creative and subtle use of language?

# Notes

1. Retrieved on September 28, 2003 from http://www.bartleby.com/66/33/20933.html. This quote is attributed to Ralph Waldo Emerson (1803–1882), U.S. essayist, poet, philosopher. "Social Aims," Letters and Social Aims (1876).

2. Speech retrieved on September 15, 2003 from http://www.sagawards,cin.8_speeches.html.

3. Retrieved on September 2, 2003 from http://www.hhs.gov/news/speech/2003/030724.html.

4. For additional information, see http://www.nashspeakers.com/.

# Appendices

# Appendix A: Assignments

## Speech #1 Bag Speech (Introductory Speech)

In this first assignment, you will provide further insight into who you are as a person, as well as demonstrate a basic understanding of the structure of an informative speech. First, collect three personal items that represent your past, your present, and your future. Then, find an interesting container for these objects that represents you as a whole. Organize your speech with an interesting introduction, a detailed body, and a conclusion. In describing the objects you bring, explain how they relate to you, how they are like you, and how they can help the audience to know you better.

Strive to find innovative and unique items to bring to class; objects that symbolize what's important to you: your values, interests, hobbies, work, goals, concerns, etc. The best presentations will provide a clear and thoughtful description/explanation of the objects and how they describe who you are. Additionally, a well-rehearsed extemporaneous speaking style will be demonstrated.

All audio/visual aids are subject to approval by your instructor. Visual aids such as weapons, explosives, illegal drugs, alcohol containers, or anything related to explicit sexual acts are not allowed.

**To present:**

- Speak 2-3 minutes

- Describe/explain 3 innovative items representing your past, your present, and your future. Items will be placed in an interesting container representing you as a whole.

- Make sure items are large enough to be seen, not too common, and appropriate for this classroom setting.

**To turn in:**

- Speech folder.

- Speech#1-Evaluation Form(see Appendix B).

- VHS videotape.

## Speech #2 Speech to Inform

The goal of this assignment is to inform your audience about a specific topic. This topic may be an interesting object, a person, a place, an event, or concept. Your speech must be based on at least one innovative and unique item that you will use as a visual aid at some point during your speech.

As you prepare for your speech, concentrate on the most interesting/important aspects of your topic, and clearly describe/explain those details to the audience. This speech should not be about you; the purpose of this assignment is not to help the audience get to know you. Though your insight and experience may provide useful additional information, focus on organizing your original research into a fascinating presentation that will broaden the audience's sphere of knowledge.

**To present:**

- Speak for 3-5 minutes

- Effectively inform the audience about a fascinating topic.

- Display at least 1 Audio/Visual aid.

- Provide at least 3 types of verbal supportive material.

- Cite at least 3 documented sources.

**To turn in:**

- Speech folder.
- Speech #2-Evaluation Form (see Appendix B).
- Preparation Outline.
- VHS videotape.

## Speech #3 Speech to Demonstrate

The goal of this assignment is to vividly inform your audience about a clearly defined, step-by-step process. Concentrate on the distinct steps of your process, in order to give your audience a comprehensive demonstration.

**To present:**

- Speak for 5-7 minutes
- Effectively demonstrate/explain a worthwhile process.
- Display at least 1 Audio/Visual aid.
- Provide at least 3 different types of verbal supportive material.
- Cite at least 2 documented sources.

**To turn in:**

- Speech folder.
- Speech#3-Evaluation Form (see Appendix B).
- Preparation Outline.
- VHS videotape.

## Persuasive Speech Audience Analysis

Prior to your persuasive speech, you must have a clear understanding of your audience; taking into account their interests, values, opinions, experience, etc.- Do not make assumptions based solely on the demographics of your audience.

1. Based on the specific purpose of your persuasive speech, create an audience analysis survey addressing the audience's interests, values, opinions, etc. Your questions should focus on situational variables. For the survey portion of this assignment, observe the following guidelines:

- 10 questions maximum.
- 1 page; typed or word-processed.
- Your name must appear clearly in the upper right-hand corner.
- Surveys must be anonymous; do not ask respondents for their name.
- Bring enough copies of your survey for the entire class.

2. Based on the responses to your survey, write a brief analysis addressing the following questions. Attach your analysis to the preparation outline of your persuasive speech.

- How did you adapt your introduction to gain the attention of this audience and directly relate your claim as being "significant"?
- How did you develop the main points for this audience?
- How were your supportive materials appropriate/effective for this audience?
- What steps did you take to adapt your language/wording to this audience?

## Speech #4 Persuasive Speech

The purpose of this speech is to persuade your audience to accept, confirm, or change their minds about a clearly defined issue. This issue must be presented in terms of a central claim with which the audience may, in the end, choose to agree or disagree. It must be of some significance to the audience, having some impact on their lives. Directly address your audience's predisposition to your topic as illustrated by your audience analysis. Additionally, you must demonstrate a clear understanding of Monroe's Motivated Sequence.

**To present:**

- Speak for 7-9 minutes.
- Effectively persuade the audience to accept your claim regarding a significant issue.
- Ethically use strong motivational appeals.
- Provide at least 3 types of verbal supportive material.

- Cite at least 4 documented sources.

- Audio/Visual aids are optional, but strongly recommended.

**To turn in:**

- Speech folder.

- Speech#4-Evaluation Form(see Appendix B).

- Preparation Outline (including audience analysis; attach copy).

- VHS videotape.

## Speech #5 Special Occasion Speech

In this last assignment, you will demonstrate your most refined organizational and public speaking abilities in a speech of introduction, presentation, acceptance, commemoration, or entertainment. Your instructor will provide further details for this assignment.

**To present:**

- Speak for 2-4 minutes.

- Effectively speak using vivid language in a polished, extemporaneous style, with energy and enthusiasm.

- Citing documented sources and using audio/visual aids are optional but strongly recommended.

**To turn in:**

- Speech folder.

- Preparation Outline.

- Speech #5-Evaluation Form (see Appendix B).

- VHS videotape.

## Speech #1 Introduction Speech— Self Evaluation

After viewing your videotape, respond to each of the following questions in paragraph/short-essay form. Your evaluation must be typed and double-spaced. Self-evaluations may be no more than two pages in length.

1. Discuss your self-confidence before your speech; how would you characterize you attitude/expectations in preparation for this assignment? During the presentation itself, describe hoe you felt physically and emotionally. What steps did you take to control your anxiety? What were your feelings/thoughts immediately following your speech?

2. Discuss the steps you took to prepare for this assignment including gathering objects, taking notes/speaking outline, rehearsing, etc.

3. Comment on your overall delivery. How do you feel your use of visual aids, appearance, movement, attire, voice, etc. affected your credibility/effectiveness?

4. Identify the specific aspects of your presentation that were especially strong.

5. What steps will you take to improve in the next assignment? What specific goals will you set in terms of organization, content, and delivery for the next speech? ("Doing better", Getting an A", and "Try harder" are not *specific* goals).

## Speech #2 Speech to Inform— Self-Evaluation

After viewing your videotape, respond to each of the following questions in paragraph/short-essay form. Evaluations must be typed, double-spaced, and not exceeding two pages in length.

1. Why did you choose your topic? How did your topic relate to your audience? Why was this topic fascinating to you?

2. Discuss the effectiveness of your introduction. Did you state the thesis statement of your speech? How did you gain the audience's attention? How did you establish your credibility as an "expert" on this topic?

3. Discuss the body of your speech; comment on the appropriateness/effectiveness of your verbal supportive material. What specific types of verbal supportive material did you include in your presentation (examples, explanations, testimonials, narratives, statistics, comparisons, definitions)?

4. Discuss the conclusion of your speech. How did you tie your conclusion to the specific purpose/thesis statement of your speech?

5. What do you feel were your strengths in preparing for this assignment? In what areas do you feel you need to improve? What specific goals will you set to improve on organization and content of your next speech?

## Speech #3 Speech to Demonstrate—Self-Evaluation

After viewing your videotape, respond to each of the following questions in paragraph/short-essay form. Evaluations must be typed, double-spaced, and not exceeding two pages in length.

1. Why did you choose this process as your topic? How did this process relate to your audience? How is an understanding of this process worthwhile to your audience?

2. Comment on the organization and content of this speech. In what areas do you feel you have improved in terms of researching and organizing information for your speech?

3. Discuss your feelings of self-confidence during the presentation. Describe how you felt both physically and emotionally while giving your speech. What steps did you take to manage any symptoms of anxiety you may have experienced?

4. Comment on your appearance. How do you feel your use of visual aids, movement, and attire affected your credibility/effectiveness?

5. Comment on your vocal delivery (rate of speech, pitch, volume, articulation, pronunciation, etc.). How do you feel your vocal delivery affected your credibility/effectiveness?

## Speech #4 Persuasive Speech—Self-Evaluation

After viewing your videotape, respond to each of the following questions in paragraph/short-essay form. Evaluations must be typed, double-spaced, and not exceeding two pages in length.

1. Why did you choose your claim? How did your claim relate to your audience? How is this issue significant to the lives of your audience members?

2. How did you justify your position with regards to this claim? What types of supportive material did you provide to support your position? Comment on the appropriateness/credibility of your documented sources.

3. What specific motivational appeals did you use to persuade your audience to accept your position? Discuss the effectiveness/appropriateness of your motivational appeals based on your analysis of the audience.

4. Comment on your overall presentation skills. How do you feel your use of visual aids, movement, attire and vocal delivery affected your credibility/effectiveness? In what areas do you feel you need improvement?

5. What specific goals will you set to improve your overall presentation skills in terms of movement, attire and vocal delivery?

## Overall Semester Self-Evaluation

Review your videotape and evaluations of all assigned speeches. In essay form, respond to the following questions addressing your experiences throughout this semester. Include specific references to your videotaped speeches. Evaluations must be typed, double-spaced, and not exceeding three pages in length.

1. Discuss your improvement or lack thereof relative to your abilities to organize a speech. Comment on your skills regarding topic selection, audience analysis, researching documented sources, outlining, etc.

2. Discuss your improvement or lack thereof relative to your ability to effectively deliver a speech. Comment on your skills regarding eye contact, voice, language, movement, etc.

3. Discuss one experience in your lab that was especially positive; in which you performed at your best, made a significant contribution to

the class, or learned something significant about yourself.

4. Regarding the content of this class, what specific skills do you feel will be of the most value to you as a future graduate of Murray State University?

5. What advice would you offer to someone who will be taking this class next semester to insure their success?

## Outside Speaker Evaluation

Throughout the semester, there are various free presentations offered throughout the university and community. For this assignment, you must attend one presentation delivered by a speaker who is neither a member of your class nor a professor (current or past). Presentations not sponsored by the university are subject to the approval by your lecture instructor. You will then submit an evaluation of the presentation based on the principles of public speaking as discussed in lecture and your textbook.

Your evaluation of the speaker's presentation should not be a verbatim report of what was said nor your reaction to the speaker's message; don't focus on whether you agreed with the speaker or not. Assess the speaker's performance as a means of demonstrating your knowledge and understanding of public speaking.

All papers must be in the following format:

- Essay format

- Typed or word processed

- 12 point font

- 2–2.5 pages, double spaced

- On the cover page:
  YOUR NAME
  Introduction to Public Speaking
  Class Section Number
  Lab Section
  Date
  Instructor Name

- Number all pages except cover sheet.

- Your discussion must be organized in essay format and address all the areas under the following headings:

**SPEAKING SITUATION:** Identify the speaker, his/her source of credibility, the topic, the audience, speaking situation.

**SPEECH PURPOSE:** Identify the speaker's general goal and specific objective. In your opinion, was the speaker successful in fulfilling that purpose? Justify.

**AUDIENCE ANALYSIS:** Identify the three areas of analysis: audience size and appropriate demographics, situation and attitude. How did the speaker adapt his/her message to the audience and the situation (i.e. language, delivery, supportive material)?

**ORGANIZATION:** Discuss the elements needed for the introduction, preview of main points, main ideas, transitions between main points, and conclusion. Was the speech well organized and easy to follow? Justify. What organizational pattern was evident in the speech?

**CONTENT:** Briefly discuss the value of the speech content. What types of supportive material were used? Did the speaker use any visual aids? Where they helpful? Explain.

**DELIVERY:** Discuss the speaker's appearance, eye contact, gestures, movement, volume, pitch, articulation, pronunciation, vocal variety, vocalized pauses, etc.

**FINAL EVALUATION:** What was the speaker's greatest strength? Greatest weakness? If this speech were delivered in a public speaking class and you were the instructor, what grade would you have assigned the speaker and why?

# Appendix B: Evaluation Forms

# Peer Evaluation Form—Speech to Inform

Your name: _____ Section: _____ Date: _____

Speaker's name: _____ Topic: _____

Answer each question in complete sentences.

1. How did the speaker get your attention? Comment on the effectiveness of the introduction. How did the speaker establish his/her credibility? Preview main points?

   _____

   _____

   _____

   _____

2. Comment on the organization/content of the speech. What were the main ideas of the body? How were main points supported?

   _____

   _____

   _____

   _____

3. Comment on the conclusion of the speech. How did the speaker summarize his/her main points? Finalize speech?

   _____

   _____

   _____

   _____

4. What aspects of the speaker's delivery were most effective?

   _____

   _____

   _____

   _____

5. What might the speaker do to improve in terms of content/organization? What might the speaker do to improve in terms of delivery?

_____

_____

_____

_____

# Peer Evaluation Form—Speech to Demonstrate

Your name: _____    Section: _____ Date: _____

Speaker's name: _____    Topic: _____

Answer each question in complete sentences.

1. How did the speaker get your attention? Comment on the effectiveness of the introduction. How did the speaker establish his/her credibility? Preview main points?

_____

_____

_____

_____

_____

2. Comment on the variety/effectiveness of supportive material?

_____

_____

_____

_____

_____

3. Comment on the speaker's selection and use of visual aids. Were the speaker's visual aids effective/appropriate for this speech?

_____

_____

_____

_____

_____

4. What aspects of the speaker's delivery were most effective?

_____

_____

_____

_____

_____

5.  Did the speaker sufficiently demonstrate a clearly defined process? Explain.

_____

_____

_____

_____

_____

# Peer Evaluation Form—Speech to Persuade

Your name: _____   Section: _____ Date: _____

Speaker's name: _____   Topic: _____

Answer each question in complete sentences.

1. What appeared to be the speaker's central claim?

   _____

   _____

   _____

   _____

   _____

2. How did the speaker justify his/her claim? What documented support material was provided to support the speaker's position?

   _____

   _____

   _____

   _____

   _____

3. What motivational appeals or supportive material were most significant in this speech?

   _____

   _____

   _____

   _____

   _____

4. What aspects of the speaker's delivery were most effective?

   _____

   _____

   _____

   _____

   _____

5. Did the speaker appear to effectively persuade the audience to agree with his/her claim? Explain.

_____

_____

_____

_____

_____

# Peer Evaluation Form—Special Occasion Speech

Your name: _____ Section: _____ Date: _____

Speaker's name: _____ Topic: _____

Answer each question in complete sentences.

1. Comment on the effectiveness of the introduction. What appeared to be the specific purpose of the speech?

    _____

    _____

    _____

    _____

    _____

2. Comment on the organization/content of the speech. What were the main ideas of the body? How were main points supported?

    _____

    _____

    _____

    _____

    _____

3. Comment on the conclusion of the speech. How did the speaker summarize his/her main points? Finalize speech?

    _____

    _____

    _____

    _____

    _____

4. Comment on the speaker's delivery in terms of eye contact, gestures, movement, appearance, etc.

    _____

    _____

    _____

    _____

    _____

5. What aspects of this speech were especially creative? Entertaining? Explain.

_____

_____

_____

_____

_____

# Speech #1 Evaluation Form—Bag Speech

Student's name: _____  Section: _____

Objects: _____

## Organization and Content

1. Introduction                                                        1     2     3

   Gains audience's attention

   Previews main points

2. Body                                                                1     2     3

   Main points clear and well developed

   Effective explanations, descriptions, etc.

   Creative, appropriate, and effective visual aids

3. Conclusion                                                          1     2     3

   Summarizes main points

   Finalizes speech

## Delivery

4. Effective use of time; delivered within 2-3 minutes                 1     2     3

5. Direct and inclusive eye contact                                    1     2     3

Score: _____/15

Notes:

_____

_____

_____

_____

_____

# Speech #2 Evaluation Form—Speech to Inform

Student's name: _____ Section: _____

Topic: _____

## Organization and Content

1. Introduction

    Gains audience's attention; establishes credibility     1   2   3   4   5

    States thesis statement; previews main points     1   2   3   4   5

2. Body

    Main points clear/well developed     1   2   3   4   5

    Appropriate/effective verbal supportive material     1   2   3   4   5

    Effective/appropriate use of visual aid     1   2   3   4   5

    Documented sources clearly cited     1   2   3   4   5

3. Conclusion

    Summarizes main points and finalizes speech     1   2   3   4   5

4. Outline in assigned format     1   2   3   4   5

5. Topic appropriate to situation and audience; creative     1   2   3   4   5

## Delivery

6. Effective use of time; delivered within 3-5 minutes     1   2   3   4   5

7. Direct and inclusive eye contact     1   2   3   4   5

8. Demonstrated vocal variety (rate, pitch, volume)     1   2   3   4   5

9. Extemporaneous, conversational delivery     1   2   3   4   5

10. Controlled vocalized pauses; clear articulation and pronunciation     1   2   3   4   5

11. Used effective gestures, movement, and facial expression     1   2   3   4   5

    OPTIONAL BONUS—Question/Answer session     1   2   3   4   5

Score: _____/75

Notes:

_____

_____

_____

_____

_____

# Speech #3 Evaluation Form—Speech to Demonstrate

Student's name: _____ Section: _____

Process: _____

## Organization and Content

1. Introduction

   Gains audience's attention; establishes credibility     1   2   3   4   5

   States thesis statement; previews main points     1   2   3   4   5

2. Body

   Main points clear/well developed     1   2   3   4   5

   Appropriate/effective verbal supportive material     1   2   3   4   5

   Effective/appropriate use of visual aid     1   2   3   4   5

   Documented sources clearly cited     1   2   3   4   5

   Effective use of transitions     1   2   3   4   5

3. Conclusion

   Summarizes main points and ties to thesis statement     1   2   3   4   5

   Strong and/or novel final statement     1   2   3   4   5

4. Topic appropriate to situation and audience     1   2   3   4   5

5. Outline typed in assigned format     1   2   3   4   5

## Delivery

6. Effective use of time; delivered within 5-7 minutes _____    2   4   6   8   10

7. Direct and inclusive eye contact     1   2   3   4   5

8. Displayed appropriate energy and enthusiasm     1   2   3   4   5

9. Effective use of vocal variety (rate, pitch, volume)     1   2   3   4   5

10. Extemporaneous, conversational delivery     1   2   3   4   5

11. Used vivid, descriptive language; appropriate grammar     1   2   3   4   5

12. Controlled vocalized pauses; clear articulation and pronunciation     1   2   3   4   5

13. Effective gestures, movement, and facial expression     1   2   3   4   5

Score: _____/100

Notes:

_____

_____

# Speech #4 Evaluation Form—Speech to Persuade

Student's name: _____  Section: _____

Central claim: _____

## Organization (Monroe's Motivated Sequence)

1. Attention

   | | | | | | |
   |---|---|---|---|---|---|
   | Innovative; original attention getting device | 1 | 2 | 3 | 4 | 5 |
   | Establishes credibility; previews central claim | 1 | 2 | 3 | 4 | 5 |

2. Need

   | | | | | | |
   |---|---|---|---|---|---|
   | Clearly establishes a problem | 1 | 2 | 3 | 4 | 5 |
   | Problem explained/described with sufficient supportive material | 1 | 2 | 3 | 4 | 5 |

3. Satisfaction

   | | | | | | |
   |---|---|---|---|---|---|
   | Clearly states attitude, belief or action desired | 1 | 2 | 3 | 4 | 5 |
   | Solution explained/described with sufficient supportive material | 1 | 2 | 3 | 4 | 5 |

4. Visualization

   | | | | | | |
   |---|---|---|---|---|---|
   | Describes conditions/impact if solution is or is not accepted | 1 | 2 | 3 | 4 | 5 |

5. Action

   | | | | | | |
   |---|---|---|---|---|---|
   | Secures assent or action on the problem; finalizes speech | 1 | 2 | 3 | 4 | 5 |

## Content

| | | | | | |
|---|---|---|---|---|---|
| 6. Clear organization and development with appropriate transitions | 2 | 4 | 6 | 8 | 10 |
| 7. Uses appropriate motivational appeals | 2 | 4 | 6 | 8 | 10 |
| 8. Audience's predisposition to topic addressed | 1 | 2 | 3 | 4 | 5 |
| 9. Documented sources cited | 1 | 2 | 3 | 4 | 5 |
| 10. Outline typed in assigned format | 2 | 4 | 6 | 8 | 10 |

## Delivery

| | | | | | |
|---|---|---|---|---|---|
| 11. Effective use of time; delivered within 7-9 minutes_____ | 2 | 4 | 6 | 8 | 10 |
| 12. Direct and inclusive eye contact | 1 | 2 | 3 | 4 | 5 |
| 13. Demonstrated vocal variety; controlled vocalized pauses; good articulation/pronunciation | 1 | 2 | 3 | 4 | 5 |
| 14. Extemporaneous, conversational delivery (minimal use of notes) | 2 | 4 | 6 | 8 | 10 |
| 15. Effective gestures, movement, facial expression, and attire | 1 | 2 | 3 | 4 | 5 |
| 16. Used vivid, descriptive language; appropriate grammar | 1 | 2 | 3 | 4 | 5 |
| 17. Displayed appropriate energy and enthusiasm | 1 | 2 | 3 | 4 | 5 |

Score: _____/125

Notes:

_____

_____

_____

# Speech #5 Evaluation Form—Special Occasion Speech

Student's name: _____  Section: _____

Specific purpose: _____

## Organization and Content

1. Introduction

   Gains audience's attention; identifies thesis statement    1    2    3    4    5

   Relates to audience                                          1    2    3    4    5

2. Body

   Main points clear/well developed                             1    2    3    4    5

   Appropriate/effective verbal supportive material             1    2    3    4    5

3. Conclusion

   Summarizes main points and ties to thesis statement          1    2    3    4    5

   Strong and/or novel final statement                          1    2    3    4    5

4. Message appropriate to situation and audience                1    2    3    4    5

5. Outline typed in assigned format                             2    4    6    8    10

## Delivery

6. Effective use of time; delivered within 2-4 minutes_____    2    4    6    8    10

7. Direct and inclusive eye contact                             1    2    3    4    5

8. Displayed appropriate energy and enthusiasm                  1    2    3    4    5

9. Demonstrated effective vocal variety (rate, pitch, volume)   1    2    3    4    5

10. Extemporaneous, conversational delivery                     1    2    3    4    5

11. Used vivid, descriptive language; appropriate grammar       1    2    3    4    5

12. Controlled vocalized pauses; clear articulation and pronunciation   1    2    3    4    5

13. Effective gestures, movement, and facial expression         1    2    3    4    5

14. Evidence of creativity and originality                      2    4    6    8    10

Score: _____/100

Notes:

_____

_____

_____

_____

_____

## Speeches that Create Concern for Problems

The text of this speech was provided by President Cesar Chavez's office at the national headquarters of the United Farm Workers of America.

From *Contemporary American Speeches*. Ninth Edition. Eds. Richard L. Johannesen.et al. Dubuque, Iowa: Kendall/Hunt, 2000: 144-147

## Cesar Chavez

### *Pesticides Speech*

Noted speakers—whether they are presidents of large corporations, heads of public service organizations, major government officials, or leaders of social movements-frequency are called upon to speak on the same general topic to numerous but varied audiences. Politicians during major campaigns often face the same demand. One approach such speakers sometimes take is to present a "generic" speech—a speech containing the same general information and arguments regardless of audience but with opportunities in the speech for a modest amount of concrete adaptation to each specific audience. For one discussion of such generic or "stock" political campaign speeches, see Judith S. Trent and Robert V. Friedenberg, *Political Campaign Communication* 3rd ed. (Prager, 1995), pp. 156-160.

This speech by Cesar Chavez is a generic speech. It contains standard or basic arguments on the topic suitable for diverse audiences and occasions with two places noted for specific audience adaptation: "insert names" (1) and "insert additional pitches" (18). There are no mentions in the text of the speech of a specific audience or occasion. The text simply is dated 1-9-90 and labeled as "Pesticides Speech for Cesar Chavez." Other texts of speeches presented by Chavez provided by his office indicate specific audiences and occasions and some of the speeches make numerous adaptations to the audiences.

Cesar Chavez was born in 1927 in Arizona and in 1962 in California founded the National Farm Workers Association (later called United Farm Workers of America). This was a labor union noted for its aggressive but nonviolent advocacy of the rights and safety of migrant farm workers. In numerous social protest efforts spanning four decades, Chavez often has utilized the pressure tactic of consumer boycott of the purchase of farm produce such as lettuce or grapes. Although in this speech he does urge adoption of a policy—the boycott of table grapes—and he does indicate its potential effectiveness (15-18), the bulk of the speech primarily aims at creating concern for a problem rather than describing in detail a program of action. Cesar Chavez died on April 23,1993.

In presenting a compelling view of the problem, Chavez answers the question—Why grapes?—By demonstrating the scope of the problem. He employs statistics to show how widespread the problem is (4, 10) and argues that the problem threatens farm workers, their children, and consumers (5-6,10). Statistics such as 800 percent and 1200 percent above normal index the intensity of the problem (8-9). Expert testimony is used in several places, including use of so-called "reluctant" testimony from grower and government sources (2,6,14). What are the causes of the problem? Chavez clearly identifies two: grape grower greed (2-3,12, 18) and inaction and misaction by state and federal governments (12-14). For Chavez, government " is part of the problem."

Chavez attempts to generate audience concern for the problem by vividly depicting the danger, degradation, and suffering of people who directly experience the problem. First, he lists the general physical harms: "cancer, DNA mutations, and horrible birth defects" (6). Second, and at length, he "humanizes" the "technical problem of pesticides with examples of real people and groups (7-11). Note his skillful use of alliteration to make his argument memorable: "*children* are dying . . . *slow, painful cruel* deaths in towns called *cancer clusters*" (8). And note his use of parallel phrasing to summarize his point (11).

Of special interest to the rhetorical critic is Chavez's strategy of associating the pesticides and policies he condemns with so-called "devil terms" that carry intense negative force because they represent violations of fundamental human values. He establishes associations with nerve gas (6-World War I German use and use by Saddam Hussein against Kurds in Iraq in 1988); with agent orange (6-a chemical with harmful physical side-effects used to strip leaves from trees during the Vietnam War); with killing fields (10-allusion to the 1984 film of the same name that depicted mass slaughter of

Cambodian civilians by Communist terrorists); and, sarcastically, with Idi Amin (Uganda's bloody dictator) and Adolf Hitler (13). How adequately and legitimately do you believe that he establishes these associations? In what ways and to what degree might the lack in a generic speech of arguments and appeals specifically intended for a specific audience lessen Chavez's, or any speaker's, ability to create concern for the problem she or he describes? Here recall the discussion of the second suggested criterion for evaluating speeches that create concern for problems: Has the speaker shown the significance of the problem for the specific audience? In addition, are there any ethical issues involved in the use of generic speeches? If so, what might they be and on what grounds? For an analysis of Chavez's rhetoric, see John C Hammerback and Richard J. Jensen, *The Rhetorical Career of Cesar Chavez* (Texas A 9 M University Press, 1998).

Thank you very much, I am truly honored to be able to speak with you. I would like to thank the many people who made this possible for their kindness and their hospitality, (insert names)

Decades ago, the chemical industry promised the growers that pesticides would create vast new wealth and bountiful harvests. Just recently, the experts learned what farm workers, and the truly organic farmers have known for years. The prestigious National Academy of Sciences recently concluded an exhaustive five-year study which showed that by using simple, effective organic farming techniques, *instead of pesticides*, the growers could make *more money*, produce *more crops*, and *protect the environment*.

Unfortunately, the growers are not listening. They continue to spray and inject hundreds of millions of pounds of herbicides, fungicides, and insecticides onto our foods.

Most of you know that the United Farm Workers have focussed our struggle against pesticides on table grapes. Many people ask me "Why grapes?" The World Resources Institute reported that over three hundred thousand farm workers are poisoned every year by pesticides. Over half of all reported pesticide-related illnesses involve the cultivation or harvesting of table grapes. They receive *more* restricted-use application permits, which allow growers to spray pesticides known to threaten humans, than *any* other fresh food crop. The General Accounting Office, which does research for the U.S. Congress, determined that *34 of the 76*

types of pesticides used *legally* on grapes pose potential human health hazards and could *not be detected* by current multi-residue methods.

My friends, grapes are the most dangerous fruit in America. The pesticides sprayed on table grapes *are killing America's children*. These pesticides *soak* the fields, *drift* with the wind, *pollute* the water, and are *eaten* by unwitting consumers. These poisons are designed to kill life, and pose a very real threat to consumers and farm workers alike.

The fields are sprayed with pesticides like captan, a fungicide believed to cause cancer, DNA mutation, and horrible birth defects. Other poisons take a similar toll. Parathion and phosdrin are *"nerve gas"* types of insecticides, which are believed to be responsible for the majority of farm worker poisonings in California. The growers spray sulphites, which can trigger asthmatic attacks, on the grapes. And even the growers own magazine, *The California Farmer*, admitted that growers were *illegally* using a very dangerous growth stimulator, called *Fix*, which is quite similar to *Agent Orange*, on the grapes.

This is a very technical problem, with very *human* victims. One young boy, Felipe Franco, was born without arms or legs in the agricultural town of McFarland. His mother worked for the first three months of her pregnancy picking grapes in fields that were sprayed repeatedly with pesticides believed to cause birth defects.

My friends, the central valley of California is one of the wealthiest agricultural regions in the world. In its midst are clusters of children dying from cancer. The children who live in towns like McFarland are surrounded by the grape fields that employ their parents. The children contact the poisons when they play outside, when they drink the water, and when they hug their parents returning from the fields. *And the children are dying*. They are dying *slow, painful, cruel* deaths in towns called *cancer clusters*. In cancer clusters like McFarland, where the childhood cancer rate is *800 percent* above normal.

A few months ago, the parents of a brave little girl in the agricultural community of Earlimart came to the United Farm Workers to ask for our help. Their four-year-old daughter, Natalie Ramirez, has lost one kidney to cancer and is threatened with the loss of another. The Ramirez family knew about our protests in nearby McFarland and thought there might be a similar problem in their home town. Our union members went door to door in Earlimart and found that the Ramirez family's worst fears were true. There are at least four other children suffering from cancer and similar diseases which the experts believe were caused by pesticides in the little town of Earlimart, a rate *1200 percent* above normal. In Earlimart, little Jimmy Caudillo died recently from leukemia at the age of three.

The grape vineyards of California have become America's Killing Fields. These *same* pesticides can be found on the grapes you buy in the store. Study after study, by the California Department of Food and Agriculture, by the Food and Drug Administration, and by objective newspapers, concluded that up to *54 percent* of the sampled grapes contained pesticide residues. Which pesticide did they find the most? *Captan,* the same carcinogenic fungicide that causes birth defects.

My friends, *the suffering must end. So many* children are dying, *so many* babies are born without limbs and vital organs, *so many* workers are dying in the fields.

The growers, and the supermarket owners, say that the government can *handle* the problem, can *protect* the workers, can *save* the children. It *should,* but it *won't.* You see, agribusiness is *big business.* It is a *sixteen billion* dollar industry in California alone. Agribusiness contributed very heavily to the successful campaign of Republican Governor George Deukmajian. He has rewarded the growers by turning the Agricultural Labor Relations Board into a tool for the growers, run by the growers. The Governor even vetoed a bill that would have required growers to warn workers that they were entering recently sprayed fields! And only *one percent* of those growers who *are caught* violating pesticide laws were even fined in California.

President Bush is a long-time friend of agribusiness. During the last presidential campaign, George Bush ate grapes in a field just *75 miles* from the cemetery where little Jimmy Caudillo and other pesticide victims are buried, in order to show his support for the table grape industry. He recently gave a speech to the Farm Bureau, saying that it was up to the *growers* to restrain the use of dangerous pesticides. That's like putting *Idi Amin,* or *Adolf Hitler,* in charge of promoting *peace* and *human rights.*

To show you what happens to pesticides supposedly under government control, I'd like to tell you more about captan. Testing to determine the acceptable tolerance levels of captan was done by Bio-Tech Laboratories, later found *guilty* of falsifying the data to the E.P.A. The tolerance level set was *ten times* the amount allowed in Canada. Later, government agencies tried to ban captan, but were mysteriously stopped several times. Finally, the government banned captan on 42 crops, but *not on grapes.* Even the General Accounting Office found that the government's pesticide testing is wholly inadequate. The government is *not* the answer, it is part of the problem.

If we are to protect farm workers, their children, and consumers, we must use *people power.* I have seen many boycotts succeed. The Reverend Martin Luther King, Jr., who so generously supported our first fast, led the way with the bus boycott. And with *our* first boycott, we were able to get DDT, Aldrin, and Dieldrin banned, in our first contracts with grape growers. Now, even more urgently, we are trying to get deadly pesticides banned.

The growers and their allies have tried to stop us with *lies,* with *police,* with *intimidation,* with *public relations agencies,* and with *violence.* But *we cannot be stopped.* In our *life and death struggle* for justice, we have turned to the court of last resort: the American people.

At last we are winning. Many supermarket chains have stopped selling or advertising grapes. Millions of consumers are refusing to buy America's most dangerous fruit. Many courageous people have volunteered to help our cause or joined human chains of people who fast, who go without food for days, to support our struggle. As a result, *grape sales keep falling.* We have witnessed truckloads of grapes being dumped because no one would stoop low enough to buy them. As demand drops, so do prices and profits. This sort of economic pressure is the only language the growers understand.

We are winning, but there is still much work to be done. If we are going to beat the greed and power of the growers, we must work *together. Together,* we can end the suffering. *Together,* we can save the children. *Together,* we can bring justice to the killing fields. I hope that you will join our struggle, for it is *your* struggle too. The simple act of boycotting table grapes laced with pesticides is a powerful statement the growers understand. *Please, boycott table grapes.* For your safety, for the workers, *we must act,* and *act together.* (insert additional pitches)

Good night, and God bless you.

Reprinted by permission of The Cesar E. Chavez Foundation.

## Toni Morrison—Nobel Lecture

### December 7, 1993

"Once upon a time there was an old woman. Blind but wise." Or was it an old man? A guru, perhaps. Or a griot soothing restless children. I have heard this story, or one exactly like it, in the lore of several cultures.

"Once upon a time there was an old woman. Blind. Wise."

In the version I know the woman is the daughter of slaves, black, American, and lives alone in a small house outside of town. Her reputation for wisdom is without peer and without question. Among her people she is both the law and its transgression. The honor she is paid and the awe in which she is held reach beyond her neighborhood to places far away; to the city where the intelligence of rural prophets is the source of much amusement.

One day the woman is visited by some young people who seem to be bent on disproving her clairvoyance and showing her up for the fraud they believe she is. Their plan is simple: they enter her house and ask the one question the answer to which rides solely on her difference from them, a difference they regard as a profound disability: her blindness. They stand before her, and one of them says, "Old woman, I hold in my hand a bird. Tell me whether it is living or dead."

She does not answer, and the question is repeated. "Is the bird I am holding living or dead?"

Still she doesn't answer. She is blind and cannot see her visitors, let alone what is in their hands. She does not know their color, gender or homeland. She only knows their motive.

The old woman's silence is so long, the young people have trouble holding their laughter.

Finally she speaks and her voice is soft but stern. "I don't know", she says. "I don't know whether the bird you are holding is dead or alive, but what I do know is that it is in your hands. It is in your hands."

Her answer can be taken to mean: if it is dead, you have either found it that way or you have killed it. If it is alive, you can still kill it. Whether it is to stay alive, it is your decision. Whatever the case, it is your responsibility.

For parading their power and her helplessness, the young visitors are reprimanded, told they are responsible not only for the act of mockery but also for the small bundle of life sacrificed to achieve its aims. The blind woman shifts attention away from assertions of power to the instrument through which that power is exercised.

Speculation on what (other than its own frail body) that bird-in-the-hand might signify has always been attractive to me, but especially so now thinking, as I have been, about the work I do that has brought me to this company. So I choose to read the bird as language and the woman as a practiced writer. She is worried about how the language she dreams in, given to her at birth, is handled, put into service, even withheld from her for certain nefarious purposes. Being a writer she thinks of language partly as a system, partly as a living thing over which one has control, but mostly as agency—as an act with consequences. So the question the children put to her: "Is it living or dead?" is not unreal because she thinks of language as susceptible to death, erasure; certainly imperiled and salvageable only by an effort of the will. She believes that if the bird in the hands of her visitors is dead the custodians are responsible for the corpse. For her a dead language is not only one no longer spoken or written, it is unyielding language content to admire its own paralysis. Like statist language, censored and censoring. Ruthless in its policing duties, it has no desire or purpose other than maintaining the free range of its own narcotic narcissism, its own exclusivity and dominance. However moribund, it is not without effect for it actively thwarts the intellect, stalls conscience, suppresses human potential. Unreceptive to interrogation, it cannot form or tolerate new ideas, shape other thoughts, tell another story, fill baffling silences. Official language smithereyed to sanction ignorance and preserve privilege is a suit of armor polished to shocking glitter, a husk from which the knight departed long ago. Yet there it is: dumb, predatory, sentimental. Exciting reverence in schoolchildren, providing shelter for despots, summoning false memories of stability, harmony among the public.

She is convinced that when language dies, out of carelessness, disuse, indifference and absence of esteem, or killed by fiat, not only she herself, but all users and makers are accountable for its demise. In her country children have bitten their tongues off and use bullets instead to iterate the voice of speechlessness, of disabled and disabling language, of language adults have abandoned altogether as a device for grappling with meaning, providing guidance, or expressing love. But she knows tongue-suicide is not only the choice of children. It is common among the infantile heads of state and power merchants whose evacuated language leaves them with no access to what is left of their human instincts for they speak only to those who obey, or in order to force obedience.

The systematic looting of language can be recognized by the tendency of its users to forgo its nuanced, complex, mid-wifery properties for menace and subjugation. Oppressive language does more than represent violence; it is violence; does more than represent the limits of knowledge; it limits knowledge. Whether it is obscuring state language or the faux-language of mindless media; whether it is the proud but calcified language of the academy or the commodity driven language of science; whether it is the malign language of law-without-ethics, or language designed for the estrangement of minorities, hiding its racist plunder in its literary cheek—it must be rejected, altered and exposed. It is the language that drinks blood, laps. vulnerabilities, tucks its fascist boots under crinolines of respectability and patriotism as it moves relentlessly toward the bottom line and the bottomed-out mind. Sexist language, racist language, theistic language—all are typical of the policing languages of mastery, and cannot, do not permit new knowledge or encourage the mutual exchange of ideas.

The old woman is keenly aware that no intellectual mercenary, nor insatiable dictator, no paid-for politician or demagogue; no counterfeit journalist would be persuaded by her thoughts. There is and will be rousing language to keep citizens armed and arming; slaughtered and slaughtering in the malls, courthouses, post offices, playgrounds, bedrooms and boulevards; stirring, memorializing language to mask the pity and waste of needless death. There will be more diplomatic language to countenance rape, torture, assassination. There is and will be more seductive, mutant language designed to throttle women, to pack their throats like paté-producing geese with their own unsayable, transgressive words; there will be more of the language of surveillance disguised as research; of politics and history calculated to render the suffering of millions mute; language glamorized to thrill the dissatisfied and bereft into assaulting their neighbors; arrogant pseudo-empirical language crafted to lock creative people into cages of inferiority and hopelessness.

Underneath the eloquence, the glamor, the scholarly associations, however stirring or seductive, the heart of such language is languishing, or perhaps not beating at all—if the bird is already dead.

She has thought about what could have been the intellectual history of any discipline if it had not insisted upon, or been forced into, the waste of time and life that rationalizations for and representations of dominance required—lethal discourses of exclusion blocking access to cognition for both the excluder and the excluded.

The conventional wisdom of the Tower of Babel story is that the collapse was a misfortune. That it was the distraction, or the weight of many languages that precipitated the tower's failed architecture. That one monolithic language would have expedited the building and heaven would have been reached. Whose heaven, she wonders? And what kind? Perhaps the achievement of Paradise was premature, a little hasty if no one could take the time to understand other languages, other views, other narratives period. Had they, the heaven they imagined might have been found at their feet. Complicated, demanding, yes, but a view of heaven as life; not heaven as post-life.

She would not want to leave her young visitors with the impression that language should be forced to stay alive merely to be. The vitality of language lies in its ability to limn the actual, imagined and possible lives of its speakers, readers, writers. Although its poise is sometimes in displacing experience it is not a substitute for it. It arcs toward the place where meaning may lie. When a President of the United States thought about the graveyard his country had become, and said, "The world will little note nor long remember what we say here. But it will never forget what they did here," his simple words are exhilarating in their life-sustaining properties because they refused to encapsulate the reality of 600, 000 dead men in a cataclysmic race war. Refusing to monumentalize, disdaining the "final word", the precise "summing up", acknowledging their "poor power to add or detract", his words signal deference to the uncapturability of the life it mourns. It is the deference that moves her, that recognition that language can never live up to life once and for all. Nor should it. Language can never "pin down" slavery, genocide, war. Nor should it yearn for the arrogance to be able to do so. Its force, its felicity is in its reach toward the ineffable.

Be it grand or slender, burrowing, blasting, or refusing to sanctify; whether it laughs out loud or is a cry without an alphabet, the choice word, the chosen silence, unmolested language surges toward knowledge, not its destruction. But who does not know of literature banned because it is interrogative; discredited because it is critical; erased because alternate? And how many are outraged by the thought of a self-ravaged tongue?

Word-work is sublime, she thinks, because it is generative; it makes meaning that secures our difference, our human difference—the way in which we are like no other life.

We die. That may be the meaning of life. But we do language. That may be the measure of our lives.

"Once upon a time, . . ." visitors ask an old woman a question. Who are they, these children? What did they make of that encounter? What did they hear in those final words: "The bird is in your hands"? A sentence that gestures towards possibility or one that drops a latch? Perhaps what the children heard was "It's not my problem. I am old, female, black, blind. What wisdom I have now is in knowing I cannot help you. The future of language is yours."

They stand there. Suppose nothing was in their hands? Suppose the visit was only a ruse, a trick to get to be spoken to, taken seriously as they have not been before? A chance to interrupt, to violate the adult world, its miasma of discourse about them, for them, but never to them? Urgent questions are at stake, including the one they have asked: "Is the bird we hold living or dead?" Perhaps the question meant: "Could someone tell us what is life? What is death?" No trick at all; no silliness. A straightforward question worthy of the attention of a wise one. An old one. And if the old and wise who have lived life and faced death cannot describe either, who can?

But she does not; she keeps her secret; her good opinion of herself; her gnomic pronouncements; her art without commitment. She keeps her distance, enforces it and retreats into the singularity of isolation, in sophisticated, privileged space.

Nothing, no word follows her declaration of transfer. That silence is deep, deeper than the meaning available in the words she has spoken. It shivers, this silence, and the children, annoyed, fill it with language invented on the spot.

"Is there no speech," they ask her, "no words you can give us that helps us break through your dossier of failures? Through the education you have just given us that is no education at all because we are paying close attention to what you have done as well as to what you have said? To the barrier you have erected between generosity and wisdom?

"We have no bird in our hands, living or dead. We have only you and our important question. Is the nothing in our hands something you could not bear to contemplate, to even guess? Don't you remember being young when language was magic without meaning? When what you could say, could not mean? When the invisible was what imagination strove to see? When questions and demands for answers burned so brightly you trembled with fury at not knowing?

"Do we have to begin consciousness with a battle heroines and heroes like you have already fought and lost leaving us with nothing in our hands except what you have imagined is there? Your answer is artful, but its artfulness embarrasses us and ought to embarrass you. Your answer is indecent in its self-congratulation. A made-for-television script that makes no sense if there is nothing in our hands.

"Why didn't you reach out, touch us with your soft fingers, delay the sound bite, the lesson, until you knew who we were? Did you so despise our trick, our modus operandi you could not see that we were baffled about how to get your attention? We are young. Unripe. We have heard all our short lives that we have to be responsible. What could that possibly mean in the catastrophe this world has become; where, as a poet said, "nothing needs to be exposed since it is already barefaced." Our inheritance is an affront. You want us to have your old, blank eyes and see only cruelty and mediocrity. Do you think we are stupid enough to perjure ourselves again and again with the fiction of nationhood? How dare you talk to us of duty when we stand waist deep in the toxin of your past?

"You trivialize us and trivialize the bird that is not in our hands. Is there no context for our lives? No song, no literature, no poem full of vitamins, no history connected to experience that you can pass along to help us start strong? You are an adult. The old one, the wise one. Stop thinking about saving your face. Think of our lives and tell us your particularized world. Make up a story. Narrative is radical, creating us at the very moment it is being created. We will not blame you if your reach exceeds your grasp; if love so ignites your words they go down in flames and nothing is left but their scald. Or if, with the reticence of a surgeon's hands, your words suture only the places where blood might flow. We know you can never do it properly—once and for all. Passion is never enough; neither is skill. But try. For our sake and yours forget your name in the street; tell us what the world has been to you in the dark places and in the light. Don't tell us what to believe, what to fear. Show us belief's wide skirt and the stitch that unravels fear's caul. You, old woman, blessed with blindness, can speak the language that tells us what only language can: how to see without pictures. Language alone protects us from the scariness of things with no names. Language alone is meditation.

"Tell us what it is to be a woman so that we may know what it is to be a man. What moves at the margin. What it is to have no home in this place. To be set adrift from the one you knew. What it is to live at the edge of towns that cannot bear your company.

"Tell us about ships turned away from shorelines at Easter, placenta in a field. Tell us about a wagonload of slaves, how they sang so softly their breath was indistinguishable from the falling snow. How they knew from the hunch of the nearest shoulder that the next stop would be their last. How, with hands prayered in their sex, they thought of heat, then sun. Lifting their faces as though is was there for the taking. Turning as though there for the taking. They stop at an inn. The driver and his mate go in with the lamp leaving them humming in the dark. The horse's void steams into the snow beneath its hooves and its hiss and melt are the envy of the freezing slaves.

"The inn door opens: a girl and a boy step away from its light. They climb into the wagon bed. The boy will have a gun in three years, but now he carries a lamp and a jug of warm cider. They pass it from mouth to mouth. The girl offers bread, pieces of meat and something more: a glance into the eyes of the one she serves. One helping for each man, two for each woman. And a look. They look back. The next stop will be their last. But not this one. This one is warmed."

It's quiet again when the children finish speaking, until the woman breaks into the silence.

"Finally", she says, "I trust you now. I trust you with the bird that is not in your hands because you have truly caught it. Look. How lovely it is, this thing we have done—together."

# Index